SEEING STRAIGHT

SEEING STRAIGHT

An Introduction to Gender and Sexual Privilege

Jean Halley and Amy Eshleman

ROWMAN & LITTLEFIELD
Lanham • Boulder • New York • London

Published by Rowman & Littlefield
A wholly owned subsidiary of
The Rowman & Littlefield Publishing Group, Inc.
4501 Forbes Boulevard, Suite 200, Lanham, Maryland 20706
https://rowman.com

Unit A, Whitacre Mews, 26-34 Stannary Street, London SE11 4AB,
United Kingdom

British Library Cataloguing in Publication Information Available

Library of Congress Cataloging-in-Publication Data Available
ISBN 978-1-4422-3353-9 (cloth : alk. paper)
ISBN 978-1-4422-3354-6 (pbk. : alk. paper)
ISBN 978-1-4422-3355-3 (electronic)

♾ ™ The paper used in this publication meets the minimum requirements of
American National Standard for Information Sciences Permanence of Paper
for Printed Library Materials, ANSI/NISO Z39.48-1992.

Printed in the United States of America

For our parents, by blood and by heart,
Lore Segal, Kathleen O'Malley, Richard Holland,
Lorraine Eshleman, and David Eshleman

and to our students, may they live in a more just world.

CONTENTS

ACKNOWLEDGMENTS

Many more people were helpful in writing our book than we can possibly acknowledge. We are deeply thankful to so many. Among them, Nicholas P. Richardson encouraged us to write the book that matched the title he liked. Jacob Segal carefully read and gave us very thoughtful feedback on numerous drafts as well as suggested some of our favorite discussion questions.

We are very thankful for the inspiring work of all of our research assistants, who gathered sources, wrote discussion questions, and provided critical evaluation of much of the book. Isaiah Halley-Segal helped us to find important and relevant research material. Joey Sergi assisted us in rethinking our book's structure and clarifying our arguments. Danielle Lucchese brought us concrete examples from the news and challenged us to make our descriptions more accessible. Through research inspired by seeking to understand a powerful experience of her dear friend, Tiffany Turner helped to frame the way we addressed bullying—in addition to supporting us in innumerable ways. We are also very grateful to Stephanie Capellan, Laura DiSarro, Melissa M. Digregorio, David M. Jordon, and Samantha Otero.

We have learned so much from the scholarly work of and countless conversations with our students. Among the many students who have influenced us, we are grateful to Rej Joo, Emily Scotti, and Shayne Zaslow for critical analysis of our plan for this project. We thank Georgia Brooke Guinan and Gina Sportiello for critical discussion in (and outside of) the classroom. Bryan Bickford, Naveena Waran, Stephanie

Gangemi, Julia Hardman, Erin Bernstein, and Kristen Woodbury regularly draw our attention to new ideas. Carly Schmidt and Rebecca Barrett inspire us to think beyond traditional categories of sexual identity. We remember K. Justin Stevens for encouraging everyone to rethink labels for sexual identity. We owe a deep debt to all of our students who, over the years with great insight and patience, discussed gender, sexuality, race, class, and social power with us.

For their helpful suggestions, we are very thankful to several anonymous reviewers of our proposal.

Dennis Schaub, librarian extraordinaire, found missing pieces for us that helped make this project complete. Melissa Hope Ditmore, Jeremiah Jurkiewicz, Danielle Lucchese, Pauline Park, and Shayne Zaslow generously gave hours of their time to enlightening interviews and conversations. Isaiah Halley-Segal and Kathleen Halley-Segal were very gracious in allowing us to share their insights and experiences.

PREFACE

As professors dedicated to undergraduate education, we are delighted to offer this interdisciplinary text as an introduction to power and privilege afforded heterosexuality and gender normativity in the United States. This text will encourage students to think critically about heteronormativity, feminism, and cultural materialism by providing accessible explanations of theory and empirical research. Through reading aspects of sociology, psychology, gender studies, sexuality studies, and history, students will gain insight into these disciplines and how they can be combined to offer a more complete understanding of a social problem. Our intersectional approach examines ways that identity is affected by interactions among gender, sexuality, race, ethnicity, religion, disability, and economic resources.

We use concrete examples to illustrate critical theoretical concepts, to exemplify evidence from qualitative and quantitative research, and to foster empathy. Each chapter begins with an anecdote of a child, often an example of resistance to heteronormativity and gender privilege. Stories of children offer surprising and alternative ways of thinking about sex and gender; they provide examples of human beings in our society who have not yet fully become socialized to accept heteronormativity and sexism. Many of these anecdotes reveal ways that today's young people may become adults who think differently, and more justly, about gender and sexuality. The first chapter begins with a description of the son of one of the authors negotiating assumptions about gender. The final chapter culminates with a description of a gender-fluid child's celebration at a queer pride march. Rhetorical questions within each chapter and discussion questions at the end of each chapter encourage readers to examine their understanding of sexuality and gender. These questions provide students with opportunities to connect social scientific perspectives to their personal experiences.

In our classrooms, heterosexual and cisgender students offer us hope in that they support equal rights for lesbian, gay, bisexual, transgender, and queer (LGBTQ) sexualities and gender identities. Often, these students quickly recognize discrimination experienced by others and identify the unfairness of presumptions that queer individuals are abnormal, but our students do not usually notice how they personally benefit from the privilege of having their sexual and gender identity commonly considered to be "normal." Our focus in *Seeing Straight: An Introduction to Gender and Sexual Privilege* gives students—regardless of gender or sexual identity—tools to engage in respectful, thoughtful discussion of fundamental social and political changes necessary for justice.

The first three chapters help readers to build vocabulary and theoretical foundations on which to base a critical discussion of gender and sexuality. In chapter 1, we introduce a social constructionist perspective. We distinguish biological sex from gender, both of which, we explain, are distinct from sexual desire and sexual behavior. This book challenges binary thinking about sex, about gender, and about sexuality. Through recognition of individuals who are intersex, we reject sex as a binary. We describe cultures that recognize more than two genders. Binary thinking, which would simplify sexuality into heterosexual or queer, is challenged, for example, by recognition of asexual identity.

Beginning in chapter 1 and continuing across multiple chapters, we explore conceptions of what is "normal" and abnormal in a family. And, again and again, we consider the power and privilege that comes with being understood to be normal. Within explanation of shifting perspectives on queer sexuality, *Seeing Straight* includes descriptions of Sigmund Freud's powerful theoretical contribution and Alfred Charles Kinsey's prescient empirical work.

Chapter 2 draws on the works of Peggy McIntosh and Michael S. Kimmel to clarify the concept of privilege. We inspect social norms, institutions, and ideology with a focus on Adrienne Rich's conceptualization of compulsory heterosexuality. Romantic love is compared to sexual desire. Readers are encouraged to make thoughtful choices to use respectful language, and we explain our choice to use LGBTQ and queer as inclusive terms.

By chapter 3, we prepare our readers to explore the theory of cultural materialism by examining and unpacking quotes from Michael Warner and Judith Lorber on heteronormativity. Terminology, such as heterosexism and microaggression, is placed in a historical context. Gender as performance is explained with clear references to Judith Butler and to Candace West and Don H. Zimmerman. We introduce Michel Foucault's theory of normalization and evaluate the metaphorical closet as it relates to Erving Goffman's work on stigma.

In the following chapters, we apply the theoretical concepts to contemporary institutions. Chapter 4 offers further challenges to dualistic thinking and to heteronormativity. The roles of LGBTQ centers as safe havens are described. We present a sex-positive perspective on the potential of sex work, for some individuals, to be an avenue for empowerment. The NCAA's guidelines for inclusion of transgender athletes are celebrated as exemplary. In chapter 5, we focus on the social institutions of the military, law, and religion. Policy and legislation reveal historical privilege and discrimination but also potential for an inclusive present and future. Chapter 6 analyzes popular culture and media myths about normality, sexual agency, and sexual objectification. Film and television portrayals of queer lives—past and present—reveal implicit and explicit messages about gender and sexuality. Diversity within feminism is presented through contrasting perspectives on pornography. Readers are encouraged to set personal standards for clear communication regarding sexual consent.

We acknowledge that the examination of violence and aggression in chapter 7 may be emotionally challenging for readers. Readers are likely to feel painful connections to bullying and other forms of violence examined in the chapter. Many college students in the United States have experienced or deeply care about someone who has experienced relational aggression, intimate partner violence, or sexual aggression. Sadly, mass killings of queer people range from the state-sponsored violence of the Nazi regime to the mass shooting at a nightclub in Orlando, Florida, in 2016. Reading Leelah Alcorn's suicide note, which she posted online to reveal the horrors of conversion therapy, is heartbreaking.

As social scientists, we maintain that an understanding of the problems of violence is important for discovering solutions. Chapter 8 offers a celebration of successes in feminism and queer rights movements, as well as a call to social action. Throughout the book, we hope readers enjoy meeting some of the courageous, brilliant, and fabulous people who model for us a demand for justice. It is on their shoulders we stand.

I

PRIVILEGED THINKING

Sex, Gender, and Sexuality

We invite readers to imagine meeting a nine-year-old child. How quickly do you think you would make an assumption about the person's sex? At first meeting, regardless of age, a person is likely to be clothed, and therefore primary sexual characteristics are not visible. A child of age nine is unlikely to show secondary sexual characteristics that develop at puberty, such as full breasts (which are more likely but not exclusively traits of females) or facial hair (a trait more often associated with men but one that can develop for women). Assumptions about a person's sex are often based on cultural markers for gender.

For example, hair, whether it is long or short, acts as a primary clue of a person's gender in our society. From around age eight to age twelve, a boy close to the authors wore his thick, brown hair long. When Isaiah had long hair, people regularly assumed that he was a girl. If Isaiah gently corrected someone, often the person in error would be quite upset by the mistake, apologizing profusely. People seemed to think that it would—or should—bother Isaiah very much to have them get his sex and gender wrong. Nonetheless, Isaiah did not mind being considered a girl—or a boy. Neither was an insult, and he was fine with either one.

In the current culture of the United States, there are strong, unwritten rules for socially acceptable displays of masculinity.[1] Boys and men are expected to express gender in a way that avoids any semblance of femininity. While changing fashions might make long hair on a boy more or less acceptable, a boy is expected to be recognizable as a boy, even if he wears his hair long. A boy mistaken for being a girl is expected to take offense.

Because it seemed to bother people so much when they mistook him for a girl and he corrected them, Isaiah decided to stop correcting people in most cases. For example, if he judged that he was unlikely to have an ongoing relationship, Isaiah decided it was easier and kinder to go with whichever gender assumption the new person made about him.

In one striking example, Isaiah signed up to run a one-mile competitive race. Because awards would be given to the fastest boy and the fastest girl, the registration form included check boxes to indicate male or female sex. A woman helping to organize the race offered to register Isaiah. Given what happened next, we assume that she perceived him as a girl as soon as he approached the registration table.

The woman patiently listened to Isaiah spell his name for her and accurately transcribed it. Masculine or feminine names often indicate sex and gender, but it seems Isaiah's traditionally masculine name did not sufficiently challenge the woman's assumption. After writing his name, she checked the box for female without asking for his sex. Because sex of the runners factored into the rules for the race, Isaiah judged that he should politely correct the woman. Consistent with his anticipation, she seemed disconcerted and upset about her error as she crossed out her checkmark. A moment later she was distracted by a question from another contestant. When she returned to Isaiah and his registration form, she looked confused at her own mark and circled the female box. Apparently, Isaiah's hair continued to indicate for her that he was a girl.

When meeting a new child or adult, we effortlessly use social cues, such as hairstyle and clothing, and biological traits, including shape and size, to make assumptions about the person's sex and gender. Infants are sometimes dressed to provide social cues about femininity or masculinity—a headband with a big bow for a girl or an outfit that looks like a miniature football uniform for a boy.

When a person's sex and gender are not immediately obvious, many people find it disconcerting. Social expectations for interacting with boys differ from how one is expected to interact with girls.[2] We act differently toward women than we do toward men. When sex and gender are unknown, normatively appropriate social interaction is unclear. When introduced to an infant dressed in yellow or green, we often ask, "Is it a boy or a girl?" Looking closely at the first part of the question, "it" is used to refer to a human being with the implication that one is an object—an "it"—until the person's sex is known (or assumed). The second part of the question suggests that all infants are easily classified into one of two clear categories—male or female.

In the United States, if a baby is born with a vagina, she is understood to be female and normatively expected to have the gender of a girl. Babies with penises are identified as male and assigned the gender of boy. It is normative to assume that human infants with vaginas will one day be sexually attracted to humans with penises, and vice versa. As we will further describe in chapter 2, the word *normative* refers to what people in a given society assume to be normal. What people assume to be normal is not necessarily normal, or natural, or correct. In other words, the normative assumption maintains that an infant's sex (vagina or penis) corresponds to gender (girl or boy) and sexual orientation (desiring the other sex). Yet in human experience, this assumed link between genitals, gender, and sexual orientation does not necessarily bear out.[3]

Sex is a biological category that is socially understood, in the United States and many other cultures, to be critically important—central to who one is and simple to categorize as male or female. *Gender* is social and psychological—an aspect of how an individual is perceived within social groups, how one is expected to interact, and how one comes to understand oneself. *Cisgender* individuals identify with a gender that is normative for their biological sex—as occurs when biological females identify as girls and women, and when biological males identify as boys and men. *Transgender, trans,* or *trans** are terms that describe people whose gender identity challenges traditional notions for the biological sex identified at their birth.[4] For example, *transgender men* or *trans men* are people who were born with vaginas or intersex genitals who identify with masculine gender.[5] *Genderqueer* people do not identify as traditionally masculine or feminine. For example, genderqueer activist Mattilda Bernstein Sycamore expresses gender through choices of clothing and hairstyle that challenge the notion that people neatly fit into either a masculine category or a feminine category. In other words, Sycamore disrupts a *binary conception of gender*—an assumption that gender has exactly two categories and that every person fits neatly into one of the two. *Gender-fluid* individuals experience gender identity in different ways across situations. DJ Ruby Rose's short film *Break Free* explores gender-fluid identity by showing a person transition in a matter of minutes from a woman to a man. People who identify as *bigender* experience their gender as both masculine and feminine, either at different times or simultaneously. People who do not experience themselves as having gender, such as rap artist Angel Haze, might identify as *agender*.

We will focus on two of the competing perspectives about gender and sexuality. We will critique an *essentialist perspective* (sometimes called *deterministic perspective*), which suggests that gender and sexuality are simple, central, and immutable. In contrast, we will present evidence that supports a *social constructionist perspective* that gender and sexuality are responses of the individual to cultural pressures and expectations of the social environment. Individuals experience their own feelings and desires, and their responses to cultural pressures and expectations range from completely accepting the assumptions of the culture as normal to fully rejecting the pressures and expectations, and therefore facing the social consequences.

Feminist psychologist Sandra Lipsitz Bem and social psychologist Daryl Bem applied a critical social constructionist perspective to parenting. Beginning with the birth of their first child in 1974, the Bems raised their daughter and son in ways that allowed the children to express gender as they chose. Compared to the norms of the culture in the United States, the Bems' parenting choices introduced more options for each gender. One of their techniques for challenging essentialist thinking about gender was to use art supplies to alter the books they read to their children so that a prince in peril was saved by a brave princess as often as a princess was saved by a prince. They regularly communicated with their children about biological sex and gender, which helped the children to understand these concepts and to resist stereotypes that pressure boys to act one way and girls to behave in an opposite way.

Developmental psychologists demonstrate that children predictably develop cognitive skills, including understanding of the concepts of boy and girl, at specific points of maturation. With patient guidance from an adult, children can often master a skill more quickly than their peers.

Children around the age of four tend not to be able to mentally reverse an action. As an example, please imagine a situation in which an adult wants to give juice to two thirsty children—one aged four and the other seven. There is just enough juice in the container for a small serving for each child, and there are two glasses available—one is wider, the other taller. Because of the children's past concerns regarding fairness, the adult finds a measuring cup and carefully measures an equal portion for each child. The cognitive maturation of a typical seven-year-old yields the ability to mentally reverse an action. In this case, the seven-year-old can imagine pouring the juice back into the measuring cup and therefore understands that the taller cup has the same amount of juice as the wider cup. If readers ever face a situation like this, our advice is to allow the four-year-old to select between the glasses. The four-year-old is unlikely to be able to mentally reverse the pouring of the juice into the glass and therefore is likely to perceive one of the two glasses as containing more juice. A typical four-year-old can focus on one aspect—height or width—but is unlikely to be able to take both into account at the same time. A patient adult could help a four-year-old to master the concept that the amount of liquid stays constant even as its shape changes in different containers, but the children in this scenario are thirsty.[6]

The Bems worked with their children to understand sex and gender, including *gender constancy*, the cognitive ability to mentally reverse actions that might affect perceptions of gender. For example, mastering gender constancy would mean understanding that a boy who dresses one time in feminine attire is still a boy. One day their son, Jeremy, asked his mother to put barrettes (decorative hair clips) in his hair. At his preschool, another boy had not mastered gender constancy and had very strong feelings about feminine attire. The teacher later shared the following with Sandra Lipsitz Bem: "Several times that day, another little boy had asserted that Jeremy must be a girl, not a boy, because 'only girls wear barrettes.'" Jeremy insisted multiple times, "Wearing barrettes doesn't matter; I have a penis and testicles." Eventually Jeremy "pulled down his pants to make his point more convincingly. The other boy was not impressed. He simply said, 'Everybody has a penis; only girls wear barrettes.'"[7] Sometimes one side of an argument has all the evidence in its favor, but it is impossible to prevail if the other side is not ready to understand. In this case, essentialist thinking about barrettes has no reliable evidence to support it, but an essentialist thinker is unready to hear or see young Bem's evidence regarding the social construction of barrettes as gendered behavior.

Feminist psychologist Janice D. Yoder shares a story about trying to teach the concept of gender constancy to her son: "Dan, at age 3 declared that he wanted to be a mom when he grew up (undaunted by the fact that he'd have to change his sex). When we challenged him on this, he thought for a moment and conceded that if he couldn't be a mother, he'd settle for being a lion."[8] While the queer rights movement has opened ways that a boy might grow up to be a mom, we share Yoder's confusion about how to even begin to address a child's lack of species constancy! We find social constructionist arguments about family roles and gender identity to be valuable, but in comparison to young Dan Yoder, we might be essentialist thinkers when it comes to species identification.

Although we will highlight the two opposing perspectives of essentialism and social construction, we do not mean to imply that there are only two points of view. We invite readers to explore gender and sexuality as complicated and nuanced. We will challenge arguments that use a false binary, or *dualism*, to present a complicated matter in an overly simplified way. Binary, or dualistic, thinking suggests that an issue can be understood in terms of exactly two straightforward and contrasting categories. We strive to reveal that gender, sexuality, and even sex should not be treated as binary; none of these are truly dualisms. Indeed, we will recognize that there are more than just two genders, that sexuality is more complex than can be captured by suggesting that people are either heterosexual or not, and that there are more than two sexes.

THE BIOLOGY AND SOCIAL UNDERSTANDING OF SEX

Biological sex is often presented as a straightforward binary. In simplified descriptions, the twenty-third chromosome in the ovum of the biological mother is always a single X, and the twenty-third chromosome of the biological father's sperm is either a single Y to create a male (XY) or a single X to produce a female (XX). Binary thinking about sex ignores genetic variations that occur in an estimated seventeen of out every one thousand births.[9] Individuals traditionally classified as male might receive two Y chromosomes from their father (XYY) or two X chromosomes from their mother (XXY, Klinefelter syndrome). Individuals traditionally classified as female might receive two X chromosomes from one of the parents (XXX) or a partial or completely missing twenty-third chromosome from either parent (XO, Turner syndrome).[10]

Variations can result in individuals who are *intersex*—difficult to classify as either male or female. Biologist and women's studies scholar Anne Fausto-Sterling estimates that approximately one of every thousand or two thousand births defies the binary conceptualization of male and female. For example, congenital adrenal hyperplasia "leads to a baby with masculinized external genitalia who possesses two X chromosomes and the internal reproductive organs of a potentially fertile woman."[11] Treating sex as a male-female binary ignores the evidence of human diversity.

Traditionally in western culture,[12] individuals who were not easily classified as male or female would be assigned to one of the two sexes. Surgery and hormone treatments have often been prescribed in an attempt to force individuals to fit into a false binary. Later in the book, we will identify ways that this has been deeply problematic.

THE SOCIOLOGY AND PSYCHOLOGY OF GENDER

Sex is a matter of social interpretations of genes, organs, and hormones (a matter that is more complicated than is often acknowledged). In contrast, gender is sociological and psychological, related to social interactions and personal identity, including how one engages with the social world and understands oneself.[13] Similar to sex, gender has been traditionally treated as a binary, breaking people into boys or girls, men or women. Some transgender activists have challenged this categorization by expressing gender in ways that defy traditional masculinity or femininity. As noted above, Sycamore expresses her trans identity through her choices of clothing and hairstyle in ways that force passersby to recognize that not all people in the United States desire to fit clearly into a stereotypical masculine or feminine expression of gender.

We agree with social constructionist arguments regarding gender identity, that is, that expression of gender is connected to culture and historic time. In some cultures, only two genders are acknowledged, and all individuals are assumed to fit into the expectations of one.[14] Other cultures recognize more than two genders, such as the socially accepted fa'afafine of Samoa[15] or the often-derogated hijras of India.[16]

What it means to be a given gender can be remarkably different across cultures. As early as 1935, anthropologist Margaret Mead revealed dramatically different expectations of what it means to be a man or a woman across diverse groups. For example, in her study of cultural groups in New Guinea, she highlighted three groups that perform gender very differently than in the contemporary United States. Both women and men of the Arapesh had traits that might be considered stereotypically feminine when compared to expectations in the United States. Men and women cared for children and focused on being sensitive to the needs of others. In contrast, women as well as men of the Mundugumor displayed violence and withheld emotional expression. In a third group, the Tchambuli, men and women played very different gender roles from each other and from expectations of men and women in the United States. Tchambuli women were assertive, whereas the men were submissive.[17]

In addition to cultural differences, expectations regarding gender can vary considerably within a given culture over historical time. For example, today in the United States, there are many more socially acceptable careers for middle-class mothers than there were decades ago, when these women were expected to forgo a career to focus on raising children. Cultural and historical differences reveal diversity in the understanding of and expectations for each gender.

In contrast to the social constructionist view on gender, the essentialist perspective suggests that gender is determined by biological sex. Alternatively, social constructionists note that gender is an interaction between an individual and the compelling power of the social world regarding what is accepted and what is derogated.[18] Within a given culture at a given time, certain ways of expressing gender will be encouraged while others will be discouraged. Individuals perform gender within cultural constraints, sometimes defying social pressure.

At this time in the United States, the *hegemonic form of masculinity* demands that boys and men convey gender—be gendered—in a way that is expressed as the opposite of femininity. This conceptualization of masculinity is based on false binary thinking about gender. Given that boys are often raised primarily by women, young boys often develop their masculinity by doing the opposite of what they see their feminine caretakers doing. Their male peers and cisgender, heterosexual men in their lives tend both to value and promote this antifeminine form of masculinity.[19] Mothers, regardless of their sexual identity, and queer fathers often encourage hegemonic masculinity because they want their sons to fit in and be perceived as normal.[20]

Boys and men who fulfill the demands of hegemonic masculinity are often privileged with the respect of other boys and men, while those who reject cultural pressures, or who fail to meet the expectations of masculinity, risk bullying and bashing that range from ridicule to violent attacks.[21] Isaiah experienced mild bullying in instances when other students, passing him in the hall on their way to class, shouted at him to cut his hair. Isaiah challenged the demands of hegemonic masculinity merely by growing his hair.

David Shneer and Caryn Aviv have focused their scholarship on lesbian, gay, bisexual, transgender, and queer experiences. They note that assumptions about a person's sexuality are often made based on how that person expresses gender, rather than knowledge regarding the person's sexual attraction.[22] Any hint of femininity in a boy's way of walking, speaking, or interacting with friends might give the impression of homosexuality. Pressures toward hegemonic masculinity are based on assumptions that gender reveals sexuality.[23] In contrast, we argue that gender and sexuality are separate constructs.[24]

Hegemonic masculinity confines boys and men. In gender studies classes, our students have told us that two men who are friends with each other might cancel their plans if they cannot find a third person to join them, for fear that others might mistake them as a romantic couple. The two women authors of this text enjoy attending films together when our busy schedules allow us this treat. We often sit elbow to elbow without any concern for how this might appear. It is ideal for sharing popcorn. But our students tell us that two men will keep an empty seat between them so that they will not be mistaken as a gay couple.

Tragically, hegemonic masculinity often encourages boys and men to act violently to demonstrate their masculinity. Antiviolence activists Jackson Katz and Byron Hurt emphasize the importance of challenging men to think critically about the confining demands of hegemonic masculinity. Through their Mentors in Violence Prevention Project, they work with male college athletes—often meeting in locker rooms—to encourage men to consider ways they can be authentic to themselves and more caring. Through this program, college athletes can become mentors who spread this critical thinking about masculinity to youth.[25] Social movements and support groups can create environments that transform lives.

A TRAGIC CASE STUDY: ENFORCING SEX AND GENDER AS BINARY

Interventions such as the Mentors in Violence Prevention Project can be the focus of research to see how changing one or more aspects of a situation can influence thoughts, feelings, and behavior across large groups. In contrast, the *case study* is a detailed examination of the complexities of a single individual, group, or event. The case study may be applied when an extreme or highly unusual situation occurs. In some cases, an individual has experienced an event that no ethical researcher could ever create but that might reveal valuable information. Caution must be used when attempting to draw conclusions about human nature from a single person, especially one whose experience is unlike those of others.

Before their infant son's catastrophic accident, the Reimer family of Winnipeg, Manitoba, Canada, would have been perceived as a normal family and perhaps of little interest for a case study. Janet and Ron Reimer were a married couple and the parents of identical twin boys, Bruce and Brian Reimer, who were born in 1965. At seven months old, the infant boys were scheduled for routine circumcisions. Bruce was the first of the twins to undergo the procedure. Disastrously, the equipment—a cauterizing tool that used electrical current—malfunctioned and burned off Bruce's penis. Twin brother Brian was spared from the procedure.[26]

Bruce's parents searched for advice regarding the best way to help their injured child. Months later, Bruce's mother became hopeful when she saw psychologist John Money and a transgender woman interviewed on television. Money confidently discussed this woman's satisfaction in transitioning from being a man to a woman. Bruce's mother wrote to Money to see whether he might be able to help her family.

Money was confident that he could solve the Reimer family's problem. Like contemporary gender studies scholars with a social constructionist perspective, Money and his colleagues argued that the biological category of sex is distinct from the cultural, social, and psychological concept of gender.[27] Sex is an issue of how chromosomes relate to genitals, organs of reproduction, and hormones. Gender develops through socialization within a culture and includes one's understanding of the self in terms of masculinity and femininity as well as the assumptions of others regarding these concepts.[28]

Unlike today's social constructionists, Money enforced binary thinking about gender, and he did not recognize the role of the individual in the development of gender. In terms of binary thinking, Money was a person of his time; he assumed gender should be performed and understood as either masculine or feminine. In contrast, contemporary social constructionists recognize genderqueer identity. Further, the social constructionist perspective now perceives gender development as an interaction between an individual and the social demands of the historical moment, culture, and family. Money did not anticipate the role of Bruce Reimer as an individual in the development of gender identity.

Money convinced Bruce's parents that their injured child would be more likely to live a happy life if raised as a girl rather than as a boy. Money and his colleagues in psychiatry, Joan G. Hampson and John L. Hampson, argued that any individual can develop successfully into either masculine or feminine gender if treated consistently as that gender, as long as this assignment occurs no later than eighteen months of age.[29] At seventeen months old, Bruce was renamed Brenda. Four months later, the child's testicles were removed as a first step toward surgical reassignment to female sex, with plans for further surgery and hormone treatments when Brenda reached puberty. Money emphasized that it was critically important to be consistent in raising Brenda as a girl. She must never know that she started life as Brian's identical twin brother.

Because of challenges raised by the intersex rights movement and support from social constructionists who recognize that gender develops as an individual response to historical, cultural, and familial demands, Money's approach would not be followed today. Rather than insisting on quick surgery to remove the gonads and insistence on raising the child as a girl, the Reimer family would be offered multiple

options. Given the catastrophic damage to the penis, the option of raising the child as a girl would likely be suggested today with the understanding that the child's gender development might not conform to
social demands. Therapy would encourage self-discovery of the child's
gender. Progressive therapists would be open to any of multiple gender
identities, such as genderqueer, masculine, or feminine. Any surgery
would be performed only at puberty or later, and then only with the
assent of the adolescent.

In contrast, for decades starting in the 1950s, the sex and gender
binary was strictly enforced, and the role of the individual in the social
construction of gender was ignored. The argument that an individual
could be assigned either gender was the basis for sex-reassignment
surgery for many intersex infants. When an individual was born with
external genitals that did not match the gonads, Money and colleagues
advocated for physicians to make a decision based on what surgery
would have the greatest likelihood of clearly assigning either male or
female sex. Physicians were encouraged to tell parents of intersex infants that nature intended for the child to be a boy or to be a girl and
that surgery would finish the job. For example, physicians might have
insisted on removing an unusually long clitoris. While removing sensitive tissues became less common over the decades, early surgical reassignment—based largely on the arguments of Money and colleagues—
continued until challenged by a movement of intersex individuals and
their advocates.

In 1973, when the Reimer twins were nine years old, Money published a case study in which he claimed that Brenda's sex reassignment
had been completely successful. In his writing, Money used the
pseudonym of John/Joan to protect Brenda's identity. In contrast to
Money's published claim, Brenda was deeply unhappy. At thirteen
years old, Brenda refused further visits with Money. Her parents eventually confessed that she was born male. Just weeks after learning she
had once been Bruce, Brenda became David. David chose to undergo
procedures to produce male physiological characteristics. As an adult,
he married a woman and adopted the children she mothered prior to
their relationship.

Money and colleagues' belief that gender is malleable was not shak-
en by the revelation that Brenda Reimer became David. Money
switched from focusing on the John/Joan case as the strongest evidence

of gender malleability to arguing that the Reimer family must not have been successful in consistently raising Brenda as a girl. To combat Money's claims, as an adult, David Reimer spoke anonymously about his experience multiple times. Journalist John Colapinto, a gender essentialist, was attracted to David's story as evidence that sex determines gender. In other words, essentialists such as Colapinto argue that Bruce was born with a penis, and that is why David became a man. In contrast, as social constructionists, we argue that Reimer's gender developed within a social system that demanded femininity. Research with trans individuals reveals that it is not terribly unusual for an individual to develop gender that does not match social demands.

Colapinto pressed David to break his anonymity and reveal his identity.[30] Unlike the happy trans woman who gave David's mother hope, David struggled with deep unhappiness. At age thirty-eight, David was mourning his brother Brian, who had died of a drug overdose two years earlier. David and his wife separated; he lost his job. When David's parents heard the news that he had committed suicide, they were devastated.

As noted above, the intersex rights movement has advocated for physicians to listen to the experiences of intersex individuals who were assigned a binary sex and gender as infants. Medical ethicist Laurence B. McCullough encourages physicians to fully inform parents regarding their child's physical condition and to focus on therapy rather than quick surgery.[31] Fausto-Sterling discourages surgery before puberty except when required for the child's physical health. She argues that physicians working with parents might choose to socially categorize an intersex individual as a boy or as a girl, but they should be aware that social construction reveals the individual's role in developing gender in response to social demands.

THEORIES OF SEXUALITY

When describing gender and sexuality, we will use *queer* as an inclusive term that encompasses not only diverse expressions of sexuality but also nonnormative gender. Shneer and Aviv traced the history and contemporary use of the term queer from playful by insiders in the early 1900s through derisive by outsiders in the 1950s and to resurgence among activists and theorists in the 1980s. "Queer theory encourages people to look at things differently, invites readers to pick up on subtle cues, unpack hidden messages, and make texts more complicated. Others have taken the word 'queer' as an identity label and a politics, a way of making an epithet yelled at someone on the playground into a word that screams 'We're different, that's good, and if you don't like it, that's your problem.'"[32]

If asked to define *sexuality*, to what extent would you include sexual desire, sexual experience, and romantic love in your definition? In chapter 2, we will explore the example of normatively acceptable romantic love between women in the late nineteenth century. Yet within that social and historical context, heterosexual oral or anal sexual activity would have been considered deviant—one might even say queer.[33] Following the sexual revolution of the second half of the twentieth century, heterosexual oral sex is a prevalent form of sexual activity in the United States. Today, heterosexual anal sex is not uncommon.[34] As you develop your definition of sexuality, we invite you to consider social constructionist evidence that understanding of sexuality shifts across historical time and culture. We further challenge readers to consider the complexity of sexuality. We encourage individuals to avoid binary thinking that suggests people are either queer or heterosexual, with the category of queer encompassing anyone who does not fit a narrow definition of what it means to be heterosexual and cisgender.[35] We argue that sexuality is much too complicated for binary classification.

If asked to determine who is heterosexual, who is queer, and who defies binary classification, is sexual activity with a person of the same gender sufficient to identify someone as queer? Campaigns seeking to encourage condom use among men who meet for anonymous sex have been more successful if they use the words "men who have sex with men" than if they refer to "gay" men. Public health advocates Gary Goldbaum, Thomas Perdue, and Donna Higgins identified seventy-three categories of men who have sex with men while not identifying as gay.[36] Will your definition of sexuality allow individuals the right to define their own sexual identity?

HISTORICAL SHIFTS IN THINKING ABOUT SEXUALITY

As best as research can tell, those whom today we call queer have always been around. Only the terminology, social understandings, and historical context of queerness have changed. As journalist and historian Neil Miller notes, there is "rich documentation of the 'ancestors' of the modern homosexual."[37] In ancient times and around the globe, we have extensive evidence of people who took part in same-sex sexual relations, who lived in a gender role that did not correspond to social expectations for the sex assigned to them at birth, and who took members of their own sex and/or gender as husbands or wives. In many cultures, it seems that queer people were not understood to be "queer," different, or deviant. For example, Miller writes,

> In general, it can be assumed that the gay prototypes of antiquity did not view themselves as a minority (and in ancient Athens, they were apparently *not* a minority). They were not stigmatized, not perceived as different or deviant. Above all, they were not defined by their sexual orientation or attractions; the homosexual of the ancient world was Everyman, not a specific "type."[38]

In later years, starting around 1300, historian John Boswell argues,[39] Christian churches used their power to place bans on "sodomy" that were "rigorously enforced" and "gay subcultures that may have been more similar to our own were repressed and forced underground."[40] In Europe, homosexuality became a sin—against God and against the church.

As a founder of *queer theory*, social theorist Michel Foucault challenges binary thinking about sexuality. Foucault notes that slowly, sexuality became a topic of obsessive discourse in the form of the religious confession. Foucault writes that the church imposed "meticulous rules of self-examination" and "attributed more and more importance in penance."[41] Whereas we often think of sexuality in the nineteenth-century western hemisphere as restricted, in particular kinds of conversations like that of the confession, people reviewed their own sexual experiences and desires—be they mere dreams or physical sensations—near compulsively. Foucault argues that the "guiding principle" regarding sexual experience and desire of the past several centuries "was the fact of recounting them all, and in detail, from day to day." This guiding principle was "lodged in the heart of modern man."[42] Thus Foucault continues, "Toward the beginning of the eighteenth century, there emerged a political, economic, and technical incitement to talk about sex."[43]

From sinful, sexuality moved easily to criminal in Europe and the United States. Indeed, one of the early demands of queer people, and others interested in queer causes, involved abolishing laws that criminalized sexual acts understood to be queer. The very language used to describe queer people developed around the goal of decriminalization of queer sexual relations. A German-Hungarian man, Karl Maria Kertbeny, campaigning for the "abolition of Prussia's laws that criminalized sexual relations between men," first used the term "homosexuality" in 1869.[44]

At times more restrictive and at times less so, laws have supported broad social abuses against nonnormative sexuality in the United States. Early in the making of the nation, states invested immense energy and attention in defining and identifying "sodomy," and ensuring it was criminal. Sodomy laws banned a diversity of sexual acts at different times and places (further discussed in chapter 2). For example, in Virginia, the death penalty was the maximum punishment for sodomy. In 1779, Thomas Jefferson proposed a reform. Rather than the death penalty, Jefferson suggested castration as the harshest punishment for men convicted of sodomy. Ultimately, the state of Virginia opted to maintain the option of the death penalty.[45]

Usually the idea behind the laws was to criminalize sexuality between people of the same sex, but these laws could apply to any sexual acts other than those intended by heterosexual married couples for procreation. It was a legal problem to determine which sexual acts were criminal and whether these acts were criminal only with same-sex partners or whether the acts were criminal without regard to who did them. So in the nineteenth-century United States, while oral sex between any pair of adults was criminal in some places, legal opinions commonly determined that sodomy laws did not apply to oral sex.[46] When the law was interpreted this way, ostensibly everyone could have oral sex without fear of legal repercussions. Some states responded by creating laws that specifically identified certain sexual acts, such as oral sex, as criminal behavior. For example, in the 1930s Michigan revised its penal code twice to specify that "gross indecency"—including oral sex—was a felony. In 1931, "gross indecency between male persons" was codified. In 1939, "gross indecency between female persons" and "between male and female persons" were added so that any oral sex between any persons could be punishable by up to five years in jail or a hefty fine.[47]

A century and a half later in Europe, when the Nazis persecuted queer people, they did so under the rubric of Paragraph 175, a German law enacted in 1871 that made "male homosexual acts" illegal.[48] This persecution is further discussed in chapter 7.

FROM CRIMINAL SIN TO ILLNESS

Foucault argues that over the course of the nineteenth century, people decreasingly referred to sodomy or sinful actions—what one does—and increasingly referred to homosexuals as a "kind" of person and a medical category. Foucault writes,

> As defined by the ancient civil or canonical codes, sodomy was a category of forbidden acts; their perpetrator was nothing more that the juridical subject of them. The nineteenth-century homosexual became a personage, a past, a case history, and a childhood, in addition to being a type of life, a life form. . . . The sodomite had been a temporary aberration; the homosexual was now a species.[49]

Thus before the nineteenth century, sodomy was an action committed by a person, not an aspect of the person. The acts were sinful but did not alter the perceived identity of the people involved. During the nineteenth century, ways of thinking changed, and the person who engaged in sodomy became something else, something distinct from other people, like a separate species. He or she became a "homosexual."

By the end of the nineteenth century, physician Henry Havelock Ellis, psychiatrist Richard von Krafft-Ebing, and other early sexologists were studying same-gender sexual interest as a medical or psychiatric condition.[50] Queer sexuality continued to socially evolve from being perceived as a chosen sin to an illness that involuntarily afflicted the person. This shift in ideological understandings of sexuality came with the hope of creating greater empathy for queer people, but the new way of thinking continued to suggest that something was deeply wrong with same-gender sexual interest.

Radclyffe Hall lived in England from 1880 to 1943. She identified as a lesbian or, in the language of her time, an invert. Notoriously, Hall dressed in the male clothing of her day and went by the name of John. Miller writes about Hall, "She was famous for her 'mannish' appearance—plain tailored jackets, ties and skirts; she wore a monocle and, at one point, smoked a pipe."[51] In our time, perhaps Hall would have transitioned and identified as a heterosexual trans man. In her time, sexuality and gender were treated as inherently linked rather than separate concepts. Many believed that the sexual orientation of homosexuality or inversion was the same thing as having a gender expression in opposition to one's genitals.

Already a well-known author when she wrote *The Well of Loneliness*,[52] Hall openly claimed her political agenda in producing what became "the most influential lesbian novel of the twentieth century."[53] As Miller notes, Hall communicated in a letter to her publisher, "I wrote the book from a deep sense of duty. . . . I am proud indeed to have taken up my pen in defence of those who are utterly defenceless, who being from birth set apart in accordance with some hidden scheme of Nature, need all the help that society can give them." In this work of fiction, Hall tells the story of Stephen Gordon, a woman in many ways like herself.

Before the character's birth, Stephen's family anticipated a boy, and for this reason Hall had them give the character a traditionally male name. Born into a wealthy and landed English family, Gordon expressed herself like a contemporary boy and had a childhood crush on one of her family's maids. Due to her inability to fit into her traditionally gendered world, Gordon grows up largely friendless and even unloved by her mother. However, Gordon did have a strong and close relationship with her father. He spent much time over the years of her childhood trying to understand his boy-like daughter. Through her father's eyes we learn about the progressive and influential work of sexologists, including Richard von Krafft-Ebing and Havelock Ellis.

The sexologists of the late nineteenth century theorized about the causes of queer sexuality. As noted above, Kertbeny coined "homosexuality," still in use today. Another sexologist, Karl Westphal, devised terms that were even more popular at the time. In binary thinking, an *invert* expressed the gender of the "opposite" sex—a man or a woman who performed gender "inversion." As noted above, gender expression was understood as inherently linked with sexuality. Although our contemporary social constructionist perspective challenges this thinking, we acknowledge the important historical role the sexologists played in helping to move popular thinking on queer lives from the realm of sinfulness to question queerness as a crime and to promote considering queerness as part of the medical sphere of illness.

In this time, there were a number of medical theories about the origins of homosexuality. Krafft-Ebing taught psychiatry at the University of Vienna in the late 1800s, and early in his career, he argued that homosexuality came from degeneracy. Albeit varying in its definition from one scientist to another, in general, degeneracy theory often held that disabilities—physical disabilities such as a cleft palate, intellectual disabilities like developmental delay, and psychiatric disabilities such as the then-common hysteria—sprang from a genetic decline in the familial lineage of a person. Krafft-Ebing argued that inverts or homosexuals were merely another example of the possible degeneration of humans. Krafft-Ebing claimed, "In almost all cases [of homosexuals] . . . where an examination of the physical and mental peculiarities of the ancestors and blood relations has been possible, neuroses, psychoses, degenerative signs etc. have been found in the families."[54] Later in his career, Krafft-Ebing argued that inversion sprang from "congenital anomaly" rather than from degeneration. Believing it to be a medical problem, Krafft-Ebing, like other sexologists, worked to decriminalize homosexuality.[55]

In contrast to Krafft-Ebing's work to understand homosexuality through science and scientific theorizing, Ellis focused on gaining social tolerance for homosexuals. Ellis published his comprehensive *Sexual Inversion* in English in 1897.[56] In it, Ellis argued that homosexuality was not a sin, crime, or disease. According to Ellis, homosexuality was simply an abnormality of nature that current inverts inherited from earlier inverts in their family. Ellis believed that between 1 and 10 percent of the population was homosexual. And Ellis's lesbian wife, Edith, was among them. (Ellis himself enjoyed nonnormative sexual experiences.[57] According to historian Peter Gay, "The most arousing sight, to [Ellis], was a woman urinating."[58])

Also in contrast to Krafft-Ebing and other sexologists of the time, Ellis did not believe male homosexuals were men with stereotypically female characteristics. In other words, Ellis believed that the sexuality of men might be inverted but that men's sexuality was not necessarily reflected in their expression of gender. Oddly however, he did believe (like other popular thinkers on the topic) that female homosexuals by and large expressed both inverted sexuality and inverted gender, that is, women like Radclyffe Hall, who behaved and dressed like men.[59] Miller notes that some of Ellis's views were amusing (as well as harmful), at least from today's perspective. For example, Ellis believed:

- Green is the favorite color of inverts (but not of the general population, who, according to Ellis, prefer blue or red).
- A large percentage of male inverts are unable to whistle (a manly trait, in Ellis's estimation); female inverts, on the other hand, can whistle "admirably."
- Inverts of both sexes are often characterized by youthfulness of appearance and childlike faces.[60]

Inspired by the writing of Ellis and Krafft-Ebing and her personal experience, Hall's semiautobiographical character, Gordon, referred to herself as an invert. Gordon had a long-term relationship with a woman named Mary Llewellyn, who in Gordon's terms was "normal." As was believed by many at the time, Hall indicated that inverts were often involved with non-inverts, "normal" people who happen to fall in love with an invert as though the invert were simply a member of the "other" sex.

Hall exposed the immense difficulty of living as a lesbian couple in the early twentieth century. She ended her novel with Gordon's tragic and selfless act of pushing Llewellyn away, away and into the arms of a male suitor so that Llewellyn can live a "normal" life free from the suffering born of facing profound social prejudice and isolation.

Albeit perhaps not the best writer in literary history,[61] Hall made an immensely courageous choice to speak out for queer people, people like herself. This is the only novel in which she explicitly explored queer themes, maybe disappointingly without any explicit sexuality. Even so, Hall faced a powerful backlash of social outrage. *The Well of Loneliness* was confronted with extensive legal battles, including an obscenity trial in the United Kingdom. The trial resulted in the order that all copies of the novel be destroyed. Perhaps in spite of the intentions of those persecuting Hall, the legal and highly public uproar made lesbianism

more, not less, visible. The unintentional publicity inspired more people to read Hall's novel and experience the presentation of lesbianism
as natural.

SIGMUND FREUD AND (QUEER) HUMAN DEVELOPMENT

The founder of psychoanalysis, Sigmund Freud, made a radical depar-
ture from other thinkers of his time on homosexuality. At the turn of
the twentieth century, in 1905, Freud wrote *Three Essays on the Theory of Sexuality*, including the first chapter of the book and his earliest
work on sexuality, "The Sexual Aberrations." In this work, Freud challenged the common idea of his time that homosexuality was a sign of
degeneracy in a family. Freud noted that inversion could be found in
otherwise "normal" people. Indeed, he argued many inverts are "distinguished by specially high intellectual development and ethical culture."
Thus he claimed that it was "impossible to regard inversion as a sign of
degeneracy."[62] Further, instead of the thinking of the time that sexuality was something set and inflexible, Freud believed that sexuality was a
"drive" and that it was shaped through the person's individual and social
development. Social theorist Nikki Sullivan writes, "Freud's work was
ground-breaking" insofar as he claimed that "heterosexuality (as a culturally and historically specific institution) may well be a cultural necessity, but it is not something that is naturally preordained."[63] About this
Freud wrote, "From the point of view of psychoanalysis the exclusive
sexual interest felt by men for women is also a problem that needs
elucidation and is not a self-evident fact based upon an attraction that is
ultimately of a chemical nature."[64]

FROM ABERRATION TO COMMON EXPERIENCE

In 1948, Alfred Charles Kinsey and his three research associates, Wardell B. Pomeroy, Clyde E. Martin, and Paul H. Gebhard, shook the
world with the publication of *Sexual Behavior in the Human Male*.
Kinsey, a biologist, and his associates interviewed thousands of men
about their sexual experiences and practices and, using their extensive
data, shattered conventional ideas about men's sexuality. Five years and

thousands of interviews later, Kinsey and his colleagues published the second volume from their study, *Sexual Behavior in the Human Female*. In all, Kinsey himself interviewed approximately eight thousand men and women about their sexual histories. Pomeroy interviewed another eight thousand or so, and Martin and Gebhard completed about two thousand interviews for a total of approximately eighteen thousand.[65] In these two enormous and enormously thorough books, Kinsey illuminated the gap between what people thought other people did sexually and what people actually said they themselves did.[66]

Before applying the scientific method to the study of human sexuality, Kinsey's meticulous studies of the gall wasp earned him recognition as a leading global authority on that animal. Regardless of many differences between his two primary subjects, gall wasps and humans, Kinsey's dedication to the scientific method was consistent across his career. He refused to take a moral position, examined his subjects calmly and rationally, and gathered enormous amounts of data. Indeed, Kinsey eventually gave his vast gall wasp collection to the American Museum of Natural History in New York, and it was "the largest collection of any kind ever given to that institution, numbering more than four million different specimens."[67]

Kinsey and colleagues' eighteen thousand in-depth interviews actually fell short of their goal to garner one hundred thousand human sexual histories.[68] Contemporary researchers with a goal of representing a group of interest—such as all men or all women in the United States—would likely employ a system of random sampling. A representative group can be constructed by recruiting participants in a way that ensures all relevant individuals have an equal chance of being selected. Kinsey's approach of amassing enormous amounts of information can be criticized because a large sample might not reflect the group of interest.

There existed one interesting similarity between Kinsey's wasps and his human participants: both are extremely hard to categorize. Each time he collected a new wasp, hoping to collect evidence of each major type, he struggled with locating the tiny creatures in categorical sets. Gall wasps, it turns out, come in endless variety. And so, it seems, does human sexuality. Kinsey found that humans do all kinds of things sexually. The possibilities of "normal" sexual behavior, he claimed, were endless. The more he studied, the more variety he found. And he argued that all the variety of sexual activity he encountered is healthy. The only limit Kinsey advocated was that the behavior be consensual.

Upsetting all kinds of mainstream ideas about human sexuality, Kinsey showed that women regularly had and regularly enjoyed having sex. Women as well as men had sexual relations outside of marriage. Twenty-five percent of women and 50 percent of men challenged marital monogamy in this way.[69] Further, both men and women took part in high rates of homosexual behavior. Kinsey revealed that behavior assumed to be an aberration was actually fairly common. Kinsey's findings included the following figures:

- 37 percent of the total male population has had at least some overt homosexual experience to the point of orgasm, since the onset of adolescence.
- 50 percent of males who remained single until age 35 have had overt homosexual experience to the point of orgasm. . . .
- 28 percent of females reported erotic responses to other females.
- 13 percent of females have achieved orgasm in homosexual relations, while 20 percent have had some homosexual experience.[70]

Kinsey asked his participants direct, face-to-face questions like, "How old were you the first time you had sexual contact with another person of your own sex?" His classification of "homosexual experience" came from the participant when she or he answered, for example, "Ten years old," and then upon further questioning described the homosexual experience. As his research progressed, Kinsey became increasingly convinced of how common homosexual behavior is among humans. About the commonness of homosexuality, Kinsey explained to a critic, "We are not particularly interested in any sexual aspect of human sex behavior. We are interested in the entire story. The homosexual is a very much larger portion of human sexual behavior than most people realize, and consequently, we have an abundance of data on it."[71]

Kinsey effectively revealed that homosexual behavior was much more common than people had believed. Kinsey divulged homosexuality to be normal in practice. Through demonstrating its commonness, Kinsey challenged the notion that homosexuality was pathological. Miller writes, "Could so many Americans—who were apparently having homosexual relations with regularity, at least at some point in their lives—really be 'sick'?"[72]

Kinsey developed a rating scale with eight categories ranging from zero to six plus a category labeled X, with zero being entirely heterosexual, six being entirely homosexual, and X for asexual individuals who had no sexual interest. Thus, Kinsey wrote, "Individuals are rated as 0's if all of their psychologic responses and all of their overt sexual activities are directed toward individuals of the opposite sex. Such individuals do not recognize any homosexual responses and do not engage in specifically homosexual activities."[73] Kinsey argued that most people would fall between zero and six if it were not for "social condemnation and legal penalties."[74] He noted:

> In our American culture there are no types of sexual activity which are as frequently condemned because they depart from the mores and the publicly pretended custom, as mouth-genital contacts and homosexual activities. There are practically no European groups, unless it be in England, and few if any other cultures elsewhere in the world which have become so disturbed over male homosexuality as we have here in the United States.[75]

Kinsey and his colleagues' research was revelatory. Queer behavior was much more common than many had assumed. Kinsey did not assume that queer behavior was a sin or an illness. His research team presented same-sex sexual interest and experience as normal variations in human desire and behavior.

ESSENTIALIST AND SOCIAL CONSTRUCTIONIST PERSPECTIVES ON SEXUALITY

A lasting legacy of the work of Kinsey and his colleagues is the seemingly endless variation they found in human sexuality. Some recent scientific approaches to studying sexuality have sought physical evidence that sexual behavior defined as queer in our culture is concretely located in physiology.[76] These researchers seem to want to support queer rights by demonstrating that the variation identified by Kinsey and colleagues is rooted in biology. Other activists for queer rights argue that the goal of acceptance for queer people hinges on acceptance of queer sexuality and queer gender expression as valid choices. Activists might argue biological evidence is irrelevant to the social movement for acceptance of queer people.

On the topic of gender, the essentialist perspective is problematic because men and women are boxed into limiting roles. Essentialism disregards evidence of social construction of gender, such as diversity in expectations for each gender across cultures and over historical time.[77] Yet when examining sexuality, some activists who promote greater rights for and acceptance of queer people have been drawn to essentialist arguments regarding sexuality that highlight evidence of same-sex sexual experience across cultures and over historical time. Essentialist arguments have claimed that diverse sexual desire and experience are normal because they are inherent. Other activists focus on social constructionist arguments to explore ways that culture and history influence the types of sexual interest and behavior that are considered normal or abnormal, and how individual understanding of sexuality develops within a social context.

The essentialist perspective has inspired research searching for genetic and other biological evidence for sexuality. Researchers have examined whether identical twins, who share all genes in common, are more likely to have the same sexual orientation than are fraternal twins of the same gender, who are no more genetically related than any two siblings. Biological evidence has been sought in structures of the brain by comparing men and women who identified as gay, lesbian, bisexual, or heterosexual.[78]

The essentialist perspective has often been perceived as consistent with men's reports of being aware of their sexual orientation from a young age and having consistent sexual desire for one gender, with fewer men identifying as bisexual than as gay. Yet the social constructionist perspective seems to offer a better explanation for women's reports of changes in their sexual identity over the course of their life and the greater number of women than men who identify as bisexual.[79] Developmental psychologist Phillip L. Hammack suggests an approach that integrates the essentialist and social constructionist perspectives— sexual desire is connected to biology yet influenced by cultural understandings of oneself within a social context.[80]

Acknowledging a socially constructed aspect to queer identity suggests that the rapid changes within our culture at this historical time will affect how people understand their own sexuality. While our culture still has much work to do to increase acceptance, a look at our recent past and hopes for our possible future help us to keep our present in perspective.

PERSPECTIVES

In our previous book, focusing on racism and white privilege,[81] we shared that we were dismayed by a conversation in which an academically successful college graduate admitted that she had never considered that real people write textbooks; she treated textbooks as "Truth" rather than as a perspective created by humans. We are keenly conscious throughout this book that we have the privilege of framing the arguments. While we have been careful to present information as clearly and accurately as possible, we acknowledge that our work—like that of all thinkers—will be influenced by our cultural understandings. Like all authors of textbooks (or writing of any form), we present a particular perspective and have selected to focus on specific issues.

As a genre, textbooks have a tendency to present material as though it is simple, objective fact. We take issue with this tendency. Indeed, we argue there is no way out of opinion in argument. Everyone's arguments, ideas, and claims—including ours in this book—are just that, arguments. We work to offer readers the clearest argument possible with strong supportive evidence as we seek to *problematize* issues of privilege, gender, and sexuality. We maintain that privileged perspectives often treat complex issues as though they are simple and straightforward.

Our goal is to challenge readers to critically examine expressions of gender and sexuality that have been privileged by major social institutions, including schools, workplaces, and religious organizations. We will expose laws and governmental support that have privileged heterosexual, cisgender men who perform masculinity in prescribed ways and heterosexual, cisgender women who conform to expectations of femininity. We will present evidence of privilege garnered through normative romantic attachments and expressions of sexual desire.

We invite you to carefully consider our arguments and to use this material to inform your own perspective. Given that these issues are complex, we acknowledge that your perspective may differ from ours. We recognize that some will disagree with us, and we look forward to an ongoing conversation.

DISCUSSION QUESTIONS

1. When you are asked on official documents to indicate your sex or your gender, such as at your school or workplace, are questions asked in a way that readily allows expression of nonbinary sex or gender? What assumptions are implied on these forms regarding binary sex and cisgender identity?

2. How might common cultural understandings of sexuality as a matter of biology and/or a matter of social construction influence social policy, such as the ability to marry, to foster parent, or to adopt? Historical and contemporary understandings vary in terms of assumptions about possible causes of sexual orientation, such as genes, early environmental influences outside of an individual's control, and individual choice. How might social constructionist or essentialist understandings of sexuality influence acceptance of queer individuals?

3. Given the description of the current intersex rights movement and current guidelines for treating intersex individuals, how do you think a case would be treated today if an infant boy's penis were physically destroyed in an accident?

4. Historical sexuality experts John Money, Sigmund Freud, and Alfred Charles Kinsey are briefly described in the chapter. Choose one of these figures and identify how he used his privileged status as an expert to influence thinking about sexuality. Does the evidence suggest that he sought to extend rights to those who have been stigmatized or to maintain privileged status for some groups over others?

5. In your perception, is women's sexuality understood to be more fluid than men's in the contemporary culture of the United States? What might this reveal about essentialism or social construction of sexuality? Why might heterosexual men be concerned about behaviors that culturally prompt observers to wonder whether they have sexual interest in another man?

6. What assumptions might you make if you saw two men sitting in adjacent seats at a movie theater? Would you make a different assumption than if you saw two women sitting next to each other? How do expectations about gender influence how we perceive behavior and how we choose to behave? Why is it not questioned for two women to spend time together while men face pressure to be seen in a group?

2

PRIVILEGED ASSUMPTIONS

Heterosexuality and the Normative Expression
of Gender

Shortly before he started to grow his hair long (as described in chapter 1), seven-year-old Isaiah was overheard reading a picture book about a farmer and the farmer's wife to his toddler sister, Lena. He regularly paused to explain the meaning of what he had read and discuss the family in the story. At one point he noted, "We know that the farmer's wife is a woman because 'wife' means woman, but the book does not tell us whether the farmer is a man or a woman." Isaiah's parents are committed to critically examining families as places where expectations about gender and sexuality are reproduced. Years of thoughtfully, patiently, and honestly answering Isaiah's questions about gender, family, and careers had culminated in this moment, revealing that this child did not assume heterosexuality or automatically assign a man to the term "farmer."

As you read the phrase "farmer and the farmer's wife," did you picture the farmer's gender? Both the authors of this text surmised immediately, without intentional bias, that the farmer was a man. Isaiah's response revealed that we automatically assumed heterosexuality and a traditional association of "farmer" as a man's role. Markie L. C. Blumer and Megan J. Murphy, marriage and family therapy experts, identify that assumptions regarding the normality of heterosexuality and of traditional gender roles are "so embedded in our language, laws, institutions, media, policies, and overall culture" that one must actively seek to become aware of unintentional bias in order to attempt to counteract it.[1] In Isaiah's case, his parents' dedicated work to counteract prevailing assumptions—to combat prejudice—yielded a truly open mind.

WHAT IS A (NORMAL) FAMILY?

One of the authors of this book, Jean Halley, regularly teaches a sociology course on the family. At the beginning of the semester, she asks the class how they define family. What does it mean to be a "normal" family? Who is included in this category? Do families always involve a married pair? Who should be allowed to marry? In years prior to the 2015 Supreme Court decision in favor of marriage equality, *Obergefell v. Hodges*, Halley asked students whether only heterosexual couples should be allowed to marry or whether we should allow couples to marry regardless of gender.

For some people, families are economic institutions, social structures that help people with their daily economic needs, food, housing, clothing, and the money needed to purchase these things. For some, families reproduce society. In families, people retreat from the work world, rest, and rejuvenate so as to go back to work again. And families produce the future workers. In families, children are born and raised and upon adulthood will enter the workforce and potentially make their own families. For many, an important function of family is as a place where one experiences intimacy and love. And for the mainstream United States, that love involves marriage.

Regarding marriage, legal scholar Martha Nussbaum argues:

> Marriage is both ubiquitous and central. All across our country, in every region, every social class, every race and ethnicity, every religion or non-religion, people get married. For many if not most people, moreover, marriage is not a trivial matter. It is key to the pursuit of happiness, something people aspire to—and keep aspiring to, again and again, even when their experience has been far from happy.[2]

As Nussbaum notes, "To be told 'You cannot get married' is thus to be excluded from one of the defining rituals of the American life cycle."[3] This issue, what is a family and who should be allowed to partake in this significant institution of marriage, is an important one in the larger political debates going on in our society. Although most people see marriage as central to family, what families are and what they mean vary across political, religious, and cultural groups in the United States. We will continue to explore families and these debates in this text.

SOCIAL NORMS AND INSTITUTIONS

Social psychologist Muzafer Sherif defined *social norms* as "values, customs, stereotypes, conventions."[4] Norms are socially constructed from interactions and relationships within a group and become expected ways of thinking, feeling, or behaving that express the group's social values.[5] Social psychologists identify *injunctive norms*—ideals for how a person should feel, believe, or behave based on what is accepted within a social group or expected within a society—and *descriptive norms*—common social perceptions of the ways individuals in a group regularly feel, believe, and behave.[6] Individuals often face a conflict when reconciling injunctive norms, which describe what ought to be, with the descriptive norms of what is known to typically happen. For example, injunctive norms suggest that a person's wedding day should be one of the most joyous of one's life, but descriptive norms acknowledge that many people feel stressed about the details and frustrated with common mishaps at their wedding.

Injunctive and descriptive norms can be distinct from common but unacknowledged practice. The sexuality research of Alfred Charles Kinsey and his colleagues in the 1940s and 1950s (described in chapter 1) exposed that private experience often contradicted injunctive norms that one ought to desire and experience sexual behavior only within heterosexual, married couplings and descriptive norms that assumed heterosexuality and sexual activity only after marriage. In contrast, the interviews revealed that same-sex erotic feelings and behavior were much more common than the injunctive and descriptive norms would suggest.

Our social world is filled with injunctive and descriptive assumptions and expectations. For example, if prompted to think about a high school's prom, what comes to mind? How would you expect participants to dress? What sort of music would you assume would be played? What actions would you anticipate from someone who is not dating as prom approaches? Injunctive norms might suggest that prom attendees ought to find the event to be a romantic experience that one relishes. Meanwhile, descriptive norms acknowledge that many prom dates are disappointingly platonic, while others are barely tolerated by two people who would have ended a relationship much earlier if the injunctive norms of the prom had not been looming. Individuals often *internalize* norms—injunctive norms are internalized by fully accepting an expectation of the group as part of one's own value system, and descriptive norms are internalized by taking what is perceived as common to be "normal."[7]

Social scientists have developed the concept of the *social institution* to refer to the ways that larger systems of multiple rules and expectations are organized to meet the basic needs of a society. Social institutions include family, religion, military, education, law, politics, medicine, and the economy.[8] All social institutions encompass a collection of injunctive norms (specific rules or expectations) as well as descriptive norms (common practices). For example, as a school prepares for the prom, we can perceive the school as an institution. What injunctive norms and descriptive norms influence whom is welcome at the prom, appropriate locations for the prom, and ideal timing for the prom? Social institutions influence *actors*—individuals taking action and interacting with others.[9] Who attends the prom, who supervises the prom, who plays the music at the prom?

Political scientists James G. March and Johan P. Olsen have defined institution as "a relatively stable collection of practices and rules defining appropriate behavior for specific groups of actors in specific situations."[10] In this text, we will explore schools, workplaces, religious groups, and families as social institutions. March and Olsen identify that the rules and practices of institutions are connected to commonly held beliefs and social power, to the ways groups understand and interpret the social world to "explain and legitimize particular identities and the practices and rules associated with them."[11] Social institutions influence which expressions of gender and sexuality are accepted.

Many high schools have a practice of voting for one prom king and one prom queen. This system implicitly promotes heterosexuality. Some schools have used their institutional power to state explicit rules that attendees at proms must be heterosexual couples. [12] These practices and rules reveal how sexuality is understood within a school. Heterosexuality is promoted as legitimate and appropriate. While schools may explicitly reach out to lesbian, gay, bisexual, and transgender students as welcome at proms, [13] heterosexuality maintains a privileged status through the common practice of electing a prom king and prom queen. We invite you to imagine that you were a visitor from another culture that does not hold high school proms. In addition to promotion of heterosexuality, what assumptions regarding sexuality and expression of gender are common within the institution of the prom? How is gender expressed or performed at the prom in terms of the expectations for how young women and men expend resources and prepare for the event? At prom, what practices related to gender and sexuality are normative? Following the tradition of Michel Foucault, we reserve the term *normative* to communicate expectations that are dominant in a society and that often reflect and reinforce the culture and values of groups in power. What practices would be considered *deviant*—behaviors, attitudes, desires, and even ways of thinking that directly contradict normative expectations?

Whereas it used to be deviant based both on injunctive norms and descriptive norms for a white girl to go to prom with an African American boy, contemporary injunctive norms would encourage acceptance of such a couple, even if interracial couples were uncommon at the school (and therefore an interracial couple did not follow descriptive norms). Injunctive norms on interracial romantic relationships have shifted dramatically over the past century. In the 1950s in southern parts of the United States, injunctive norms for whites encouraged racism as a social value, and laws in some states prohibited marriage between a white person and an African American person (further discussed in chapter 5). Over the decades, injunctive norms have shifted to discourage open expressions of racism. [14]

Injunctive norms describe what is socially approved by a group or expected based on the standards of a society (but not necessarily practiced), and descriptive norms identify what people believe to be common practice. Injunctive and descriptive norms of prom can be positive—such as celebrating with friends—or deeply problematic—such as the unfortunately common practice of girls of healthy weight trying to drop pounds to fit an unrealistic ideal. Norms have the strongest influence when injunctive norms are consistent with descriptive norms.[15]

In the work of Foucault, normative is a related but distinct term that conveys social power and addresses expectations based on injunctive or descriptive norms that are dominant—that is, expectations both springing from and reinforcing the power of the dominant within a historical time and culture. For example, high school students face intense social pressure to find a normative date for prom based on gender and height. Boys are expected to pair with girls—not other boys. Specifically, boys are expected to pair with girls who are shorter than they, even when the girls wear high heels. When one deviates from the normative, the individual will often face social pressure to conform or experience social rejection.[16]

What is normative and what is deviant change across historical time and within a given culture. The thoughts and behaviors that are understood to be deviant change as cultures change, and some things that used to be deviant eventually become accepted. Deviant acts range from laudable to despicable. An example of admirable deviance from a descriptive norm would be two young trans men attending prom as a couple. Contemptible deviance from an injunctive norm might come in the form of sexual coercion of an intoxicated seventeen-year-old girl in the wee hours after prom. We ask readers to think critically about norms, the normative, and deviance, and we acknowledge that changes are likely to occur in terms of what is promoted, accepted, tolerated, rejected, or punished.

Social power, rules, and practices of institutions change over time in response to social movements and historical changes.[17] Depending on social power and the importance of a norm within a given context, those who counteract it may be celebrated as individuals or derogated as deviant.[18] For example, a senior in high school who seeks to bring her girlfriend to prom might face responses as distinct as being banned from attendance by school administrators, discouraged by peers who might claim that prom is only for heterosexual couples, or lauded for being true to herself. Some norms, like a heterosexual couple going to prom, are so pervasive, so taken for granted, that they become invisible assumptions. Only deviance from such a norm becomes visible.

We will explore how systems of power—social power—influence social norms and institutional practice as well as the thoughts, feelings, and behaviors of individuals. Our goal is to critically analyze privilege based on heterosexuality and normative gender. Privileged status, such as being part of a heterosexual couple at prom, is often unexamined. In our work to reveal social power and privilege, we follow social psychologist Gregory M. Herek, who encourages us to develop a thoughtful understanding of how heteronormative and gender normative bias are "expressed through society's structure, institutions, and power relations" and internalized by individuals who "express, reinforce, and challenge them."[19]

BEING "NORMAL"

In our society, heterosexuality is understood to be "normal." We ask readers to examine what they consider to be normal for each gender. If someone were described as a "normal girl," what assumptions, if any, would you make about her? How would your assumptions differ when picturing a "normal boy"? For example, it is "normal" for teenage girls to cry and talk about their feelings. It is not "normal" for teenage boys to cry and talk about their feelings. It is "normal" to associate beauty with thinness and to admire thinness. It is not "normal" to associate beauty with fatness and admire fatness. In many spaces, such as a locker room, it is "normal" for boys to brag to each other about their sexual experiences with girls. It is not "normal" for boys in a locker room to brag to each other about their sexual encounters with other boys.

In this book, we challenge normal ways of thinking about sexuality and gender and ask readers to think critically about ways of being sexual and ways of doing gender that have not been considered normal in our culture. We explore the privilege that comes with being considered normal, and we critique the ways that privilege both harms those outside of the "normal" and binds those considered normal to limiting constraints.

Those who do not benefit from a privilege tend to be much more aware of it. When a person examines one form of privilege, other forms—even ones from which the person does benefit—are easier to see. In an earlier book on privilege—focusing on white privilege and racism[20] —we credited Peggy McIntosh, who was inspired by her work in feminist studies to identify ways that white individuals, including herself, are systematically advantaged (privileged) over people of color.[21] As a feminist, McIntosh is accustomed to thinking critically about power, privilege, and injustice. Her awareness of gender privilege, from which McIntosh does *not* benefit, helped her to see how she *does* benefit, unfairly, from racial privilege.

Similar to the diversity of approaches to queer rights, *feminism* encompasses multiple critical perspectives that share a common focus on promoting women's status, well-being, and freedom from violence and discrimination. Barbara Smith, a Black, lesbian, feminist scholar, clarifies that feminism must address the experiences of all women: "Feminism is the political theory and practice that struggles to free all women: women of color, working-class women, poor women, disabled women, lesbians, old women, as well as white, economically privileged heterosexual women. Anything less than this vision of total freedom is not feminism, but merely female self-aggrandizement."[22] Branches of feminism focus on equal consideration for women as well as women's economic, political, sexual, personal, and social rights.

Feminist perspectives can be starkly different from each other, and feminists from different orientations often have passionate disagreements. For example, early and more conservative feminists understood differences between men and women as something to acknowledge and respect. More recent, liberal feminists have understood gender differences as evidence of inequality. Contemporary, socialist feminists are profoundly concerned about issues of oppression. In other words, feminist approaches often disagree regarding how to understand the problem and therefore the ideal way to achieve feminist goals. For the purposes of this book, one particularly interesting feminist debate involves the ways that the social phenomena of sexuality and sexism inform, reinforce, and challenge each other.[23]

When McIntosh sought to reveal to men the ways they were privileged in comparison to women, she observed that men often focused on women as disadvantaged rather than seeing their own privilege. Aware of racial disadvantages for people of color, she challenged herself to consider the ways she experienced racial privilege, white privilege.

McIntosh identified that privilege unfairly keeps one group dominant over others. This often means that the advantaged group feels in the right when choosing to maintain ignorance of the history, current events, values, and ways of communicating of less privileged groups. Privilege often takes the form of not wanting to learn about the experiences of others or of ignoring the evidence of injustice. Unfortunately, privileged groups, including groups of people who are heterosexual and cisgender, "can remain oblivious of the language and culture" of other groups "without feeling . . . any penalty for such oblivion."[24]

A subset of privileges would ideally be extended to all people. No one should have reason to fear that one's race, sexual identity, or way of expressing gender might lead to being unwelcome in a neighborhood or mistreated by police officers. In an accepting and fair society, all individuals would find positive role models of their race, sexual identity, and gender identity in literature, films, and television.

Across media and in many everyday circumstances, heterosexuality is often treated as so normal that only exceptions are stated.[25] When sexual orientation is remarked on, it is often employed to refer to lesbian women, gay men, or bisexual individuals, but this term is rarely applied to describe heterosexual people. Heterosexuality has a privileged status of being assumed if not mentioned.

Sociologist Michael S. Kimmel provides a helpful analogy for visualizing the way that privilege is often made invisible. Please consider web addresses on the Internet that represent companies. A business in the United States will likely have an address that ends with .com, while a company from another country will often include a country code as well, such as .co.uk or .com.au. The United States holds such a privileged status on the Internet that it is taken for granted without mention.[26] Heterosexuality is similarly privileged—assumed unless an exception is explicitly stated. As suggested by the story that opened this chapter, many in our culture would automatically think a phrase such as a "farmer and the farmer's wife" refers to a man and a woman. One might expect additional clarification to convey an exception to the assumption, such as a "lesbian farmer and her wife." Similarly, traditional gender roles are often presumed unless someone identifies an unexpected pairing of gender with occupation, such as a "woman farmer" or a "male nurse."

SEEING SEXUALITY

Heterosexual couples are often perceived as "normal." Heterosexual privilege includes communicating openly about relationships and expressing affection in public without concern of ridicule or bullying regarding sexual orientation. Katie Hill and Arin Andrews are close friends who were a heterosexual couple.[27] They met as teens when they both participated in a community group.[28] Neither Andrews nor Hill felt privileged before they joined the support group for transgender youth. Their love story is remarkable because they supported each other as each transitioned from the gender assigned at birth (male for Katie Hill and female for Arin Andrews) to the gender that matches each of their identities. In the case of Hill and Andrews, one can quickly see the power of finding a partner who has an uncommon ability to offer understanding.

While our attention is often drawn by unusual stories, it can be much more challenging to critically analyze what is common and privileged. We often accept "normal" cases as though they are correct, right, and the way things should be. Seeing "normal" as something specific to one's own time and culture can be hard. Looking at another context, one that is different from our own, often helps to reveal that "normal" is specific to a historical time and place.

What does it mean to be heterosexual? What exactly does this identity and label indicate? In the case just described, Andrews identifies as a man who was in love with Hill, who identifies as a woman. While their transgender identities challenge normative gender expectations, they were clearly a heterosexual couple.

When defining heterosexuality, we often make assumptions about sexual desire based on public expressions of romantic love. Should heterosexuality be defined by *sexual desire*, based on interest in physical sexual acts? What role should *romantic love*, which includes infatuation and companionate love, play in sexual orientation? Can a woman be heterosexual if she feels *infatuation* for another woman through "intense desires for proximity and physical contact, resistance to separation, feelings of excitement and euphoria when receiving attention and affection from the partner, fascination with the partner's behavior and appearance, extreme sensitivity to . . . her moods and signs of interest, and intrusive thoughts of the partner"?[29] How about if a woman feels a romantic attachment through *companionate love*: "feelings of calm, security, mutual comfort seeking, and deep affection"?[30]

The history of women having romantic friendships shows that romantic and sexual identities might not always carry the same meaning in different cultures or historic moments. For example, in the late nineteenth century in western Europe and the United States, middle-class and elite women's lives were changing. What historians now describe as the first wave of feminism coincided with increasing opportunities for women, both financial and educational, that opened up the possibility of new power dynamics and greater independence for women. With changes in the economic realities of their lives, the normative ideas about what it means to be a woman also changed. Simultaneously, romantic friendships between women thrived. Journalist and historian Neil Miller notes, "The tradition of female romantic friendships, combined with women's growing economic independence, created the possibility of two women living together in a primary relationship without men."[31] These relationships between women often lasted a lifetime and might even involve women who were legally married to men.

It seems that these romantic friendships were not perceived as particularly abnormal in spite of the fact that the women in the relationships do not appear to be heterosexual to us today. Indeed, the very language between women in romantic friendships reads like the words of lovers in contemporary society. For example, Miller quotes a letter from Louise Brackett, herself married to a male Boston artist, to her unmarried romantic friend, actor and activist Anna E. Dickinson. Brackett wrote, "How much I want to see you: as your letter gave me such exquisite pleasures indeed! I will marry you—run off any where with you, for you are such a darling—I can feel your soul—if not your body sweet Anna—do I offend your delicacy?"[32] And Miller quotes suffrage leader Susan B. Anthony's letter to the same Anna E. Dickinson, "Now when are you coming to New York—do let it be soon—I have plain quarters—at 44 Bond St—double bed—and big enough and good enough to take you in— . . . I do so long for the scolding and pinched ears and every thing I know awaits me—what worlds of experience since I last snuggled the wee child in my long arms. . . . Your loving friend Susan."[33]

Another example of romantic friendships between women occurred at women's colleges in the 1800s, such as Vassar and Smith. In what people called *smashing*, a female student would fall for another female student and romance her with letters, flowers, chocolates, poetry, and other signs of the advancer's love and admiration. The romanced woman might or might not return the affection, but if she did, according to a formerly smashed woman cited by Miller, the two would become a devoted pair. Miller quotes an 1873 letter to the Yale Courant that describes smashing:

> When a Vassar girl takes a shine to another, she straightaway enters upon a regular course of bouquet sendings, interspersed with tinted notes, mysterious packages of "Ridley's Mixed Candies," locks of hair perhaps, and many other tender tokens, until at last the object of her attentions is captured, the two become inseparable . . . smashed.[34]

Was this practice sexual? We do not know. Yet the words, stories, and letters sound very much like words of love between two romantic, potentially sexual partners today. Miller offered the story of one woman who described her experience of being smashed at Smith. She claimed that, a "veteran smasher . . . soon deserted her for someone else." This smashed woman "used to cry herself to sleep night after night, and wake up with a headache in the morning." The woman noted that while together she and her "veteran smasher" would "write each other the wildest love-letters and send presents, confectionery, all sorts of things, like a real courting of the Shakespearean style."[35] When we read these words, do we consider this "smashed young woman" to be a lesbian? Were these women sexual with each other? And does a woman have to be actively sexual with, or at least sexually desire, other women to be considered lesbian? What do you think?

Around the same time as smashings, women practiced what came to be called *Boston marriages*. In these alternative "marriages," often college-educated, politicized, generally feminist women who were involved with progressive social movements remained outside of heterosexual marriages. Instead they lived and made a home with a long-term female partner. Again, as with smashing, we do not know if some, perhaps most, of these marriages included sexual behavior between the two life partners. Nonetheless, many women, including influential people, had such partnerships. For example, Jane Addams, the founder of the United States settlement house movement and, some claim, of the field of social work, partnered for forty years with Mary Rozet Smith.

Novelist Willa Cather also had a long-term "marriage" of forty years with Edith Lewis. And after living together in New York City during life, Cather and her partner are buried together in a graveyard in New Hampshire. In spite of the fact that Lewis lived for twenty-five years after Cather died in 1947, she still found her way back to Cather's side in death in 1972.[36] In the interim, Lewis remained committed to Cather, devoting her life to developing public recognition of Cather's work and keeping their Manhattan home "exactly as it had been when Cather was alive."[37]

In the early part of the twentieth century, Boston marriages were socially acceptable romantic relationships between women. Scholars today debate whether it is appropriate to apply our current historical and cultural understandings of sexuality to women of a different time. Is it befitting to use a contemporary perspective and claim that women in Boston marriages were lesbian? Or should we seek to understand these relationships within their context and refrain from what might be an ahistorical understanding? This debate challenges us to consider romantic love as complex and distinct from sexuality.[38]

ADRIENNE RICH AND COMPULSORY HETEROSEXUALITY

This question regarding what constitutes being a lesbian came up in the 1970s too, during what is called the second-wave feminist movement in the United States. Springing from the 1960s and the many radical social movements of that time, an important branch of the feminist movement called radical feminism argued that women as a group were oppressed by men. Radical feminists saw this oppression everywhere, including in social phenomena like the low pay women workers earn, the limited educational and job opportunities for women, and the extensive violence women experience.

Ideologies—commonly held beliefs and ways of thinking in a culture—emerge from the lived, material reality of a culture in a given time. (We will return to this idea, cultural materialism, in chapter 3.) The ideologies of that time maintained that women were meant to be in the home and were naturally bad at most kinds of wage work, especially that involving science, mathematics, management, finance, business, writing, technology, and physical labor. Radical feminists argued that these ways of thinking helped to reproduce women's oppression. Yet ultimately for radical feminists, it was violence against women that represented the most important way women's oppression was reproduced. They illuminated all kinds of violence against women, including rape, incest and child sexual abuse, sexual harassment at work and on the streets, and domestic and intimate partner violence. For the first time, people in the mainstream United States began to recognize the extent of the sexual and other violence women faced in their daily lives.

In part in response to this new awareness, a lesbian feminist element within second-wave feminism pushed for lesbian separatism. *Women-identified women* made other women the central relationships and commitments in their family, friendships, and work. Feminist, activist, writer, and poet Adrienne Rich argued that to be a women-identified woman, with or without sexually desiring other women, meant that one was lesbian.

In her formative work first published in 1980, Rich challenges readers to acknowledge heterosexuality as normative, indeed as "compulsory."[39] As a radical feminist, Rich argues that we live in a society where women have significantly less power than men. Rich identified male heterosexual privilege as reproducing this gendered power imbalance, in part, by demanding women's heterosexuality and making lesbianism invisible in order to maintain male power. Rich explains that the way women are expected to live their lives recreates and reinforces male power. Ideologies such as the ones that women are better at caring for children and are naturally heterosexual are often perceived within our culture as normal. Women are expected to marry a man, have children, and invest selflessly in, and for the good of, a nuclear family—father, mother, and their children. In chapter 3, we will further explore how these expectations reinforce the privilege, power, and relative freedom of men at a cost to women.

In her exploration of women-identified women, Rich proposes the use of the term *lesbian continuum*. By this Rich means "to include a range—through each woman's life and throughout history—of woman-identified experience, not simply the fact that a woman has had or consciously desired genital sexual experience with another woman." Rich argues for expanding the meaning of the lesbian continuum "to embrace many more forms of primary intensity between and among women, including the sharing of a rich inner life, the bonding against

male tyranny, the giving and receiving of practical and political support."[40] Many women who identify as lesbian perceive their sexual identity as a political and emotional "choice," and not a biological "nature"
into which one is born. Additionally, by the terminology introduced in
chapter 1, many lesbian women conceive of their sexuality as socially
constructed rather than as essentialist.

Women gain a limited kind of privilege by seeking to live in accordance with heteronormative expectations, such as working to be attrac-
tive to men, connecting with men in romantic and sexual relationships,
and honing an image as demure, quiet, sweet, and gentle. In contrast,
Rich challenges us to consider rejecting such privilege that comes at a
cost to oneself and other women. Being a women-identified woman
means to connect with women in spite of women's lack of privilege
outside of heteronormativity and in that connection to come together in
solidarity and strength. Being a women-identified woman means refus-
ing heteronormative privilege that excludes some. It means demanding
social change.

LET'S TALK ABOUT SEX(UALITY AND GENDER)

When discussing sexuality, a person's choice of terms within a context
communicates messages about how sexuality is understood. We invite
readers to consider their goals when communicating about sexuality,
and we suggest terms that convey respect.

Sexual orientation is regularly used in western cultures to indicate a
pattern of sexual attraction (or lack of attraction), such as heterosexual,
gay, lesbian, bisexual, or asexual. The term is often used in cultures that
identify sexuality as an important aspect of who the individual is. While
diverse sexual behaviors exist across cultures, the concept of sexual
orientation—of sexuality as an enduring trait of a person—does not
exist in all cultures.[41] Psychologist Phillip L. Hammack notes that some
cultures conceive of sexuality as actions one does rather than as part of
who a person is. Indeed, Foucault argues this is how western cultures
before the nineteenth century used to understand sexuality (discussed
in chapter 1). How have you conceived of sexuality? Do you perceive an
individual's sexual attraction and sexual activity to be part of a person's
identity?

Sexual identity is similarly linked to western notions of sexuality as an aspect of who a person is. This term describes a personal understanding of one's own sexuality, including how individual awareness and acceptance develop over one's life.[42] Sexual identity is often chosen as a term when one wants to focus on how an individual understands his or her own sexuality and the way that understanding develops.

In contrast, *sexual preference* has been a controversial term within western discourse. Although used by some scholars to explore possible links between biology and sexuality,[43] those who promote acceptance of sexual diversity have roundly rejected "sexual preference" as a substitute for sexual orientation. The term has been criticized for implying that sexuality is a matter of individual volition, of personal and simple choice.[44]

Queer rights movements have often been driven by the banding together of people with diverse sexual and gender identities. Although transgender identities are aspects of gender orientation or gender identity rather than sexual orientation or sexual identity, trans identity is recognized as a queer identity. With the goal of embracing multiple identities, many have adopted *LGBTQ* as an inclusive term that incorporates lesbian, gay, bisexual, transgender, queer, and questioning.[45] The Q addresses the more all-encompassing term "queer," and in LGBTQ it also welcomes individuals who are *questioning*, considering or exploring their sexual or gender identity. In an attempt to be inclusive, some scholars and activists have included additional letters and symbols, such as I for intersex (explored in chapter 1), A for asexual (discussed in chapter 4), and 2-S for two-spirit (described in chapter 4). As authors, we have chosen to use LGBTQ and queer as inclusive terms, but we acknowledge that terms intended to be respectful sometimes inadvertently exclude individuals or fail to capture the complexity of an issue.

Adding letters and symbols to LGBTQ communicates an intention to be respectful and unifying that we, as authors, respect. In our writing, we prefer the term queer because of its immediate inclusiveness of anyone rejected from a narrow definition of straight. Queer has been reclaimed to demand consideration of gender and sexuality as complex and nuanced. Queer encompasses any person who differs from limiting assumptions that binary sex should match narrow cultural expectations for gender and restrictive prescriptions for sexual desire and experience.

False cultural binaries tend to claim that cases fall clearly into either a good side or a bad side. A valued side is presented in contrast to a devalued side. Correct is on one side and wrong on the other. A seemingly reasonable side is differentiated from a side depicted as irrational. One side is honorable; the "opposite" is understood to be shameful. "Normal" is distinguished from "abnormal." Queer theory challenges this binary and demands rethinking the meaning of normal. The term queer bursts through the false binary by acknowledging the diversity among individuals within the term. Similarly, the term LGBTQ recognizes multiple identities within the very wording of the term. In other words, binary thinking should not be applied to categorize people as either straight or queer. Rather, diverse experiences should be acknowledged for heterosexual and cisgender individuals as well as queer individuals.

Partly because of our concern about the tendency to slip into false binary thinking, we find the term straight to be problematic. While the term queer explicitly demands that one question what is normal, the term straight does not directly challenge binary thinking. Further, the word straight might imply being correct, rational, and normal. For example, "straightforward" suggests honesty. In contrast to calling someone "straight," referring to someone as "heterosexual and cisgender" might prompt one's audience to think more critically about sexuality and gender.

When considering how terms are being used, context is a critical indicator of intention. Referring to "gay rights" as an important aspect of social justice is dramatically different from a derogatory comment of "That's so gay." Similarly, context is important in determining whether queer is used as a term of respect and empowerment or as an insult. Like Shneer and Aviv, we acknowledge that some activists and their supporters might reject the use of queer. Following media strategist Kimberley McLeod, we urge that reclaimed terms should be used with care and with an awareness of how one's privilege might influence context.[46]

Heterosexual and cisgender individuals might be confused if they overhear an activist for queer rights playing with terms that are generally only used as words of hate and to illicit shame. An ally shared that she routinely uses her privilege as a heterosexual, cisgender person to address examples of hate. She is dismayed to regularly hear acquaintances use antigay slurs that range from a thoughtless "That's so gay" to intentionally hateful expressions. As with any regularly practiced habit, her response became automatic—when she hears offensive antiqueer language, she pointedly identifies the words as offensive. One day she immediately reprimanded a friend for referring to someone as a "closet queen" before pausing to realize that her friend's identity as an out gay man provided him with a perspective very different from her own as an ally. People who benefit from privilege should use extreme caution regarding derogatory terms against a group to which they do not belong. Heterosexual and cisgender people should carefully consider their words before using a term that might sound like an antiqueer slur. Queer individuals may disagree on whether there is justification for an out gay man to express his frustration with a closeted man through the use of a slur, but heterosexual and cisgender people should stay away from words that are not intended as terms of respect.

Gender activists have expanded how some institutions refer respectfully to gender—breaking through the traditional false binary that assumed all people would identify as either male or female and cisgender. As a result, on February 13, 2014, the social media site Facebook began allowing users to customize the label they use to describe their gender. Facebook officially recognizes that users might identify their gender in ways other than a binary. Backlash in comments on Facebook and in other media revealed that for many, the normative and binary system seems simpler; many find the "queering" of gender and sexuality to be confusing.[47] For example, individuals have expressed distress regarding the effort required to try to keep track of which gender pronoun to use with each person.[48]

Oberlin College, a liberal arts college and conservatory in Ohio, has published recommendations for use of pronouns. Students are invited to express whether they would prefer masculine pronouns (he/him/his), feminine pronouns (she/her/hers), or gender-neutral pronouns (across different publications on the college's website, multiple options are offered, including ze/hir/hirs, zie/zir/zirs, and using the traditionally plural they/their/theirs to refer to a single person).[49] We invite readers to consider the local culture of a college that would institutionalize allowing individuals to express their preference for pronouns. What ideologies regarding acceptance are likely to be at play in such an institution?

Sexual advice columnist Dan Savage, a queer activist, admits that he found it confusing when he attended a meeting where everyone went around the table and introduced themselves via their name and preferred gender pronoun. Savage notes on his podcast that he has trouble remembering his own name, much less remembering the names of a large group of newly met people. To add the preferred gender pronoun to the list of things to remember about new acquaintances was beyond Savage, but he also encourages readers to explore the goals of the preferred gender pronoun movement.[50]

After a visit to Oberlin College in which students announced their preferred gender pronouns when introducing themselves, journalist Margot Adler asked activists for their perspective on this movement. Inviting people to share their preferred gender pronoun can be perceived as acknowledging that gender is complicated, that it is not a simple binary. Given that transgender individuals have been historically marginalized even more than cisgender queer people (such as cisgender gay men, lesbian women, and bisexual individuals), some activists welcome taking a moment at the beginning of a meeting to acknowledge that gender is not a simple binary.[51]

Many reputable news organizations follow the GLAAD *Media Reference Guide*, which offers clear definitions to help writers to quickly understand the distinctions between sex, gender identity, gender expression, and sexual orientation. In response to "grossly defamatory and sensationalized" coverage of HIV and AIDS by the *New York Post* tabloid newspaper, GLAAD started in 1985 as the Gay & Lesbian Alliance Against Defamation.[52] The organization has continued to evolve as queer issues have evolved, and the group's stated goals are to be a media organization "to shape the narrative and provoke dialogue that leads to cultural change" as it "rewrites the script for LGBT acceptance."[53]

When writing about a person with transgender identity, GLAAD advises using the name the person has chosen rather than imposing a person's legal name or the name assigned at birth. For example, one would refer to Chaz Bono by the name he chose. GLAAD further advises to ask transgender people which pronouns they prefer. By June 2015, Caitlyn Jenner's identification as a woman included preferring feminine pronouns, a change that occurred following the April 2015 interview granted to journalist Diane Sawyer. At the time of Sawyer's interview, the Olympic athlete identified as Bruce Jenner, a trans woman who preferred masculine pronouns. GLAAD provided a press release to help journalists recognize that "every transgender person's journey is unique" and to encourage respecting Jenner's immediate preference for first name and pronouns (whether masculine, feminine, or gender neutral).[54] If asking is not possible, GLAAD suggests referring to a person with pronouns that are consistent with expressed gender, such as feminine pronouns for someone who wears feminine clothing or masculine pronouns for someone who has chosen a masculine name.[55]

In terms of what questions are appropriate to ask a person who is queer, we recommend considering whether one would ask a similar question of a heterosexual and cisgender person. If someone would consider it rude to ask a heterosexual person about sexual positions or use of sex toys, then that person should refrain from such questions for a gay, lesbian, or bisexual friend or acquaintance. If a person would not ask about the genitals or breasts of a cisgender person, then one should curb such questions when talking to a trans person.[56]

Finally, we urge people to be as welcoming of expressions of queer identity as they would be of heterosexual and cisgender identity. When an eight-year-old child close to the authors came out as queer or, as she put it, "gay and lesbian," her parents were happy and supportive. Yet they found the response from most other adults to be something like: "Oh, she is too young to really know." Or, "You will have to wait and see, she cannot possibly understand what this means at her age." Even people who identify as queer tended to dismiss or resist the child's disclosure. In contrast, parents of children as young as four and five have spoken with us about their child's heterosexual crush on another child. No one seems to question whether a child is too young to express heterosexuality.

PAULINE PARK AND THE LGBTQ RIGHTS MOVEMENT

Pauline Park has always lived her life with profound integrity and courage, embracing her unconventional family in addition to challenging institutionalized privilege. Park led the campaign for legal protection in New York City for transgender rights (enacted 2002),[57] cofounded the New York Association for Gender Rights Advocacy (NYAGRA), and cofounded the Queens Pride House, the LGBTQ community center in Queens, one of only two in New York City at that time. When Park and her identical twin brother were infant boys in 1960 in Korea, discrimination against queer individuals was entrenched in institutions throughout the United States. *Sodomy laws* criminalized consensual sexual activity between same-gender individuals. Park was a toddler in Wisconsin when Illinois became the first state to repeal its sodomy laws in 1961. Park was school aged when Connecticut followed in 1969. Through Park's adolescence, another twenty states decriminalized consensual sexual activity in the 1970s. Three more—including Park's current home in New York and her early home in Wisconsin—struck the laws from their books in the 1980s, followed by seven in the 1990s, and four more shortly after the turn of the twenty-first century. In 2003, when Park's activism had become her full-time work, the sodomy laws in the remaining fourteen states were declared unconstitutional by the Supreme Court's decision in the case of *Lawrence and Garner v. Texas*.[58]

The Stonewall riots in 1969 in New York City—often cited as the impetus of the queer civil rights movement—erupted when Park was a child far away in Milwaukee. The riots were a response to a perception of capricious enforcement of New York's sodomy laws. Violent raids by the police of queer gathering places were commonplace. A raid on the Stonewall Inn, an infamous bar in Greenwich Village, happened one too many times and prompted sudden outrage and subsequent civil action.[59] Despite activists in New York playing a central role in the national gay rights movement, New York lagged behind twenty-two other states in abolishing sodomy laws.[60]

Throughout Park's childhood, homosexuality was an officially recognized psychiatric disorder. It was not until Park was an adolescent in 1973 that the American Psychiatric Association voted to remove homosexuality as a disorder from the *Diagnostic and Statistical Manual of Mental Disorders* (DSM).[61] Despite risk of being prosecuted as a criminal or labeled as disordered, Park has always sought to speak the truth.

In 1961, at eight months of age, Park and her twin brother were sent from their birthplace in Korea to their new adoptive family in Milwaukee, Wisconsin. Park's conservative, white working-class adoptive parents were part of a (now revealed to be problematic) religious movement adopting babies from Korea so as to raise them as Christians.[62]

As a child, Park did not have the words for all of the ways she was different from her community—being trans, being queer. Yet by the time she came out, first as a gay man, later as a trans woman, she was already familiar with difference. Albeit loved, Park lived her childhood "feeling like the other."[63] Park was Asian in a white social world. Even when seen with her family, people challenged Park and her brother's "sense of belonging." She writes, "The striking physical difference between my adoptive parents and my brother and me made it impossible for others not to notice. 'Whose children are they?' complete strangers would often ask."[64]

At age four, Park knew she was a girl although she did not have the words to explain this. When she went to kindergarten, she saw all the other girls wearing stretch pants with stirrups and she wanted to wear them too. When she asked her mother for the pants, Park explains that her mother's "shocked response ['But those are for girls!'] made me realize that I had crossed an invisible gender boundary that I hadn't been aware of." About this, in an interview with Halley, Park said, "And at that point I hit smack dab into the sex/gender binary. Of course I didn't have the vocabulary. And so I suddenly realized that I'd been assigned to a sex and gender that I didn't necessarily identify with. I suddenly realized there were two categories, boys and girls."[65] Park notes, "My mother and society assigned me to the category 'boy' without consulting with me. I realized that neither the public space of school nor the more private space of home was a safe environment in which to explore my gender identity, so I buried it very deep inside me."[66]

Park experienced racism at school:

> My brother and I were the only nonwhite children in our elementary school. We were harassed often enough by white kids both inside and outside of school. The constant hurling of the words "Chink" and "Jap" made me feel ambivalent about my adoptive country, and also made it nearly impossible for me to think of myself as American.[67]

Yet one more way that Park was different was that she was a bookish child in a family of nonreaders. She and her twin brother would spend hours reading at their local library. When she was eight she stumbled on a small shelf of books about "homosexuals." Park explains, "I remember picking up *Transvestites and Transsexuals*. It would be hopelessly old-fashioned today, but it meant I never felt alone. They also had *The Gay Mystique*." Park notes, "I read surreptitiously. I never took them home. And I was petrified I'd be found, but I knew there were other LGBT people in the world."[68] Her cultural context and family had given her no reason to know anything about queer people. Nonetheless, although she had no reason to recognize the terms used or the people described, she knew that she had found books about herself.

Racism continued to influence Park's life. Throughout her elementary and middle school experience and even at her large urban high school, Park and her brother were among very few students of color. While she was in high school, Milwaukee was forced to integrate its schools. Park remembers and welcomed Black students being bused into her nearly all-white education.[69]

Even as a child, Park was feisty, always challenging, always pushing boundaries. While her brother worked to keep the peace, Park worked to make the world more fair. In college at the University of Wisconsin–Madison, in 1978, Park and her brother both came out as gay men. Park observes, "Though we were close over the years, we had both kept this secret hidden from each other until then."

In future chapters, we will further describe Park's experiences of coming out—first as a gay man, and later as a trans woman.[70] Throughout this text, we will follow the example of queer theory by challenging what it means to be normal and by exposing unfair examples of privilege that benefit heterosexual and cisgender people while harming those who are queer.

DISCUSSION QUESTIONS

1. Identify a major event celebrated by a social institution and the ideologies regarding sexuality and expression of gender that are common within the institution and at the event. Within the chapter, we invited you to consider prom as an event celebrated by many schools. You might consider an event that occurs within a religious institution, a ritual other than prom held by your school,

or a major national sporting event. In this event, are girls and women expected to play different roles than boys and men? Are there gendered expectations for how people should dress and act? Are there assumptions regarding sexuality?

2. In the event you explored, for the first question, identify the injunctive norms and descriptive norms. What actions would be considered deviant?

3. Before reading this chapter, how would you have described a "normal" family? Identify injunctive and descriptive norms in your description. Did you include any aspects that you would expect others to perceive as deviant? Did you mention the roles of any social institutions beyond the family, such as law, politics, economics, the workplace, or school? Evaluate what the inclusion or exclusion of social institutions suggests about how you perceived a "normal" family.

4. Use the Internet to find one of the widely available lists of heterosexual privilege inspired by Peggy McIntosh's original work on white privilege. Identify items on the list that would ideally extend to all people in a fair and welcoming society. Identify items on the list that should be abolished for all because they are based on the privileged group's ability to maintain ignorance of other groups. What examples from the list are active on your campus, in your workplace, or in your community?

5. What do the phenomena of smashing and Boston marriages reveal about sexuality? How does cultural and historical context influence how sexuality is understood? As you define it within your current culture and historical time, to what extent is sexuality based on intimate connection to members of one or more genders, on sexual desire, or on sexual experience?

6. Explain what Adrienne Rich meant by the terms compulsory heterosexuality and women-identified women. How do these terms challenge privilege?

7. A critical aspect of the present argument is that sex, gender, and sexuality are not binary categories. Using chapter 1 and chapter 2, evaluate the evidence that sex does not exist as a simple male-female binary, that gender is not a straightforward binary between masculine and feminine, and that sexuality cannot be simplified into a clear-cut binary between straight and queer.

3

PRIVILEGED POWER, HATE, AND HETERONORMATIVITY

Preschooler Lena forgot which way it went and asked her mother, "Is it when men love men or when men love women that people hate them?"

This child's question reveals that prejudice against gay men is not a natural response but one that must be learned. Lena's experience has been unusual in our society in that her parents have consciously exposed her to diverse family structures and openly discussed the problem of prejudice and discrimination against queer families and individuals. What is "normal" is taught within the context of a family, culture, and historical time. Lena's parents intentionally showed her a broad definition of a normal family.

For many of us who were raised in families with a more limited definition of normal, we may have prejudice to overcome. This prejudice may have been unintentionally bestowed upon us, or it may have been carefully cultivated. If certain conservatives had their way, many families would be invisible or not exist at all. Numerous conservatives in the United States argue in favor of injunctive norms that families mean marriage and that marriage should entail a heterosexual couple. In this thinking, families parented by single mothers and queer families are not normal. Further, in today's mainstream idealization of families, we often assume that middle-class families are normal, with a father who is the major breadwinner for the family and a mother whose career can be shaped around a caregiver role.

In contrast, to these limiting perspectives on families, many liberals have worked to broaden the concept of family, arguing that families are about love regardless of the number of parents or their gender, that families with one mother and one father should not be privileged as the only ones that are "normal." Marriage equality activists, for example, worked to promote marriage rights for any loving adult couple, same sex or heterosexual, while recognizing that choosing to become a family without marriage can also be a valid choice.

People on the conservative end of the political spectrum often argue that families are the backbone of our society in that they produce children and reproduce important heteronormative gender roles. In this framework, men and women are understood to be biologically distinct, and families are instrumental in helping each sex to fulfill its rightful and unique role in society. In this view, men are naturally aggressive, competitive, and rational providers. Women are naturally gentle, emotional, nurturing, and loving caregivers—who care for men and for their children. Women civilize and tame men and give them something to focus their competitive energies on, that is, providing for women and children.[1] Each needs the other. Women need men to provide for them so that they can focus their nurturing energies on raising children. And men need women, for without women to tame their "natural promiscuous sexuality,"[2] men tend to run wild.

George Gilder, an important conservative thinker, writes in his classic book, *Men and Marriage*,

> Modern society relies on predictable, regular, long-term human activities corresponding to the sexual faculties of women. The male pattern is the enemy of social stability. This is the ultimate source of female sexual control and the crucial reason for it. Women domesticate and civilize male nature. They can jeopardize male discipline and identity, and civilization as well, merely by giving up this role.[3]

For many conservatives like Gilder, queer families threaten civilization, such as it is, because they disrupt this important process wherein men and women fulfill their most basic social roles—men as the providers for women and children; women as the civilizers of men and nurturers of men and children. In this thinking, heteronormative families uphold our contemporary modern social order.

On the other, liberal end of the political spectrum, families matter too. Yet for many liberals, the strength of the family does not depend on the sex and gender identity of the adults involved. Liberals often understand gender to be a socially constructed phenomenon, not a biologically bound one. In this thinking, both men and women are capable of having characteristics traditionally understood to be masculine or feminine. And both men and women are capable of caring for children (and for their partners). Finally, both men and women are capable of working in the larger wage workforce.

For example, sociologist Barbara Risman has researched single fathers in their role as caretakers of their children. Contrary to conservative arguments, such as that of Gilder, evidence reveals that men do not require women to civilize them or to care for their children. When men face the demands of being a single parent, they demonstrate strengths in skills that have traditionally been considered feminine, such as connecting emotionally with children and taking care of necessary housework. Risman concludes "that men can mother and that children are not necessarily better nurtured by women than by men."[4]

Second-wave radical feminist Adrienne Rich also provides powerful criticism of conservative perspectives. Conservative arguments that women must tame men and therefore be protected by men, in effect, excuse and promote normative male domination in our society that reproduces a gendered power imbalance privileging men, in part, by demanding women's heterosexuality. From a lesbian feminist perspective, Rich argues that men "really fear" the possibility that "women could be indifferent to them altogether, that men could be allowed sexual and emotional—therefore economic—access to women only on women's terms."[5] In other words, Rich claims that lesbianism threatens male power. She writes, "The enforcement of heterosexuality for women [is] a means of assuring male right of physical, economic, and emotional access."[6] Rich views women's sexuality as socially constructed—as a product of the interaction between the individual and the powerful social context that demands heterosexuality and sexual access for men. In Rich's view, lesbianism is a political choice as well as a sexual orientation. Understanding Rich's perspective requires one to critically reflect on gender and sexuality. Rich demands an examination of cultural ideologies, taken-for-granted practices, and normalizing belief systems that often go unexamined.

In further chapters, we will explore additional feminist and queer challenges to conservative, binary thinking about families, gender, and sexuality.

CULTURAL MATERIALISM

Cultural materialism is a theory that critically examines cultural ideologies, including how expectations regarding gender and "compulsory heterosexuality"[7] emerged in the United States through a heteronormative political economy. In sociology we often employ cultural materialism to help us understand our society and social power in it. Cultural materialism reveals that ideologies considered "normal" within a society actually spring from a culture's particular ways of living and function to reproduce the position of those in power. In part this means that ideas that are considered normal are merely normal in our specific cultural context. In another society, in a different context, these ideas might not be normal at all.

In another book exploring privilege, specifically white privilege, we demonstrate how the political economy within a given time and place can make a way of life seem perfectly ordinary (or "normal"). We describe the feudal system in the Middle Ages in western Europe. In this way of living, the aristocracy, a small group of elite people, owned the land and nearly everything on that land. In sharp contrast, the vast majority of the people in feudal Europe were peasants who owned almost nothing. Peasants lived at the margin of survival by farming the land that belonged to the aristocracy. In exchange for being allowed to use aristocratic land, the peasants paid a kind of rent, or a tithe, by giving the aristocracy part of what they grew. This way of living, this political and economic system, bred ways of thinking—ideologies—that helped reproduce the social power of the aristocracy.

As far as we know, peasants rarely questioned why the aristocracy owned all of the land or why peasants had to pay a tithe to use it. Peasants and aristocracy considered this way of living to be normal and correct. Under feudalism, the ideology was that God made the elite few special and especially connected to God. Thus, the elites were meant to have all of the resources, such as the land and the power to rule. In this thinking that sprang from feudalism, people believed that peasants were lesser human beings who were meant to be poor and that their position was unchangeable. People believed, and the ideology held, that everyone lived in feudal society as they were meant to live.

In our society today, we too have common ways of thinking that spring from the political economy of our ways of living. For example, in the United States, many people believe in self-help in the form of "pulling oneself up by one's bootstraps" and that one can do anything one wants to do if one simply tries hard enough. This belief in our capacity to make whatever we like of our lives stands in sharp contrast to feudal beliefs in the unchangeability of people's situation and status. The individualistic focus often propagated in the United States today has grown from the political economy, but it is no more a factual truth than beliefs that grew from feudalism.

In cultural materialist terms, ideologies spring from the political and economic systems within a culture that enforce a particular way of life. The aristocracy benefited from feudalism, and its power was reproduced within this economic structure. Looking at feudal ideology helps to reveal that ideology arises from the material culture of a system of living. In other words, a way of thinking about the social world emerges from the way lives are lived.

We argue that today in our society, as in any society, we have many ideologies that spring from our ways of living and that communicate normative ways of thinking—dominant cultural expectations that typically reflect the values of groups that hold social power. Normative ways of thinking benefit those with social power over others. Ideologies related to human sexuality and expression of gender dictate normative expectations that privilege some—those with more social power, who are considered to be "normal"—over others—those with less power, who are considered to be "abnormal." In other words, like in feudal Europe, we argue that what a society sees as normal in terms of sexuality and gender is bound up with social power and privilege.

We see cultural materialism in what anthropologist Gayle Rubin calls the *sex/gender system*, which Rubin defines as "the set of arrangements by which a society transforms biological sexuality into products of human activity, and in which these transformed sexual needs are satisfied."[8] In other words, drawing from anthropology's exploration of kinship (family) systems, Rubin explains that sex/gender systems involve a myriad of social phenomena, including kinship, productive labor, and the economy. Further, Rubin notes that every society has a sexual division of labor but "the assignment of any particular task to one sex or another varies enormously. In some groups, agriculture is the work of women, in others, the work of men. Women carry the heavy burdens in some societies, men in others."[9] The specifics of the sexual division of labor spring from culture, not biology. Rubin argues that while sex is biological, "the social organization of sex rests upon gender, obligatory heterosexuality, and the constraint of female sexuality."[10] Because they challenge normative gender and sexual roles, queer members of our society offer a powerful challenge to the sexual division of labor.

As with the cultural materialist framework described above, ways of thinking in a society spring from the ways that we live. We argue that profound and even deadly bigotry against queer people (ways of thinking) springs in part from the political economic system within which we live. Prejudice can keep queer people hidden and afraid, thereby hiding the challenge queer people might offer to the sexual division of labor. Prejudice happens in many ways; these include ugly name-calling on a playground, gay bashing, and the medicalization of queer people as abnormal, as mentally ill.

DYLAN SCHOLINSKI: TREATED FOR A DUBIOUS "MENTAL ILLNESS"

As we noted in chapter 2, homosexuality was treated as a diagnosable mental illness until 1973, when the American Psychiatric Association removed it from the *Diagnostic and Statistical Manual of Mental Disorders* (DSM). Until 2012,[11] transgender individuals could be diagnosed with gender identity disorder, which classified gender expression that was not typical for one's biological sex as a mental illness.[12] With the latest version of the DSM, gender identity disorder has been replaced with gender dysphoria. The updated diagnosis focuses on severe psychological distress regarding one's gender rather than atypical gender, but we find this diagnosis problematic because of potential to continue to pathologize transgender individuals.[13]

Before trans man Dylan Scholinski transitioned as an adult, Scholinski had been assigned the gender of a girl and given the name Daphne. Scholinski's childhood and early adolescence were filled with trauma, including a physically abusive father and sexual abuse from multiple older perpetrators. Scholinski's father was himself traumatized by his military experience in the Vietnam War. Scholinski's mother was depressed and neglectful. In 1980, at fifteen years old, Scholinski identified as a girl who was suicidal, depressed, and rebellious. Scholinski's parents admitted their adolescent to a psychiatric institution, Michael Reese Hospital, in 1981. Scholinski was institutionalized in psychiatric facilities for the next three years and subjected to "girly lessons." [14] Among other diagnoses, Scholinski was treated for gender identity disorder. Scholinski's psychiatrist, Dr. Browning, said Scholinski was "not an appropriate female" and did not "act the way a female is supposed to act." [15]

Scholinski grew up being asked, "Why don't you act more like a girl?" [16] While hospitalized, Scholinski tried desperately to act feminine in order to gain privileges that came only by complying with the expectations of the hospital staff. Scholinski writes,

> I turned control of my face over to my roommate Donna, a fluffy-haired girl with major depression. She wanted to help. She tried to pinpoint exactly why my fifteen-year-old girl-face looked boyish. This turned out to be a bigger question than we could answer.
>
> So we settled for the superficial: A jawline that needed shading? Eyes that needed definition?
>
> Donna wasn't given the strong drugs, at least not early in the morning, so her aim was true. She came at me with a black wand and drew a thin line on the edge of my eyelid.
>
> Every morning I lowered my eyelids and let Donna make me up. If I didn't emerge from my room with foundation, lip gloss, blush, mascara, eyeliner, eye shadow and feathered hair, I lost points. Without points I couldn't go to the dining room, I couldn't go anywhere. . . . Without points, I was not allowed to walk from the classroom back to the unit without an escort. [17]

Scholinski hated both the makeup and being constantly and closely supervised. "It didn't take me long to figure out that a half-moon of blue on my eyelids was a better decision. This was how I learned what it means to be a woman." [18]

For Scholinski, this way of being a woman was literally and figuratively a lie. "I know that later my counselor would put a check mark next to my morning treatment goal: 'Spend 15 minutes with a female peer combing and curling hair and experimenting with makeup.'"[19]

The staff at the hospital regularly inspected and dissected Scholinski's gender performance. "Getting better" for Scholinski meant becoming feminine according to mainstream ways of thinking about femininity. Scholinski writes that they studied "the way I walked, the way I sat with my ankle on my knee, the clothes I wore, the way I kept my hair."[20]

After three years spent in three different hospitals, Scholinski had reached the insurance maximum of one million dollars and was released. As a young adult, Scholinski came out as a lesbian and then later chose the bigender name Dylan when coming out as a trans man.[21] Through art and activism, Scholinski challenges people to consider how expectations for appropriate gender and sexuality permeate our social world. This arduous work is compounded by the difficulty inherent in trying to critically examine one's own culture and its assumptions about how individuals should behave or what they should want.

HATE

Young Lena's question at the opening of this chapter suggests that hating queer people is an ideology that must be taught. In the late 1960s in the United States, this was a prominent lesson that psychotherapists and law enforcement officials had learned well. As we have noted, in the late 1960s, homosexuality was listed as a psychiatric disorder,[22] and same-gender sexual activity was criminal in forty-nine states (only Illinois had repealed sodomy laws by that time, and Connecticut would be the second state to follow in 1969).[23] In contrast to rampant legal discrimination and professional prejudice against queer people, psychotherapist and ally George Weinberg coined the first term to focus attention on the problem of hate directed at queer individuals.[24] Weinberg defined *homophobia* as "the dread of being in close quarters with homosexuals—and in the case of homosexuals themselves, self-loathing."[25]

Naming a phenomenon can have a powerful effect for changing ideology regarding it. Weinberg's creation of the term homophobia challenged the society to become aware of bigotry directed against queer individuals as an important social problem.[26] Homophobia can be used to describe prejudice against any queer person, yet its history has tended to focus on heterosexual and cisgender men's discomfort with men who are not perceived as stereotypically masculine or who identify as bisexual or gay. Social psychologist Gregory M. Herek lauds Weinberg's effort to raise awareness regarding prejudice but acknowledges that the term homophobia does not feel inclusive to all hate of queer people because it is often used in an *androcentric* way—centered on men's experiences while disregarding or devaluing the experiences of women.[27]

Another criticism of the term homophobia is linguistic.[28] Since 2012, the Associated Press has discouraged journalists from using any term rooted in "phobia" when discussing political or social issues, because *phobia* refers to "an irrational, uncontrollable fear, often a form of mental illness."[29] In other words, homophobia focuses on prejudice as if it is an unusual problem experienced by an individual person rather than a systematic problem that is pervasive in a culture.

As an alternative to homophobia, radical lesbian feminists in the 1970s and 1980s, inspired by the work of Adrienne Rich, began using *heterosexism*, a term that consciously connects to sexism and racism.[30] These terms—sexism, racism, and heterosexism—acknowledge forms of prejudice that are systemic within a culture, rooted in social power, codified in institutional practice, connected to cultural materialism in the way lives are lived in a culture, and inherent in ideology.[31] Radical feminists argue that systemic male power, *patriarchy*, leads to heterosexism. To address oppression and hate, they call for an overhaul of the ways normative gender is produced and reproduced. They identify this as a challenge to abusive power. Radical feminists argue that normative gender—the expected ways of being women and men—reproduce the greater social power of men in society.[32] Scholars who focus on heterosexism recognize "systems that provide the rationale and operating instructions for that antipathy. These systems include beliefs about gender, morality, and danger by which homosexuality and sexual minorities are defined as deviant, sinful, and threatening."[33] Heterosexism is used to justify "hostility, discrimination, and violence" when queer identity is visible.[34]

Gregory M. Herek proposes an additional term to describe hate toward people with queer sexuality. Herek suggests *sexual prejudice* as an alternate term "to refer to individual heterosexuals' hostility and negative attitudes . . . toward homosexual behavior; people who engage in homosexual behavior or who identify as gay, lesbian, or bisexual; and communities of gay, lesbian, and bisexual people."[35] We suggest that *queer prejudice* could function as a term that acknowledges prejudice based on queer sexual or gender identity.

Overt hate for queer people can be described by the terms homophobia, heterosexism, or queer prejudice. *Microaggression* can be used to refer to subtle, often unintentional forms of indignity directed toward an individual based on membership in a marginalized group.[36] Psychiatrist Chester Pierce coined the term microaggression in the 1970s. Counseling psychologists Derald Wing Sue[37] and Kevin L. Nadal[38] apply the concept of microaggression to understand invalidation and insults that range from insensitivity to rudeness. Nadal notes that microaggression can come in many forms, including use of language that excludes trans people, assumptions of heterosexuality, and expectations that individuals will follow normative rules for gender expression. Indignities can come in the form of treating queer individuals as exotic, such as the stereotypes of a heterosexual woman assuming that a gay man will make an ideal best friend or a heterosexual man hoping for a bisexual girlfriend who will invite additional women for sexual experiences. Microaggression—even when unintentionally offensive—communicates exclusion, inferiority, and abnormality.[39]

NORMALIZATION

Social theorist Michel Foucault developed the idea of normalization as a critique of modern society. In some ways similar to social constructionism (see chapter 2 for our initial description of social constructionism), Foucault argues that the process from which we come to make the choices we make, to do what we do, and to think what we think springs from our society. We make choices, have feelings, and develop ideas about ourselves and the world through a social process of interaction. Through this process, some ways of acting, feeling, and thinking are normalized—they become that which is considered normal. Other ways of acting, feeling, and thinking become deviant. Foucault explains that *normalization* results from social forces that act on us, but these forces do not merely act on us from the outside of ourselves. We also internalize these influences, and they become a part of who we are. They act on us from inside of our bodies, inside of our embodied experience.

To explore how social forces become internalized and normalized, Foucault uses the example of students in school following rules that involve much more than simply studying or reading from books or listening to lectures. Students must sit in a particular place with their feet on the ground and their eyes on the teacher. They must not fidget, play, or squirm. They must sit upright and be focused. The students' bodies are disciplined, as is their time. In other words, power over individuals is exerted through *discipline* via surveillance within controlled times, and in particular spaces such as classrooms, hallways, and the cafeteria. Classes happen in special places and last a set number of minutes, and lunch, too, is regulated by space and time. School happens in a unique building and starts and ends at a particular time. Students must adhere to all of this each day.

In this example, we see how human bodies have become the focus, the object of—and thus gripped by—a kind of discipline. For Foucault, this discipline springs from modern institutions such as schools, factories, prisons, hospitals, and the military. Discipline works to control and contain the body as well as to increase its usefulness. As a historian focused on social power, Foucault describes the shifts over time that brought increasingly detailed control over the way human bodies moved and acted. As Foucault argues, this made people more obedient and more efficient within this capitalist political economic system.

As another example of obedience and efficiency, Foucault describes the ways that militaries became more regulated. Foucault quotes from a French book on the military written in 1636: "Accustomed soldiers marching in file or in battalion to march to the rhythm of the drum. And to do this, one must begin with the right foot so that the whole troop raises the same foot at the same time."[40] Foucault compares this early seventeenth-century instruction to the marching orders of the mid-eighteenth century. Over one hundred years later, French army regulation explaining the proper way to march has become even more controlled, even more detailed, even more demanding. The description as to how to march directs troops to control each tiny part of the body:

> The length of the short step will be a foot, that of the ordinary step, the double step and the marching step will be two feet, the whole measured from one heel to the next; as for the duration, that of the small step and the ordinary step will last one second, during which two double steps would be performed; the duration of the march step will be a little longer than one second. . . . The ordinary step will be executed forwards, holding the head up high and the body erect, holding oneself in balance successively on a single leg, and bringing the other forwards, the ham taut, the point of the foot a little turned outwards and low, so that one may place one's foot, in such a way that each part may come to rest there at the same time without striking the ground.[41]

Foucault notes that these instructions, as with the growing discipline throughout western Europe, brought greater restraint and even more degrees of "precision in the breakdown of gestures and movements, another way of adjusting the body to temporal imperatives."[42]

Within institutions, such as schools and the military, power is exerted not only from outside by external surveillance but also from within each individual through internalization. About this, Foucault writes, "The historical moment of the disciplines was the moment when an art of the human body was born, which was directed not only at the growth of its skills, nor at the intensification of its subjection, but at the formation of a relation that in the mechanism itself makes it more obedient as it becomes more useful, and conversely."[43] The social power that flows in and around us grips us tighter and tighter, making us more dutiful and compliant.

Using Foucault's ideas about normalization, feminist philosopher Sandra Lee Bartky argues that girls and women experience great pressure to be thin in our culture. This is not a natural, biological pressure but a social pressure. And she claims this pressure, these "disciplinary practices," help to "produce a body of a certain size and general configuration," a body made to meet the socially constructed definition of feminine.[44] About this, Jean Halley writes, "US women experience this pressure all around them, for example, in mainstream ideas of what is beautiful and what is ugly, and in popular fitness programs. Women succumb to these pressures, and pressure themselves to be thin. Women watch themselves closely for fault, 'do I look fat in this?' and in eating practices where they monitor themselves closely, and in an ongoing way, about how many calories they consume."[45] This is a form of Foucault's normalization. Like many others, we argue that the standard of beauty in the United States is socially constructed and becomes normalized when members of that society internalize the social expectations of beauty.

Women and girls are not born worrying about thinness. Nor is worrying about thinness "normal" or normative in all cultures and historical time periods. This worry is imposed on and internalized by girls and women from the larger contemporary social world in the United States (among other places). Girls and women come to believe in and be obsessed by thinness. Similar to the worry over, the obsession with, thinness, we are normalized to assume heterosexuality (predominantly in monogamous dyads). However, in sharp contrast to our society's normalization of heterosexuality, humans have a multitude of ways of being sexual. Different ways are normative in different cultures and time periods. In our contemporary society, the process of normalization has meant that our imaginations have come to presuppose, to think in terms of being heterosexual.

We are also normalized to believe in and experience as "natural" certain ways of acting masculine for boys and men and of acting feminine for girls and women. Drawing from Foucault, social constructionists such as Candace West and Don H. Zimmerman call this *doing gender*.[46] Thus at baby showers in the mainstream (normative) culture, no one thinks it odd that baby girls are given lots of pink things and baby boys blue. This norm has been consistent since the 1940s, but a 1929 trade publication reveals the opposite used to be the norm: "The generally accepted rule is pink for the boys, and blue for the girls. The reason is that pink, being a more decided and stronger color, is more suitable for the boy, while blue, which is more delicate and dainty, is prettier for the girl."[47] In addition to following contemporary social norms for clothing color, baby girls are decorated with flowers and baby boys with footballs. As the children grow, boys are taught to be ashamed of crying while girls are comforted when they cry.

When a boy related to one of the authors, David, cried in fifth grade, he was told sharply to stop crying and that "no one likes a crying child!" Yet two days later a fifth-grade girl cried and was gently soothed by the same teacher. Exhibiting the deep grip normative gender, cisgender, roles have on us (and the confusion of fifth-graders about psychiatric disabilities), another fifth-grade boy later politely asked David whether perhaps he had schizophrenia because he had cried at school.

Social theorist Judith Butler claims that gender and gendered norms and beliefs like that of "boys don't cry" spring from a performance that produces and reproduces gender in an ongoing way. In that performance, our culture regulates and limits what gender means in a particular time and place. Butler's argument refutes belief in bootstrap theory, which would suggest we are individually free to perform gender as we choose, within a system where one's lot in life is determined by individual choices. (Elites demonstrate belief in bootstrap theory when they claim they are successful because they pulled themselves up to their wealth by their own bootstraps. Belief in bootstrap theory requires that elites remain blind to their privileges of inherited wealth and of being placed, through no action of their own, in situations with rich opportunity.) In contrast, Butler clarifies that gender is "never fully self-styled, for styles have a history, and those histories condition and limit the possibilities."[48] We become gendered and reproduce the gender system of our society through our repetitive performances of gender.

NORMALIZATION AND THE POLITICAL ECONOMY

As cultural materialists, we argue that normalization entails, springs from, and reproduces particular political economies. Feudalism (discussed above) is a *political economic system* that benefits some over others and makes normative the ways of living within and thinking about each person's position in that system. Another example closer to home, slavery in the United States, involved both an economic structure of wealthy whites owning people of African descent and thus owning and profiting from their labor. In this political economic way of living, normalization happened such that whites believed themselves to be and experienced themselves as fundamentally superior to all people of African descent. Whites benefited economically from this racist system, and they believed in the racism as a way of thinking, too. Whites believed themselves to be deserving of the benefits they garnered through slavery. In this society where racism was normative, whites thought they were and experienced themselves as more intelligent, more civilized, more rational, more scientific, more spiritual, more beautiful than people of African descent.[49]

Heterosexuality also supports a political economic system that benefits some over others. Since industrialization in the United States, women's largely unpaid domestic labor, the labor of cooking, cleaning, bearing and caring for children, has produced and reproduced the adults in the wage workforce. That is, women in sexually monogamous, married dyads with men have reproduced and largely continue to reproduce the workers, who are the source of labor in our capitalist economy. The wealthy benefit from that labor, as do men, regardless of social class, who depend on women's domestic labor and assume that women will—and should—do it. For women, this political economy has often meant that divorce from a heterosexual marriage results in a loss of social[50] and economic privilege.[51] When many of us reflect on the homes we grew up in or the homes of adults we know today, we see the extensive domestic labor done, often alone and usually unpaid, by women and their daughters.

HETERONORMATIVITY

In 1991 social theorist Michael Warner developed the idea of *heteronormativity* in his seminal article and later book, "Fear of a Queer Planet."[52] Warner argued that a social world that assumes and promotes heterosexuality is a heteronormative world. The normality of heterosexuality is not a biological reality but a way of thinking, an ideology, an expression of culture springing from and helping to reproduce a way of living that privileges some—those who are cisgender, those who are heterosexual, and those who are men—over others. This way of living demands both normative gender and normative sexuality. For a woman, heteronormativity insists that she be heterosexually coupled with a man and that she act in feminine ways that reproduce unfair, unequal, and unpaid labor from her in the forms of child care and housework. Feminist sociologist Judith Lorber argues that the process of investigating heteronormativity provides remarkable insight: "Analyzing the social processes that construct the categories we call 'female and male,' 'women and men,' and 'homosexual and heterosexual' uncovers the ideology and power differentials congealed in these categories."[53] Indeed, as discussed above, some conservative thinkers are concerned about the ways in which challenges to heteronormativity will be the undoing of our society.

Included in these categories, in this body of assumptions, is the idea that sex, gender, and sexuality normally and naturally go together in a binary way; in this thinking, if one has a vagina (sex), then one is female and feminine (gender) and desires men (sexuality). If one has a penis, then one is male and masculine and desires women. Butler argues that this *heteronormative model of identity* is central to the *heterosexual matrix*, the term Butler coined for the hegemonic institutions, identities, and relations that uphold, produce, and reproduce heterosexuality in our society.[54] Heteronormative thinking assumes a marriage between a man and a woman is the best form of sexual relationship and at the heart of a "normal" and healthy family. Heteronormativity touches every aspect of our lives. Warner writes,

> Every person who comes to a queer self-understanding knows in one way or another that her stigmatization is intricated with gender, with the family, with notions of individual freedom, the state, public speech, consumption and desire, nature and culture, maturation, reproductive politics, racial and national fantasy, class identity, truth and trust, censorship, intimate life and social display, terror and violence, heath care, and deep cultural norms about the bearing of the body. Being queer means fighting about these issues all the time, locally and piecemeal but always with consequences.[55]

Warner claims, "The logic of the [hetero] sexual order is so deeply embedded by now in an indescribably wide range of social institutions, and is embedded in the most standard accounts of the world, queer struggles aim not just at toleration or equal status but at challenging those institutions and accounts."[56] For Warner, the task of queer theory is to challenge the "default heteronormativity" with a multitude of new possibilities involved in what Warner calls modern culture's "worst nightmare, a queer planet."[57] Queer theorists drew from Warner's essay on heteronormativity and began to frequently refer to and critique this important idea.

Like all social theorists, Warner drew from earlier scholars. Warner was inspired by thinkers such as radical feminist Rich, who advanced the idea of compulsory heterosexuality (discussed in chapter 2 and previously in this chapter), anthropologist Rubin, who challenged readers to consider the sex/gender system (discussed previously in this chapter), and philosopher and historian Foucault, who illuminated normalization (discussed previously in this chapter). Advancing the work of scholars like Rich, Rubin, and Foucault, Warner's heteronormativity involves compulsory heterosexuality, the sex/gender system, and normalization. In our mainstream culture, we have assumed heterosexuality to be a kind of truth, a truth that we have believed to be natural and believed to be morally correct. In much the same way, we assume "truths" about our mainstream gender roles, for example, the "truth" that women make the best caregivers.

In *Boundaries of Touch: Parenting and Adult-Child Intimacy*, Halley critically explores heteronormative "truths" regarding gender and parenting.[58]

> One example of an important—and questionable—"truth" is that for the past couple of centuries, we in Western cultures have considered women "natural" parents. In one sense, this was a self-fulfilling prophecy. Women were understood to be naturally nurturing, and were raised to be so. In another sense, of course, this thinking is incorrect, and deeply limiting to both men and women. As we begin to think of men as nurturing, too, the culture has begun to raise and socialize men to *be* nurturing. Indeed, much like that which we believe to be "truth," we *ourselves* are, as Judith Lorber writes, "transformed by social practices to fit into the salient categories of a society."[59]
>
> Another "truth" imagined to be natural, is the assumption of heterosexuality. This assumption that heterosexuality is "natural" (much like the idea that women mothering is "natural") lies at the core of mainstream United States culture. The result of this assumption is compulsory heterosexuality, a social system grounded in heteronormative ideology that reinforces (indeed, *forces*, as the penalties are severe for many who challenge heteronormativity) heterosexuality in all aspects of social life.[60]

THE CLOSET

Compulsory heterosexuality stigmatizes queer identity and calls us to question who and what is heterosexual. *Stigma* refers to an attribute of a person that has been socially constructed to be devalued in a culture. Most individuals will find themselves experiencing stigma of some kind. Stigma exists on a continuum; it might cause mild discomfort at one end and profound oppression at the other. Stigma can range from a temporary embarrassment (such as a stain on one's shirt at an important social event) to a trait that might be profoundly debased (as in tragic cases of people being assaulted and murdered for transgender identity).[61]

Being queer continues to be deeply stigmatizing within many social contexts in our culture. Indeed, compulsory heterosexuality polices the sexuality of all individuals, including those who identify as heterosexual.

When an individual faces a situation in which a stigma may harm opportunities or social interactions, one might try to *pass*—to present oneself as having an identity that is not stigmatized. Sociologist Erving Goffman recognizes that profound experiences of stigma—including being queer in many social contexts—are so powerful that it would be challenging to choose not to pass. In many situations, strong potential benefits of convincing others that one is heterosexual and cisgender can tempt queer individuals to pass.[62]

As Goffman argues, most people pass at some point in their lives by hiding a stigmatizing aspect of their identity. Goffman writes that "the problems people face who make a concerted and well-organized effort to pass are problems that a wide range of persons face at some time or other."[63] Even when an aspect of one's identity seems to be readily apparent in most situations, exceptions will arise. For example, a person who uses a wheelchair might regularly deal with expressions of pity from strangers but might have an active life on the Internet with people who are purposely kept unaware of the disability. Passing occurs on a continuum from something one does occasionally to a fundamental change of life. Examples of a queer person occasionally choosing to pass include consciously obscuring the gender of a loved one during casual conversation or laughing at an offensive anti-queer joke to avoid coming out to an acquaintance. In a way, all individuals feel pressured to fit within highly conscripted sexual and gender roles.

Writer and activist Mattilda Bernstein Sycamore argues that binary thinking about sexuality and gender is stigmatizing. While individuals who identify with queer sexuality or gender will be deeply stigmatized by binary thinking, even individuals who identify as heterosexual and cisgender will find themselves feeling pressured to express their sexuality and gender in tightly conscripted ways.[64] For example, a colleague admitted her discomfort whenever she mentioned her "partner" when talking with students. She would quickly contort the conversation to make sure the next sentence included a masculine pronoun to identify her partner as a man. Because of the social norm that men are expected to leave an empty urinal between them in a public restroom, a man desperate to urinate might find himself feeling forced to wait despite the availability of a urinal.

Dylan Scholinski's adolescent experience in the early 1980s represents an example of someone passing for an extended period. As described above, Scholinski's psychiatrist diagnosed gender identity disorder and insisted on a dramatic change in gender expression. In order to avoid punishment and increase privileges at the hospital, Scholinski learned to pass as an "appropriate female."[65]

Passing ranges from unintentional to carefully orchestrated. Gay partners on a hike in a popular park might inadvertently pass if other hikers assume they have a platonic relationship. Lesbian partners who are not out to their families might carefully "straighten up the apartment" by hiding evidence of their sexual relationship to prepare for a visit from family members.

Goffman identified *covering* as a way that people can seek to make a social situation more comfortable. Covering is distinct from passing, in that passing produces an inaccurate perception that someone does not have a stigmatized identity. In contrast, covering occurs when an individual's stigma is known. Covering occurs when a person with a stigmatized identity seeks to make others more comfortable by making choices that will make the stigma less obvious.[66] For example, a lesbian woman talking casually with heterosexual colleagues might refer to her partner as her "friend" rather than using a term that reminds everyone of the romantic connection between the women. Law professor Kenji Yoshino identifies advice he has been given to cover his gay identity by presenting himself as "a professor of constitutional law who 'happened' to be gay." He was discouraged from focusing his scholarly work on gay rights, as though that would "flaunt" his gay identity and make others uncomfortable.[67]

Queer individuals live in a constant process of choosing to come out or to pass—deciding in each situation whether to reveal their stigmatized status. As Goffman claims, "Because of the great rewards in being considered normal, almost all persons who are in a position to pass will do so on some occasion by intent."[68] Binary thinking about sexuality and gender will pressure most queer people to feel the need to pass some of the time.[69] In contrast, heterosexual and cisgender people have a profound, unfair privilege of not feeling the same pull to pass as do queer peers, for whom almost every new acquaintance presents another decision regarding whether to come out and, if so, whether to cover.

HUMOR AS A CHALLENGE TO SHAME

Covering can be a defense against shame, a way to appear to fit with a powerful group. Goffman explored the importance of identifying with a group. He distinguished between an *ingroup*—those who share an identity—and an *outgroup*—an identity to which one does not belong and does not seek to belong.[70] Humor can be hurtful or helpful, depending on one's position in a group. Humor can be a tool to disparage an outgroup or to make a connection with an ingroup. Humor can also offer a challenge to shame. For example, Pauline Park delighted that her devout, "basically fundamentalist" Christian mother hoped that Park would become an organist and have a career in the church. Park did take piano and organ lessons, and she still plays and loves the piano. It is, she disclosed, still her favorite thing to do.

With her wry sense of humor, Park joked that her mother never foresaw that having an organist in the family could mean having someone whose very business card would scream queer identity. She explained, "It's funny because the national association is called the AGO, the American Guild of Organists. If you become a Fellow of the American Guild of Organists you get to put 4 letters behind your name, FAGO."[71]

Rather than becoming an organist, Park's career is dedicated to queer activism. As a member of the queer ingroup, Park can play with humor in ways that outgroup members should seek to avoid because it could be hurtful.

DISCUSSION QUESTIONS

1. How do conservative arguments differ from cultural materialist arguments about the role of heterosexuality in families? Identify key elements that would be included in a conservative argument and a cultural materialist argument. For each type of argument, identify any direct acknowledgment of the role of privilege or ways that privilege remains invisible within the argument.

2. Select a social institution (for example, school, workplace, religious group) and identify several of the expectations for being "normal" within that context. Explore how observation of deviance might make injunctive and descriptive norms more visible. Describe to what extent queer individuals might be accepted as normal or as deviant within this institution.

3. Based on the descriptions of terms that have been used to describe prejudice against queer people, which terms might you choose to use in different contexts? Explain why you might select one term over another in a given situation. Explore commonalities and differences across terms that follow the format of racism and sexism, such as heterosexism, classism, ageism, and ableism.

4. To explore normalization, focus on a form of pressure from within to follow a norm. For example, the chapter discussed women desiring to be thin and men trying not to cry in public. Evaluate the roles of social institutions, social power, and internalization within normalization. Explain how this issue connects to the political economic system.

5. Who is privileged by heteronormativity? Explain the roles of compulsory heterosexuality, the sex/gender system, and normalization within heteronormativity. What "truths" become suspect when critically examining heteronormativity?

6. To what extent are you sympathetic to someone choosing to pass as having a nonstigmatized identity? To what extent are you sympathetic to someone who refuses to cover?

7. To what extent does the meaning of a word that could be used as a slur depend on social context? To what extent is the meaning altered by whether the user is part of an ingroup that has traditionally been the target of that slur? Is it potentially positive if a

member of an ingroup reclaims a term that would be derogatory if used by a member of an outgroup?

4

FIFTY WAYS TO BE NORMAL AND OTHER CHALLENGES TO PRIVILEGE[1]

Lena at age three explained her drawing to her mother. In it, there was a tall woman driving and a small man in the passenger's seat because, Lena clarified, women are taller than men and men do not usually drive. In contrast to her five-foot-seven mother, at five feet, two inches, Lena's father is very small for a man in the United States, and growing up in New York City, he never learned to drive. Lena's mother grew up in the Rocky Mountains, where driving borders on necessity.

CHALLENGING DUALISTIC THINKING ABOUT GENDER

Stereotypes about gender promote thinking in false binary, dualistic ways that serve to keep men in a privileged (albeit violent and stressful) place and to keep women in a supposedly protected but powerless space. Classic use of dualistic thinking has characterized men as tall, strong, and reasonable and women as petite, often frail, and usually irrational—a problematic example of stereotyping all men with one set of traits and all women as the opposite. Unlike Lena's experience of her mother as the sole driver and her father always a passenger, men are often stereotyped as good drivers, while women are stereotyped as poor drivers.[2]

Drawing from Michel Foucault, social theorist Judith Butler claims that social power happens not only to us, as when people with power

make choices that shape our lives, but also within us. We each reproduce social power by, for example, the repetitive performance of gender. We ask readers to imagine a man and a woman sitting as students
in a college classroom. Both perform gender in the clothing they choose
to wear, the physical posture of their body, the gestures they make, the
tone they use to speak, and the words they choose. In the classes we
teach, men stereotypically sit with a wider stance between their feet,
while women tend to take up much less physical space. Men and wom-
en are likely to make different gestures when they signal that they want
to speak, with men more likely to interrupt another speaker.[3] These
performances of gender recreate social messages about men and wom-
en and maintain traditional social power. Butler argues that this performance of gender brings about, or makes, gender. Our performance of
gender, genders us and our social world in a particular place and time.
Butler claims that gender is "a construction that regularly conceals its
genesis."[4]

Because cisgender performance is so privileged—considered so
"normal"—that it often becomes invisible, Butler uses the example of
drag performance to illuminate the way that gender—and she argues
the self—is constituted through performance. The television series *Ru-
Paul's Drag Race* provides a behind-the-scenes perspective on drag
performance. Journalist Julianne Escobedo Shepherd describes that
"RuPaul is exposing 'the art of drag'—the toil that goes into it, the skill
set and gumption it requires." RuPaul explains, "Drag is an extension of
the realization that, 'You mean, the thing I think I am, I'm not really?'
Exactly. So have fun with it. Change it. That's why I think drag comes
up against so much opposition from people, because the ego knows
drag is a threat to the ego." Aligned with Butler's theory, RuPaul acknowledges that examination of drag reveals how the self and gender
are performed.[5]

Butler identifies that drag performance presents a way to understand broader performance of dualistic gender in our society. Butler
writes, "In imitating gender, drag implicitly reveals the imitative structure of gender itself."[6] In her insightful overview of the work of Butler,
queer theory scholar Nikki Sullivan clarifies that for Butler, drag "suggests a dissonance between sex and performance, sex and gender, and
gender and performance, because the so-called sex of the performer is
not the same as the gender being performed." When we see drag, we

recognize that gender can be performed; we recognize in the drag performance that the human performing is not gripped in gender by the genitals. Someone with a penis can perform as a woman, and having a vagina does not limit one from performing as a man. Drag makes a dissonance, or inconsistency, visible between genitals and gender. Sullivan states, "Gender, then, is nothing but a parody."[7] Drag performance of gender reveals that all gender is performance; all gender is imitation. Indeed, in *RuPaul's Drag U*, a spin-off show that ran from 2010 to 2012, drag queens provided makeovers to tomboyish cisgender women, including lessons on feminine movement and dress.

In the performance of gender, dualisms extend to categories that are not truly opposite but are treated as such. For example, men have been associated with careers while women have been relegated to the home. In dualistic thinking, career and home are treated as opposite, with career regarded as more valuable than the work of the home. Similarly, men have been associated with the venerable possibilities of the mind while women have been associated with the base uses of the body, especially women's potential physical roles as objects of sexual desire for men (explored further in chapter 6) and as biological mothers. A common joke refers to keeping a woman barefoot and pregnant in a kitchen, implying that a man wearing shoes will be her breadwinner. In this dualistic, binary thinking, men are valued and women are devalued.[8]

The first wave of feminism began in the United States in the 1840s and extended through the early 1900s. Activist women and their male allies had been working to abolish slavery and expand the rights of African Americans. Through this work to challenge dominant norms, they were inspired to recognize male privilege as well as racial privilege. Feminists demanded greater rights for women, pressed for critical thinking about gender dualisms, and worked to expand roles for women, including greater career opportunities and the right to vote.

The founding of the science of psychology coincided with the first wave of feminism. Psychological researchers soon became interested in examining gender, with a focus on revealing differences between women and men. Critical thinking about research requires thoughtful evaluation of how historical time, culture, and other biases influence the questions researchers choose to ask, the way they seek evidence, and the meaning assigned to data. In a field dominated by men within a patriarchal cultural context, any evidence of gender differences was interpreted as demonstrating the superiority of boys and men in the world outside the home and the suitability of girls and women to the domestic sphere.[9]

From our vantage point, we can perceive bias in the ways researchers of the past sought and thought about evidence. Similarly, when we disagree with the political perspective of present-day researchers, we can often see their bias. For example, researchers who believe in gender dualism might focus on looking for differences and ignore similarities. Further, they might argue that evidence of difference supports essentialism—that women and men are inherently different—and disregard social constructionist explanations. To be a critical consumer of research, one must question what biases in the scientific work of today will be revealed in the future.

Since its start, feminism has challenged dominant assumptions. Women across the United States attained the right to vote in 1920—a major achievement of the first wave of feminism. Beginning in the 1960s, the second wave of feminism focused on attaining greater gender equality, addressing intimate partner violence, and expanding reproductive rights. Similar to the first wave of feminism emerging from the abolition movement, the second wave of feminism was sparked by the civil rights movement for racial equality. In both cases, critical examination of racial privilege aroused recognition of male privilege and inspired work toward gender equality.

As psychology continued to examine gender, the success of the feminist movements meant that more women had the opportunity to become psychological researchers and that thinking about gender was shifting. In 1974, developmental psychologists Eleanor E. Maccoby and Carol N. Jacklin applied a feminist critique of dualism in their focus not only on gender differences but also on similarities. Contrary to common dualistic thinking, they found similarity in how active or passive boys and girls are on average. Boys and girls range from active to passive, with greater differences comparing boys to one another and girls to one another than when comparing the average of the boys to the average of the girls. Maccoby and Jacklin found that the genders were similar in independence and dependence, defiance and compliance, competitiveness and nurturance. Girls were as strong as boys in intellectual analysis, goals for achievement, and planning for success.[10]

In the decades that have followed this seminal work, researchers have continued to debate whether the focus should be gender similarities or gender differences.[11] Compelling evidence continues to support that women and men are more alike than different.[12] As social constructionists, when gender differences are found, we do not perceive men and women as opposites but look for cues to how our social world might pressure boys to be different from girls, men to be distinct from women.

HETERONORMATIVITY AS BARRIER TO FRIENDSHIP

Social barriers exist that limit friendships among men and friendships among boys. To avoid giving the impression of being gay, heterosexual, cisgender boys may refrain from even casual friendships with queer boys as well as from intense friendships with heterosexual, cisgender boy peers. For example, clinical psychologist William Pollack writes, "Indeed it's this very fear—the fear of being labeled a fairy, a wuss, or a fag, of being perceived as feminine or homosexual—that often prevents boys from feeling comfortable engaging in serious emotional talks with each other." Pollack explains about this fear, "It too often inhibits boys from ever saying they care for each other. It often prevents them from expressing physical affection for other boys. It allows adults to put a low premium on the kind of tender, loving friendships among boys that, with few exceptions, we encourage among girls."[13]

Pollack recounts a story of two third-grade boys hugging at school and their teacher's and principal's striking responses. On the first day of third grade, Tommy excitedly hugged his good friend, Charlie, when Charlie arrived a little bit late at school. Their teacher, Mrs. Hutchins, saw the hug but interpreted it as "struggling and fighting" and sent them to the principal's office.

> "We weren't fighting," the boys explained to Mr. Atkins, the principal. "We were just hugging."
>
> To demonstrate, Charlie planted a kiss on Tommy's head and added, "We're best friends. We like each other."
>
> Mr. Atkins was not impressed. "I guess Mrs. Hutchins was confused in thinking you were fighting. But such sexualized behavior is

inappropriate in the classroom. I'm sending you back to class now, but I want you to take these letters home for your parents to sign."[14]

Later when telling Pollack the story, Charlie's parents explained how confused they were by the letter. They asked Charlie, "What do they mean, Charlie, that you were sexually inappropriate in class?" Charlie's response, "I just hugged Tommy," left them even more confused. These parents who had raised their child to be open and loving could not imagine what would be wrong with the boys giving each other a hug. The next day, Charlie's mother met with the principal. About the hug, she told the principal, "This is the kind of affectionate behavior we love in our son. Why are you punishing him for it?"

> "As you will see in the pupils' manual, inappropriate touching and sexual expression are explicitly forbidden," said the principal.
>
> "So you mean that if two girls in the fourth grade were working closely together on a project and one hugs the other, Mrs. Hutchins would be afraid of violence and you would send them home for sexual activity?"
>
> Mr. Atkins's eyes widened and he hesitated. "We would have to evaluate the circumstances of the specific situation," he finally said.[15]

We invite readers to speculate about what Charlie and Tommy learned from their teacher's and principal's reactions. The principal seemed surprised when Charlie's mother confronted him with a question that asked him to consider whether he had different standards for boys than for girls in terms of applying the rules of the pupil's manual. How often might different standards be applied without authority figures recognizing the unfairness?

CONFRONTING BINARY THOUGHT

Some queer movements have made powerful challenges to heteronormative binary culture. Yet even those inside the queer community struggle with what it means to challenge gender dualisms. Because of the concern that they reproduce normative binary gender, butch/femme (or fem) lesbian culture has been upsetting and confusing to some lesbians and feminists who are not part of this culture.[16] Some argue that butch/femme roles merely reproduce masculine (butch) and feminine (femme), rather than take apart, dualistic gender roles. Butch lesbian women tend to dress in more traditionally masculine clothes and behave in ways considered normative for men—more stoic and showing less emotion. Butch lesbians are more likely to open the door for other women, to ask others to dance, and to take charge in more traditionally masculine ways. Women in femme lesbian roles often dress in more stereotypically feminine ways. They more easily pass as cisgender women and are often perceived by others to be straight.

Sociologist Alison Eves argues that butch/femme can "be viewed as both structured by and exceeding normative heterosexuality."[17] She identifies that some aspects of butch/femme culture are strategic choices, while others may not be conscious or intentional. Butch/femme culture can be considered a "creative appropriation and resignification of gender." In other words, women can make gender their own through butch/femme culture. Yet Eves acknowledges that all of us are "constrained by norms, sanctions and hegemonic readings in a heteronormative context."[18] In other words, butch/femme culture is expressed within a context filled with heteronormative pressure from outside oneself, internalization of heteronormativity, and threats of social punishment if one deviates. Eves draws on Butler's revelation that all of us perform gender within a social context and on Adrienne Rich's identification that lesbianism is often made invisible. Butch lesbians and femme lesbians respond to their heteronormative social world in ways that might be perceived as reinforcing binary gender or as creating uniquely lesbian spaces and lesbian visibility.

Fem lesbian feminist Joan Nestle, who came from the working class, beautifully articulates the power and importance of the butch/femme culture in lesbian bars of the late 1950s. Describing her young adult experience, Nestle writes that she "entered gay life by finding the world of lesbian bars strung out along the narrow streets of Greenwich Village."

> Dark and dangerous, haunted by the police, these bars were places that we carved into homes, homes where we found touch and friends and learned about how to be a queer in the late McCarthy period of this country. Butch and fem women in their forties and fifties carried their worldly ways to us here. The bar was a delta, gathering the richness of lesbian experience on its smoky shores. Here we met

women who proved in their stances and in their stories that social isolation could be borne, that familial rejection could be outlived, that the state with its sexual policing laws could be outwitted.[19]

By the 1970s, many lesbian feminists wanted to challenge traditional and binary masculine/feminine gender roles. Second-wave lesbian feminists opposed the frozen and limited ways of doing gender in the United States. They defied normative femininity by, for example, dressing in comfortable, but traditionally masculine, clothes such as jeans and work boots. They saw lesbian feminism as a matter of politics as well as sexual desire and romantic relationship. Lesbian feminists believed their love undermined and challenged the oppressive patriarchy in which they had come of age.

Nestle describes overhearing two young women at a meeting of lesbian feminist activists. They complained about two older butch lesbians attending the meeting. "'Did you see those two gray-haired women who just walked in?' one said to her companion. 'Why do they have to look like men? I hope they don't come back.'" Indeed, Nestle notes, the butch women did not return for future meetings. We wonder whether they understood that they were not fully welcome. Nestle writes, "I did not speak up for them in 1971 because I wanted so desperately to be part of the new world of lesbian feminism, and I hadn't yet learned from feminism how to honor its principles by valuing my own stigmatized life and those who shared it with me."[20]

Similar to the negative response of the lesbian feminists to the butch women at Nestle's meeting, some feminists and members of the queer community have struggled to accept and support trans lives because they argue that some trans people reinforce binary gender. Some trans men identify as stereotypically masculine men, and some trans women identify as stereotypically feminine women. Some trans people, like many cisgender people, position themselves in the world in a way that supports gender dualisms. We argue that masculine and feminine, and butch and femme, gender roles in and of themselves are not the problem. There is nothing wrong with gender roles per se. We work for a world where everyone is celebrated for their gender expression and gender identity, be it masculine/feminine or some other of the infinity of ways of being gendered. Gender formations, including the binary ones of our normative culture, are only a problem if people are forced into them. They are a problem insofar as normative culture demands these binary gender roles, freezing people into them before we even have a chance to think the thought that there might be alternatives.

Indeed, rather than reinforcing binary oppression, we believe the trans movement, trans people, the celebration of trans lives, and the possibilities offered by a world that supports trans experiences, shake the foundation of false assumptions about gender as a binary even as some trans people (like some cisgender people) experience their gender as fitting a binary frame and celebrate that experience. The boundless options for being gendered that include and move beyond those hailed by normative culture—and changing for some people day by day—can be wonderfully confusing and profoundly liberating. The trans movement helps us all to see the endless array of possibilities.

HAVENS: THE ROLE OF LGBTQ CENTERS

LGBTQ or queer centers are locations where queer individuals are not expected to engage in covering. These are places where queer individuals might work together to organize political action, meet other members of the queer community, find acceptance, obtain information about queer experiences and events, and simply hang out. Jeremiah Jurkiewicz, one of the founders and the coordinator of the LGBTQ Resource Center at the College of Staten Island of the City University of New York, explained that just having a queer center on campus makes a positive difference at a university—even for students, faculty, and staff who never actually spend time at the center. Merely walking by it, seeing posters of events sponsored by the center, and hearing about it from others changes attitudes. The LGBTQ Resource Center validates and makes visible queer presence on campus.[21]

Jurkiewicz described his first time visiting a queer center. He grew up in the state of Maryland and went to Catholic school. In spite of the Catholic Church's institutionalized rejection of queer sexuality, Jurkiewicz courageously came out while in high school. He was the only student who came out at his school during his years there. When he arrived on Staten Island, he was eighteen years old, and he discovered that the borough of New York City had a center, the LGBT (now renamed Pride) Center of Staten Island.[22] He explained that he had

never been part of a queer center or group, so when he saw a flyer, he
quickly found his way there and started attending regularly. Jurkiewicz
said, "It was a way for me to feel that I belonged, that everyone around
me was just like me or going through something similar to me." About
the LGBT Center of Staten Island, Jurkiewicz said, "That's number
one, it provides a gathering space for like-minded people. It provides
that space for people to come together and bond and talk about things."
Jurkiewicz noted, "That was really instrumental for me."

Jurkiewicz joined the gay-straight alliance at his college and attended the weekly meetings regularly. Yet Jurkiewicz said, "We have
such a large, diverse campus." One club meeting once a week was not
enough. "A lot of the students agreed with me that [a campus center]
needed to exist." They needed a dedicated physical space where students could drop by more than just once a week, where events could be
planned and hosted, and where resources such as books could be
loaned and informative pamphlets could be distributed. Such a center
on a college campus usually requires a major commitment from the
administration. Jurkiewicz claimed proudly, "It really helped that the
administration was on our side." He celebrated his college as a remarkably queer and queer-friendly campus. Jurkiewicz explained, "It has out
faculty and staff who are able to function and be proud of who they are,
and advocate for such things." He noted, at other campuses, "There are
not many out faculty and staff, or they are met with resistant adminis-
trations. They might not be bigoted, but they might say that this [queer
demands for a center and other support], we don't think this is worthy
of money."

Because Jurkiewicz's campus has a visible, out, and proud queer
community and a supportive administration, it became an early college
to dedicate an LGBTQ center. After helping to found the center, Jurkiewicz became the second person to coordinate it. He uses his position
to organize events for queer students, faculty, and staff and to educate
on different issues. "A lot of students just come here to hang out,"
Jurkiewicz noted. They come to relax, to study, and to talk with Jurkiewicz. "I am just a college assistant," Jurkiewicz explained. Yet to students, "I am someone they can come and speak to. The goal from the
beginning was for the coordinator of the center to be someone who's
younger, who the students can relate to." Jurkiewicz said, "I will tell
them any day of the week, I do not have any licensing, I am not a

counselor or a psychologist. I'm not a psychiatrist. I will walk you to the counseling center if something big comes up. But I am here, you know, for their day to day conversations." Jurkiewicz continued, "When students realize that the college supports them by this center just existing, it kind of spurs them on to work harder, and to get to graduation."[23]

As places with dual goals of inclusion and political action, queer centers face difficult questions of whether to become involved in controversial issues. In February 2011 there was a great controversy at the LGBTQ Center in Manhattan. Pauline Park explained that for months a group of activists called the Siege Busters had been using space at the Center for meetings as they agitated against the Israeli government's siege on the Gaza Strip. She noted, "Palestinians there are living in dreadful conditions. The Israeli government is starving the Palestinians, blocking all sorts of aid." As a component of their work, the Siege Busters decided to have an annual event called the Israeli Apartheid Week.[24] Park explained, "They were going to hold a dance party addressing Israeli apartheid at the Center, and they were going to pay rent for the room."

Yet there was a backlash about the event and it was canceled. Michael Lucas, a pornography producer, columnist for the *Advocate*, and Israel supporter, alleged that the organizers of the event were anti-Semitic. The executive director of the Center, Glennda Testone, argued that the event would have disrupted the Center's goal of being "a safe haven for LGBT groups and individuals."[25]

Park heard about the Center's decision to cancel Israeli Apartheid Week and was outraged. She was not convinced that there was any evidence of anti-Semitism. In fact, as we note below, Park knew that many Jewish people are critical of Israeli treatment of Palestinians. "I mean, the Israeli occupation and the Palestinian occupied territory is an issue that is nearly as old as I am, right? But I did not have any desire to get involved with this issue because it's not like I don't have other work to do. It's incredibly controversial. But I was so outraged by what the Center had done."

Because of her outrage, Park went to a community forum and spoke out. In response to the forum, Glennda Testone claimed that the issue was not a queer one and, further, that it was controversial. From Park's perspective, this rationale was "ridiculous." She clarified that queer centers regularly explore controversial issues and that "the Center was founded to be a space for community organizing." Park noted that it was started as a space for activism of just the very sort that the Siege Busters engage in.

Park expressed a concern that many queer centers "have succumbed to a discourse of providing social services" at the expense of maintaining their identity as places meant in large part for activism and organizing. Park expressed a concern that "LGBT centers are more and more [staying away from] involvement with anything that is not directly LGBT and anything that is at all political or controversial." Park argued, "LGBT community centers have to be a place for community discussion of controversial issues."

Park cofounded a new group, Queers Against Israeli Apartheid, which attracted a majority of Jewish members. Park explained that today in New York City there are probably more people who are Jewish than Palestinian involved in this activism. "And so in a sense it's kind of funny because a lot of people in this country think it's Israelis versus Palestinians. That's way too binary."

The authors of this text wonder, what should be the mandate of queer centers? Historically they have engaged with very controversial issues, that is, queer lives. Should such community centers shy away from controversy now that queer existence is less controversial? And if they do take on controversial issues, what makes an issue relevant to the queer community? How do we decide whether an issue is queer?

Park believes that queer community centers have to be more than simply providers of social services. For Park, in canceling Israeli Apartheid Week, the Center in Manhattan has "fallen down on the job." Members of the Center argue that the Israeli occupation of Palestine is not a queer issue. Park strongly disagrees with this perspective. There are Palestinian queer people. And Park notes that our—queer and straight alike—United States tax dollars are going to support this occupation.[26] One organization, No Tax Dollars to Israel, estimates that United States taxpayers pay from four to six billion dollars each year to back the Israeli occupation in Palestine.[27]

What do you think?

HOW INCLUSIVE IS QUEER IDENTITY?

LGBTQ centers also face decisions regarding what identities to welcome within the concept of queer. For example, should people who identify as asexual or agender be welcomed as queer? Given the stigmatization of sexuality for individuals with disability, are all expressions of sexuality for those with disability, therefore, queer forms of sexuality?

Danielle Lucchese is strong, resilient, smart, organized, a great writer, a loving person, and very courageous. Like every human being, she lives on a continuum of ability. Yet to the larger society, Lucchese explains, instead of being seen as able, albeit it with some impairment, she is understood as disabled and not normal.

Lucchese has a visual impairment and what she calls "balance issues." Lucchese clarifies,

> I was born with Hydrocephalus, when cerebral spinal fluid (CSF) does not drain properly, resulting in built up pressure on the brain. As a result of the build up CSF on the right side of my brain, my [body's] left side is significantly weaker. Some of the fluid also went behind my optic nerve which triggered Nystagmus, an involuntary eye movement. Between both my diagnoses, doctors were unsure if I would ever talk or walk, and as a result, I received intense physical, occupational, and visual therapy until my high school graduation.[28]

Lucchese missed class time each time she went for therapy. This, she says, "marked me as different from my classmates because they never missed class." To the people close to her, Lucchese is a person like any other, but to her elementary, middle, and high school classmates, her disability made her unlike them, different.

Lucchese describes the response in our society to people with disability as binary. She argues, "One's body either conforms to society's perception of normal and able or it does not." If someone's body is "labeled disabled," then the person is understood as needing to be repaired.[29] Lucchese claims that embedded in this (dis)ability binary is a second dualism, that is, if one is understood to be able/normal, then one can be understood to be sexual. If one is understood to be on the other side of the binary, disabled/not normal, then one is also understood to be not sexual. The assumption inherent in this thinking is that if a person's body is not "normal," then the individual cannot have (normal) sex. Lucchese's experience of disability is that people do not think of her as a sexual person or a person with whom they could be romantically and sexually involved.

Cultural theorist Robert McRuer argues that stigmatization of queer individuals and of individuals who experience disability become conflated. The treatment of queerness as illness equates being queer with being disabled, while normative discomfort of thinking about the sexuality of individuals with disability makes all sexuality of individuals with disability queer sexuality.[30]

Binary thinking suggests that individuals can be clearly classified in one of the following two categories: able-bodied or disabled.[31] Normative thinking further suggests that all normal able-bodied people are sexual while it denies that people who experience disability should or could enjoy sexuality. Gender studies scholar Eunjung Kim identifies that social expectations that desexualize people with disability are deeply problematic.[32] Activists for disability rights seek to raise awareness that many people with (like many without) disability are sexual beings—people who desire and enjoy sexual activity. As experienced by Lucchese, normative *desexualization*—social assumptions and expectations that deny an individual is a sexual being—takes the forms of assuming that individuals who experience disability are asexual, that they are undesirable, or that their sexuality is deviant. Kim argues, "Desexualization produces a form of objectification and dehumanization that denies the humanity of disabled people"—in this line of thinking, people with disability have been excluded from humanity because they are not perceived as having normative sexuality that "'all' human beings" possess.[33]

Disability awareness consultant Andrew Morrison-Gurza writes, "As a queer person with a disability who is not shy about his sexuality, I find that some of the most common questions that I get are, 'Can you have sex?' 'Do you have sex?' and 'How do you have sex?' These questions arise from many different places, but predominantly from the fact that our dominant sexual discourse has left disability out in the cold."[34] Morrison-Gurza notes that one great thing about sex with someone who has disability is that "you have to communicate." Morrison-Gurza argues that we have a misconception in our culture that good sex just happens, without talking and by reading the other person in silence. He explains that discussing what will "work for both of you" actually results in a better sexual experience for sexual partners. Further, Morrison-

Gurza claims that roles one might be stuck in and one's sexual norms often dissolve by being with someone who has disability. Morrison-Gurza explains that foreplay is often inventive. He notes, "One thing that I love about how people with disabilities have sex is the fact that we have adapted our erogenous zones to respond to different stimuli. . . . Persons with disabilities are experts at using what they have around them, and the same certainly holds true for our sex lives. I know how to hit your marks, probably ones you didn't even know you had."[35]

Given shared experiences of stigmatized sexuality, LGBTQ centers may welcome all individuals with disability to identify as queer as a form of social activism. Stigmatized individuals who identify with collective social action can work together to challenge binary thinking about ability and about sexuality while promoting awareness and encouraging greater acceptance.

Kim argues simultaneously that imposed desexualization is harmful, yet an identity as asexual—as long as it is not imposed by normative pressure—is valid, regardless of ability.[36] Asexuality as a movement is often identified with the political action of David Jay, who founded the Asexuality Visibility and Education Network (AVEN) as a first-year college student in 2002 in order to create an online community for *asexual* individuals, who do not identify as experiencing sexual attraction. In addition to offering an opportunity for asexual individuals to communicate with one another about their experiences, AVEN also seeks to increase broader awareness about asexuality, such as distinguishing between *celibacy*, which is a choice regarding one's behavior, and asexuality, which is defined as a fundamental aspect of a person's identity.[37]

Individuals who identify as asexual (also called *aces*) overwhelmingly identify as queer or as queer allies. Asexual individuals have often sought connection with queer communities. The asexual movement has experienced more and more acceptance in the broader queer movement, but some resistance has occurred. Some members of queer organizations have argued that the intense stigmatization and profound risk of violence faced by lesbian, gay, bisexual, and transgender individuals is much greater and distinctly different from the experience of people who do not have sexual attraction. Yet many queer groups have welcomed asexual people, recognizing common issues in terms of identities that do not conform to heteronormativity. For example, normative gender expects a cisgender man to have strong sexual desire for cisgender women. Although the stigmatization faced by cisgender, asexual people is unlikely to be as damaging or dangerous as it is for gay men, lesbian women, or trans individuals, many LGBTQ centers have acted in generous ways by welcoming asexual people. Inclusion within the queer community is beneficial for asexuality in terms of offering community, connecting to decades of experience with political action, and raising awareness.[38]

The controversy surrounding the work of the asexual community to be recognized as queer reminds some activists that transgender identity was not always included in the gay rights movement.[39] Today, activists such as transgender advocate Brynne Tannehill tend to focus on common concerns shared by lesbian, gay, bisexual, and transgender individuals.[40] All queer individuals deviate from gender norms. For example, a cisgender man who is sexually attracted to another man will be perceived as violating gender expectations that dictate that all men should be sexually attracted to women. All queer individuals must negotiate when and how to come out of the closet. Queer individuals—regardless of whether they identify as L, G, B, or T—face stigmatization. Anthropologist Megan Davidson notes that the term transgender is often used as an inclusive term—similar to the term queer—that encompasses any individual who breaks gender norms. "This capacity of the term to encompass an unfixed group of people, both historically and currently, makes the category *transgender* useful for activists organizing people and ideas that fall outside the scope of contemporary normative cultural productions of binary sex and gender."[41]

In 1990, multiple American Indian nations began using a translation of a Northern Algonquin term to identify *two-spirit* individuals, persons who are both masculine and feminine.[42] In precolonial times, many (but not all) nations venerated individuals who were perceived to have a sacred gift of both feminine and masculine spirits.[43] The term two-spirit has been adopted by nations that wish to acknowledge similarities across cultures and distinct languages. Some nations prefer instead to continue to use traditional terms unique to their nation. Other nations have not traditionally recognized a comparable role.[44]

The movement to recognize two-spirit individuals has been described as political action to reject colonial attacks on the cultures of American Indian nations.[45] In their work to be inclusive and respectful while encouraging just this sort of political action, queer centers have been working to welcome and raise awareness about two-spirit individuals.

SEX AS WORK

In some ways, outside perspectives about sex workers have paralleled assumptions about queer people. As described in chapter 1, queer sexuality was first treated as a sin, next as a crime, and then as an illness. In the United States, prostitution is illegal in most states. And readers will easily find portrayals of sex workers as sinful and criminal. A common stereotype in our society at this time is to think about prostitution or other forms of sex work as the actions of sad, down-and-out women who were abused as children or have a drug addiction. Like queerness decades ago, sex work today is often perceived as an illness.

We acknowledge the reality that some sex workers are forced into this role, some are children, and that some resort to sex work based on financial crisis. Yet many sex workers do not fit any of the stereotypes and have not fallen victim to any form of human trafficking. Among these sex workers, many claim to enjoy their work, to find it fulfilling, interesting, and a good source of income.

In Wendy Chapkis's sociological study, Susanne claims about her and her business partner Anna's work, "There is no limit to what we can do. We're businesswomen and we have a plan. I am not a sad story. I've succeeded."[46] Susanne's work as a prostitute, or sex worker, challenges heteronormative assumptions about the roles of women and men in sexual encounters. Another sex worker, Vision, also discusses her work positively:

> I really think that if everyone had skin-to-skin and breath-to-breath contact with another human being once a day, the planet would be a very different place. And I am very happy to provide that space in the world. For me it's mostly about affection and nurturing and love, not so much a heavy sex vibe. It really helps that they [her clients] come to my environment, so the energetic [sic] is set up by me. They are walking into my game. I'm the priestess and it's my temple.
>
> I've never had a bad session in the year and a half I've been working.[47]

Carol Leigh, also known as Scarlot Harlot, describes what she calls "prostitution politics" (and offers a challenge to the virgin/whore dichotomy discussed in chapter 6). Leigh notes, "The reality of my daily life as a prostitute was a startling contrast to my prior assumptions about prostitution." About the work, Leigh explains, "I was excited and intrigued to be in this environment, working with women from all over the world, who were surprisingly strong and smart."[48] Scarlot Harlot is also interviewed in filmmaker Hima B.'s celebrated documentary, *Straight for the Money: Interviews with Queer Sex Workers*. She and other sex workers describe their work as having positives and negatives, like any job, but overall as satisfying work. Several, like Vision (quoted immediately above), even argue that sex work makes a positive difference in the world, such as by helping their clients to enjoy sexuality and to have intimate sexual connections that they might not otherwise have.[49]

In its status as wage work, work for which the worker earns a wage, sex work is similar to other jobs. In that it is work that involves a kind of intimacy, it is like other jobs involving what sociologists call emotional labor. These occupations include psychotherapy, being a minister, being a flight attendant, serving at a restaurant, and care work, for example, with children or the elderly. Emotional labor is often unrecognized labor. Flight attendants are ostensibly paid for showing people what to do in case of an emergency landing, serving food to passengers, and taking care of a limited array of physical needs while in flight. Yet sociologists argue that flight attendants also work to keep passengers feeling emotionally comfortable, happy, and calm. This work takes a conscious effort in the form of a kind of friendly performance on the part of flight attendants.

In *sex work*, sexual acts are sold to consumers in exchange for a wage. Sex work for a wage includes direct sexual contact through prostitution, suggestive sexual interaction as in the form of erotic dancing, or symbolic sexual availability such as in the case of pornography. Sex workers do not merely go through the physical motions of having sexual encounters; they also perform emotional states such as desire, happiness, and fulfillment. Interestingly, this kind of work has traditionally been understood as low status and morally problematic. Like much of traditionally female labor in our culture—child care, elder care, cleaning, and doing laundry—sex work is low status. Yet while all of these forms of female work are considered labors of love in our society, only sex work carries the weight of being understood as morally corrupt.

The historically popular understanding of sex given in exchange for a wage as immoral links sex work to queer experience. As a scholar of sex work and an activist for sex workers' rights, Melissa Hope Ditmore explains that because sex work is commonly viewed as morally wrong as well as unusual and nonnormative, many sex workers and their advocates argue that sex work and sex workers are queer.[50] Would your definition of queer include cisgender, heterosexual sex workers?

GENDER AT PLAY

By actively developing and sustaining "foundations of a diverse and inclusive culture across dimensions of diversity including, but not limited to age, race, sex, national origin, class, creed, educational background, disability, gender expression, geographical location, income, marital status, parental status, sexual orientation and work experiences," the Office of Inclusion of the National Collegiate Athletic Association (NCAA) serves as a role model for welcoming difference and combating discrimination.[51] In their work to develop a fair policy for transgender student athletes, they acknowledge a troubling history of binary thinking about sex and gender in sports.

In the twentieth century, the International Olympic Committee suspected that men might masquerade as women for unfair physical advantage in athletic competition. Early attempts to address this concern included visual inspection of the genitals of women before competition in 1966 and gynecological examination of athletes in 1967. Beginning in 1967, blood samples were taken to verify XX chromosomes.[52]

In 1985, Maria Patiño, the track hurdle champion of Spain, was shocked to learn from this genetic test that she was intersex. Androgen insensitivity caused her body not to respond to testosterone, producing a feminine physical appearance with XY chromosomes. Although her condition did not affect her athletic ability, she was banned from competition. Through her courage to publicly fight for the right to compete, she energized a movement to end genetic testing for sex verification. Her ban from competition lasted three years, but she ultimately won the right to return to the highest level of her sport. Policies instituted in

1992 allow women who were raised as girls (regardless of their sex chromosomes) to compete as women in events connected with the International Olympic Committee.[53]

Given this problematic history, the NCAA's Office of Inclusion recommends, "The apparent failure of such tests to serve their stated purpose of deterring fraud—and the terrible damage they have caused to individual women athletes—should be taken into account when developing policies for the inclusion of transgender athletes."[54] The NCAA's policy recognizes that a trans man might or might not elect to receive testosterone treatment. Athletes competing on men's teams usually cannot be treated with testosterone because it can be abused as a performance-enhancing drug. The NCAA allows a medical exception of this rule for trans men. A trans man who chooses testosterone treatment may compete on a men's team or a mixed-gender team, but not a women's team. A trans man who forgoes hormone treatment may compete on any team. A trans woman may compete on a men's team whether or not she elects for testosterone suppression. Based on medical evidence of the physical effects of testosterone suppression, a trans woman may compete as a woman following a year or more of hormone treatment.

Recommendations for welcoming transgender athletes include respecting confidentiality and providing facilities and materials—such as locker rooms and uniforms—consistent with gender identity. For example, a trans woman should be given access to a locker room for women and provided with a woman's uniform regardless of whether she competes on a men's team, mixed-gender team, or women's team.

The NCAA serves as a model of thoughtful policy based on goals of inclusion informed by careful analysis of evidence. Throughout this chapter, we explored examples of surprising and powerful ways that normative gender and heteronormativity have been reinforced and challenged—from drag performance as a window into understanding normative gender to official policies that recognize, welcome, and provide opportunities for queer people. Movements for queer rights have created spaces to play with and against normativity.

DISCUSSION QUESTIONS

1. Why does Judith Butler use the example of drag performance? What does drag performance reveal about gender as a performance?

2. In the case of third-graders Charlie and Tommy hugging at school, how do you think their teacher and principal would have understood the hug if the two boys had been two girls? Do you think a teacher would be as likely to interpret two girls hugging as a violent act? Would a principal be as likely to perceive a kiss on the head from one girl to another as sexually inappropriate?

3. If you were on the board of directors of a queer center, would you want to invest resources into political action to raise awareness and acceptance of asexuality or of the sexuality of cisgender, heterosexual individuals who have disability? Would you want to invest in resources for sex workers? Why or why not?

4. Does your campus have a student group dedicated to welcoming queer students? If so, what values does the group communicate through its name, activities, and interactions with the larger campus? Does your campus have an LGBTQ center? If so, evaluate the space of the center—to what extent is it located centrally on campus, what is the size of the space, and how does the physical space of the center meet the needs of students? What does the presence or absence of a queer center communicate about your campus? How might a queer center be good for everyone on campus, regardless of sexual or gender identity?

5. What issues are queer issues? If an issue affects queer individuals, does it become a queer issue and therefore appropriate for activism within LGBTQ centers? For example, is the Israeli government's siege on the Gaza Strip a queer issue because it affects queer individuals? Are there issues that would not be appropriate for activism in a queer center?

6. If you were on the board of directors of a queer center, would you welcome heterosexual and cisgender sex workers as queer? Why or why not?

7. Imagine that your friend's favorite NCAA team announced an out transgender student athlete on the roster. How would you explain

the history and current understanding of sex, gender, and fairness in athletic competition to your friend?

5

INSTITUTIONALIZED HETERONORMATIVITY

Military, Law, and Religion

As a preschooler, Lena was overheard planning her future with her best friend from inside a play fort they had just built. Someone suggested marriage. Lena affirmed the idea, "My mama says that one women and one women, two womens, can get married." Her wise older friend, a kindergartener, seemed to understand the reach of the law into their fort (prior to the legalization of same-sex marriage in New York in 2011 and throughout the United States in 2015). She noted realistically, "Yes, but not here. We will have to move away to get married."

For years as a toddler and preschooler, and to the chagrin of her antimarriage mother (a position discussed later), Lena regularly expressed her desire to get married and have children. Ninety-five percent of the time, but not one hundred, Lena described marrying another girl, or as in the above, a "women." What this might mean about Lena's long-term sexual orientation is unclear. Yet what is clear is that for a good three or four years, making a life commitment and having children involved another woman in Lena's young imagination. Perhaps because her access to mainstream media and its heteronormative demands was so limited, perhaps because her parents carefully described romantic relationships as involving a variety of people and a mix of genders, perhaps because her beloved grandmother was in a lesbian relationship until her partner, Lena's step-grandmother, died of cancer when Lena was five, Lena's imagined future love was not restricted to the heteronormative.

If heteronormativity did not exist, there would be no assumptions of cisgender heterosexuality. Queer individuals would not face difficult decisions regarding where, when, to whom, and how to come out. Within our heteronormative system, many people experience coming out as queer as an ongoing process. One might first come out in a safe haven, such as a queer center. A person might later come out to close friends, then to family members. As a person meets new acquaintances, there will be frequent, recurring situations that demand decisions regarding coming out.

As a young adult, Pauline Park's first coming-out experience was as a gay man. "When I went off to college in 1978 there were no transgender people." In her college town, she found

> a small gay and lesbian community, mostly gay men and a few lesbians. And I came out as gay, which was more practical. Coming out as transgender at that point was not . . . a realistic option. I joined this little support group. At the time there was no daily infrastructure [for queer people] at colleges and universities. So there was just a little gay center . . . with a couch, a desk, some volunteers answering the phone . . . in the basement of the Episcopal Church across from campus.[1]

Park remembers circling the church three times before she finally approached one of the volunteers, a graduate student. "I said I think I might be gay, and we just talked, and he invited me to join this coming out support group, which I did." Park later came out as a gay man to a member of her family: "I came out to my brother at the end of the semester and then he came out to me."[2]

As we reflect on Park's experience of preparing to come out, we are struck by the choice of this Episcopal church to use its privilege to support individuals who were completely marginalized at that time and to help provide them with a sense of community and belonging. Although the physical investment of this church was only one small room in its basement, the message was that this social institution had chosen to use its privilege to literally create a space for people who felt they belonged nowhere, for people whose consensual sexual activity was criminalized at that time.

Major institutions—religious, legal, military—have the power to extend or deny privilege. The rights of queer individuals are determined by doctrine, law, and practice. We will describe examples of ways social institutions have denied rights, have broken promises to extend rights, and have supported the rights of queer individuals.

COMBATED RIGHTS

In the United States, military prohibitions against homosexuality predated the Constitution.[3] On March 11, 1778, Lieutenant Gotthold Frederick Enslin was the first person dismissed from military service on a charge of same-sex sexual desire "for attempting to commit sodomy" and "For Perjury in swearing to false Accounts."[4] "His Excellency the Commander in Chief" George Washington endorsed the dismissal and expressed "Abhorrence and Detestation of such Infamous Crimes." Washington ordered Enslin "to be drummed out of Camp tomorrow morning by all the Drummers and Fifers in the Army."[5]

Until 1920, military members accused of sodomy were prosecuted based on civilian laws.[6] A remarkable undercover operation was conducted in 1919 to identify and prosecute men in the navy who engaged in consensual sexual acts with each other. Franklin D. Roosevelt, who served as Assistant Secretary of the Navy, wrote in a confidential letter, "The Navy Department has become convinced that such conditions of vice and depravity exist in and around Newport, R.I., as to require a most searching and rigid investigation with a view to finally prosecuting and clearing out those people responsible for it."[7] In 1920, the United States Congress amended the Articles of War to specifically identify sodomy as a punishable offense in the military.

As the United States evaluated entering World War II in 1940, President Roosevelt sought to expand the size of the military, seeking approval from Congress. Harry Stack Sullivan and other psychiatrists proposed to Roosevelt and leaders of the Selective Service System that screening of potential military members might reduce the overwhelming proportion of psychiatric casualties seen in World War I. The initial screening proposed by Sullivan and his close colleagues was unrelated to sexuality. Sullivan privately identified as homosexual, and his then-controversial perspective was that homosexuality was not relevant for predicting psychiatric problems in the military. As other psychiatrists were consulted regarding the screening proposal, they applied the justification that homosexuality was a psychiatric disorder and convinced the Selective Service to try to identify and exclude homosexuals from military service.[8]

In 1950, the army tasked all military members with being responsible for reporting evidence of homosexual activity. Those who were privileged to be considered as having "normal" sexuality were also now given the power and responsibility to inform on those considered deviant. In the updated policy, the military acknowledged for the first time that women, as well as men, might be homosexual members of the military. A three-tier classification system provided for different responses to same-sex sexual acts or desires—those who had committed homosexual acts with aggravating circumstances (such as coercion) faced court-martial, whereas those who had engaged in consensual homosexual acts could opt for an undesirable discharge, and those who had homosexual desire with no evidence of homosexual acts could opt for an honorable discharge. In all cases, those identified as homosexual were to be separated from the military, regardless of quality of service.[9]

Tens of thousands of people's lives were dramatically affected by the military's insistence on discharging people for queer sexuality. We will focus on the stories of just three exemplary service members who fought legal battles in the hopes of both continuing their service to the military and changing policy for all—Perry J. Watkins, Leonard Matlovich, and Miriam Ben-Shalom.

When the army drafted Perry J. Watkins in 1967 to serve in Vietnam, he responded honestly and affirmatively to a screening question, indicating that he had "homosexual tendencies." Although the policy clearly should have excluded him from military service, he was deemed fit to serve. Further, he was permitted to reenlist in 1971 and 1974.[10]

As Watkins was reenlisting as an openly gay man in 1974, Air Force Technical Sergeant Leonard Matlovich was preparing to come out of the closet. His decision was intended as a direct challenge to the military's policy on homosexuality. Over eleven years of outstanding service, including three tours of duty in Vietnam, he earned a Bronze Star, a Purple Heart, two commendation medals, and a Meritorious Service

Medal. His decision to come out was influenced by teaching a race relations course for officers, where he had recently expanded the curriculum to address gay men and lesbian women as stigmatized in the military. He questioned the two unfounded premises for the Department of Defense's justification for dismissal of homosexuals—that closeted gay, lesbian, and bisexual individuals posed a heightened security risk because of the potential for blackmail and that integration of heterosexual and queer troops would damage morale. Matlovich was passionate about his teaching, and he was determined to live authentically by coming out of the closet.[11]

On September 8, 1975, Matlovich appeared on the cover of *Time* magazine with a quote that read, "I Am a Homosexual." The queer rights movement had never before seen such a wide audience. Matlovich knew that he would be discharged from the air force, but he hoped that appealing his discharge might change military policy. He did not believe the military could provide any evidence of increased security risk for lesbian women, gay men, or bisexual individuals.[12]

Movements for gender and sexual rights have often been inspired by progress in combating racism. The first wave of feminism in the nineteenth century, with its major goal of gaining voting rights for women, drew inspiration from civil rights work to abolish slavery and gain voting rights for African American citizens. The queer marriage equality movement in the twenty-first century made purposeful connections to civil rights work of the twentieth century to abolish miscegenation laws. Similarly, Matlovich and others likened morale concerns regarding troop integration to arguments prior to 1948 that justified racial segregation in military service.[13]

As the United States started to pay attention to the queer rights movement, Perry Watkins, who continued to serve as an openly gay soldier, was reviewed for potential discharge in 1975. The board determined that there was "no evidence suggesting . . . a degrading effect upon unit performance, morale or discipline, or upon his own job performance." Watkins was permitted to continue to serve.[14]

Army Reservist Miriam Ben-Shalom was remarkable in 1975 for being one of only two women in her division to graduate from drill sergeant school. When a reporter asked her "how it felt to be a gay person in the military," Ben-Shalom "couldn't see any reason to lie. What kind of leader would I be if I lied?"[15] She was discharged in 1975 for "evidenced homosexual tendencies, desire or intent." She based her appeal on the grounds of freedom of speech and privacy. Following a complicated legal battle, Ben-Shalom was eventually reinstated by court order for the remaining eleven months of her enlistment.[16] Because of the slow process of the courts, Miriam Ben-Shalom did not return to military service until 1987.[17]

Matlovich pursued his appeal until 1980, when the election of President Ronald Reagan ensured that any new members of the Supreme Court would be conservative and unlikely to rule in Matlovich's favor. He and his legal team knew their chances of ultimately winning were improbable. A further disappointment was that a recent appellate court decision had not directly addressed the constitutional right for people of queer sexuality to serve in the military.[18] Matlovich accepted an offer from the air force for a generous cash settlement and an honorable discharge; he dedicated his life as a civilian to the queer rights movement.[19]

In 1981, the Department of Defense clarified its policy, emphasizing a privileged status only for heterosexual service members:

> Homosexuality is incompatible with military service. The presence in the military environment of persons who engage in homosexual conduct or who, by their statements, demonstrate a propensity to engage in homosexual conduct, seriously impairs the accomplishment of the military mission. The presence of such members adversely affects the ability of the Military Services to maintain discipline, good order, and morale; to foster mutual trust and confidence among servicemembers; to ensure the integrity of the system of rank and command; to facilitate assignment and worldwide deployment of servicemembers who frequently must live and work under close conditions affording minimal privacy; to recruit and retain members of the Military Services; to maintain the public acceptability of military service; and to prevent breaches of security.[20]

Based on this policy statement, Perry Watkins again faced discharge proceedings and was forced out of the military in 1984, following sixteen years of service as an openly gay man.

In a decision focusing on the specific case of Perry Watkins rather than the broader issue of the right of queer individuals to serve in the military, a federal appellate court determined in 1989 that Watkins should be allowed to reenlist. President George H. W. Bush appealed to the Supreme Court to try to prevent Watkins from reenlisting, but the Supreme Court maintained the earlier ruling in favor of Watkins. In the final settlement, Watkins was awarded "retroactive pay . . . , full retirement benefits, an honorable discharge and a retroactive promotion from staff sergeant to sergeant first class."[21]

Miriam Ben-Shalom's complicated legal battle resumed when she sought to reenlist.[22] The final court decision denied her right to reenlist on the basis that she identified as a lesbian. In 1990, the Supreme Court refused to hear her case.[23]

When campaigning for the presidency of the United States in 1992, Bill Clinton promised that he would end the military ban for gay men, lesbian women, and bisexual people.[24] Clinton had promised to issue an executive order, but instead, a 1993 compromise known as "Don't Ask, Don't Tell" went into effect. Although potential military members were no longer asked whether they had homosexual desire, those who were suspected of gay or lesbian sexual behavior could be investigated and discharged. The "don't tell" aspect of the policy forced queer members of the military to work and live in silence, in the closet, about this important aspect of their identity. The policy was responsible for the discharges of more than thirteen thousand people over the course of eighteen years until it was repealed in 2011 under the leadership of President Barack Obama.[25] Finally in 2016, members of the military who are transgender gained the opportunity to serve openly.[26]

LEGALIZED DISCRIMINATION

Legislative and judicial action determine rights, including whether the law allows or prohibits the formation of family through marriage, foster parenting, and adoption. From 1996 until 2013, when it was declared unconstitutional by the Supreme Court of the United States in the case of *United States v. Windsor*, the "Defense of Marriage" Act (also known as DOMA) prevented same-sex couples access to the 1,138 federal "benefits, rights and protections" of marriage such as citizenship, filing joint tax returns, and health insurance for same-sex spouses.[27] DOMA permitted states to refuse to acknowledge same-sex marriages legally performed in other states. Legal scholar Martha Nussbaum notes assertions made during the debates in 1996 that led to the adoption of this discriminatory law. Conservative Democrat and former Ku Klux Klan member Senator Robert Byrd of West Virginia argued:

> Mr. President, throughout the annals of human experience, in dozens of civilizations and cultures of varying value systems, humanity has discovered that the permanent relationship between men and women is a keystone to the stability, strength, and health of human society—a relationship worthy of legal recognition and judicial protection.[28]

Building on our discussion from previous chapters, liberal thought regarding the role and function of families differs from conservative arguments. For many conservatives, the family is considered to be an important support system for society—indeed, the family is the "keystone" of society. In this conservative thinking, our social world rests on and springs from the institution of the family, the so-called traditional (heteronormative) family in particular. In contrast, for liberals, society must not only rely upon but also support the family. This is why, for many liberals, families need social supports such as government-subsidized health care and child care, maternity and paternity leave, and welfare benefits. With social support, liberals argue, families can thrive and produce children who grow up to "give back" to society. Because liberals tend to see gender roles as more flexible, liberals often support nonheteronormative, queer families and marriage equality.

Liberals sometimes compare DOMA with historic laws against miscegenation that prohibited marriages between white people and African Americans. Some laws even made these marriages criminal. Laws against interracial marriage are now understood to be profoundly racist. Liberal thinkers argue that bans on same-sex marriage will come to be seen as deeply prejudiced. Mildred Jeter, an African American woman who married a white man, Richard Loving, in 1958 in Washington, DC, was forced to leave her home state of Virginia or spend a year in jail because state miscegenation laws made her marriage a felony. She and Loving took the case to court and gave the Supreme Court the opportunity to overturn antimiscegenation laws in 1967. In a statement made on the fortieth anniversary of the decision, Mildred Jeter Loving recognized commonalities in marriage equality rights:

Surrounded as I am now by wonderful children and grandchildren, not a day goes by that I don't think of Richard and our love, our right to marry, and how much it meant to me to have that freedom to marry the person precious to me, even if others thought he was the "wrong kind of person" for me to marry. I believe all Americans, no matter their race, no matter their sex, no matter their sexual orientation, should have that same freedom to marry. . . . I am proud that Richard's and my name is on a court case that can help reinforce the love, the commitment, the fairness, and the family that so many people, black or white, young or old, gay or straight seek in life.[29]

There are many people in the United States today who see marriage as the central, as the most important part, of a family. And certainly legally, as well as in the cultural mainstream, marriage is the institution around which the law recognizes and supports families. Prior to the Supreme Court's ruling in favor of marriage equality in 2015, the issue was hotly debated. Some argued that any adult, consenting sexual couple should be supported in a decision to marry. Others claimed that only couples consisting of one man and one woman should be allowed to marry and to thus fulfill their sacred and natural role as men and women. For these two sides, the conservative and liberal, of the pro-marriage debate, marriage matters deeply. Yet there is another perspective.

When discussing marriage in her class on the family, some of Jean Halley's students are surprised to learn that there are people within the queer community who are against marriage. This contingent argues that marriage is problematic for a variety of reasons, including, perhaps most importantly, *because* marriage is the way our government and mainstream society historically define "family." In other words, before the landmark Supreme Court decisions in 2013 and 2015 that support marriage equality, to be a family in the United States meant, and continues to mean for many people, that there is a married pair of adults, a (hetero)sexual dyad. Conversely, without a married couple at the head of a family, the family is not a "real" family. Historically and today, this way of being a family has been privileged over all other forms, allowing for the many legal and financial benefits noted above, as well as the profound social benefit of being understood as the correct, the real, family form.

Indeed, the heterosexual dyad is central to what people call the "traditional family" in the United States. The marriage equality movement, the movement that supports same-sex marriage, has worked to open up notions of the "traditional family" to include other sexual dyads, gay and lesbian dyads. The marriage equality movement fights to take part in the traditional institution of marriage and to gain the privileges garnered therein. This movement does not fundamentally challenge the institution, or the privileges gained through it—privileges denied to those in other forms of family. The marriage equality vision maintains there still must be a pair of sexually involved adults at the head of a family to be a "real" family; they just propose that the married pair could be a man and a woman, two women, or two men. Families led by single parents, families led by a grandmother and her adult daughter, or other diverse forms of family that do not include a sexual dyad of married adults are not understood to be "real" or healthy families.

Many of us who grew up in nontraditional families experienced the outsider status these nonnormative families held. Halley, for example, grew up in a family headed by a single mother. As a child, Halley was acutely aware that people saw her family as problematic, even immoral. Halley understood that without a father standing next to her mother, her family did not quite count as a family. Indeed, her family was "broken."

The antimarriage movement is not against people being in committed sexual dyads. This movement challenges the notion that to be a family, one must have such a dyad, and it further challenges that this particular form of family should be supported above other forms by the government. Some, like queer legal scholar Martha Albertson Fineman, argue that instead of sexual dyads, the government should define family as, and support families that contain, a caregiving, care-receiving pair. Fineman notes that everyone needs care in life. Given that this is a universal human need, something that infants, for example, must have to survive, this caring pair should be the dyad around which our government legally defines and supports family. Fineman makes clear that people could opt to form committed sexual dyads between consenting adults. The caring pair would not be the only way to make a family, yet the government would offer legal and social support to this caregiving, care-receiving pair.[30]

In her seminal book, *Families We Choose: Lesbians, Gays, Kinship*, anthropologist Kath Weston notes the ways queer people have often needed to form families of their own making. Historically, queer individuals were excluded from the institution of marriage and were often rejected by their families of origin. The "chosen family" might not fit into the "traditional family" of mainstream society, but Weston argues chosen family is still family, equally important, equally loving, equally sustaining.[31]

Queer people have always formed families, and expanded legal rights have created more possibilities for legal marriage, foster parenting, and adoption. Critical judicial decisions spanning from 2006 to 2016 ended discriminatory laws that prevented foster parenting or adoption for potential parents who identify as queer. The American Civil Liberties Union (ACLU) successfully worked to expand rights by demonstrating unconstitutional discrimination.[32]

In 2014, the ACLU began its representation of Greg and Stillman Stewart in their appeal of Nebraska's then-ban of "homosexual" foster parents. The Stewarts, who have been in a committed relationship for more than three decades, were residents of California before the family moved to Nebraska so that Greg could take a position as a pastor for a United Church of Christ congregation. (As noted below, this Protestant Christian denomination was the first to welcome gay pastors.) When they were California residents, the Stewarts adopted five children through the foster care system. The two fathers legally married in 2008.[33]

The Stewarts have demonstrated amazing success in parenting previously abused children. In 2014, their children, ages thirteen to twenty, had developed more independence from their fathers. The Stewarts hoped to foster new children, particularly children who have been difficult to place within the foster care system. The Stewarts' oldest child, a college student, had experienced seventeen foster homes and three adoptions that fell apart before he found his permanent family with the Stewarts. Nebraska advertised on billboards that foster parents are needed, but the Stewarts application was denied based on a ban on same-sex couples.

In 2015, in the midst of the court case in which the ACLU challenged the constitutionality of the ban in Nebraska—as well as bans that were in place concurrently in Utah and Mississippi—child welfare officials in Nebraska decided to evaluate foster care applications regardless of sexual orientation.[34] In 2016, United States District Judge Dan Jordan ruled Mississippi's law banning same-sex couples from adoption to be unconstitutional, thereby making adoption and foster parenting a legal option for same-sex couples in all fifty states.[35]

CRIMINALIZED SEXUALITY

Sexuality has been policed by legislation and court rulings since the inception of the United States. In addition to sodomy laws (described in previous chapters) and laws regulating families by marriage and becoming a family through foster parenting and adoption, laws have governed access to birth control, pornography, and other materials deemed by history and culture to be obscene.

Nurse and contraception advocate Margaret Sanger told the story of Sadie Sachs, who was living with her husband and three children in the Lower East Side neighborhood of Manhattan in New York City in 1912. When she asked her physician for advice on how to prevent another pregnancy, he callously recommended that she insist that her husband "sleep on the roof." A subsequent attempt at self-induced abortion led to severe infection and ultimately death for Sachs. Sanger nursed Sachs, and as a woman privileged with medical education, Sanger decided to risk legal battles with obscenity laws to educate working-class women about birth control.[36]

At that time, obscenity laws forbade public discussion of contraception. Medical caregivers were permitted to talk privately to their patients, but Sanger was determined to reach a broader audience, especially those who might have difficulty affording visits to a physician. Sanger started a weekly sex education column titled "What Every Girl Should Know" in a popular socialist newspaper, the *New York Call*. The column lasted for a year, until it was censored by the United States Post Office for violating obscenity law.[37]

In 1916, four years before women would be permitted to vote in federal elections, Sanger and her sister opened the first birth control clinic in the United States. They spread the word through flyers in three commonly spoken languages in local neighborhoods and saw 464 patients in a Brownsville, Brooklyn, office before the police shut it down ten days later. Sanger and her sister each served a month in prison. [38]

Sanger was not deterred. She continued to push for expansion of access to information about birth control—a term she coined. [39] Sanger used her privilege to increase the rights of women who have sex with men. She focused on helping working-class women of all ethnicities and races, including outreach specifically designed to inform and serve African American women. Sanger's critics note that she supported *eugenics*—a deeply problematic, elitist perspective that seeks to improve the human gene pool through selective breeding. While many eugenicists have also been racist, there is debate regarding whether Sanger (who came from Irish American Catholic roots) was racist or merely elitist. At the time, eugenics was commonly perceived as a scientific approach that legitimized the importance of birth control. Eugenics was widely supported by people as diverse as genocidal Nazi leader Adolf Hitler and brilliant African American labor historian W. E. B. Du Bois. From our perspective today, we can critique the horrors of eugenic arguments, and we must acknowledge that Sanger's interest in eugenics complicates her as a potential role model. [40]

Sanger started the organization that is known today as Planned Parenthood; many would argue that this legacy is laudable. Planned Parenthood annually honors activists who support reproductive health and reproductive rights. In 1966, Dr. Martin Luther King Jr. was one of the first activists to be granted the award. When Coretta Scott King delivered the acceptance speech written by her husband, she read that Margaret Sanger

> was willing to accept scorn and abuse until the truth she saw was revealed to the millions. At the turn of the century she went into the slums and set up a birth control clinic, and for this deed she went to jail because she was violating an unjust law. Yet the years have justified her actions. She launched a movement which is obeying a higher law to preserve human life under humane conditions." [41]

Sanger's legacy reveals the slippery and complicated boundaries of privilege. Privilege is not a binary that wholly increases or decreases based on membership in one group or another. In some ways, a woman in a sexual relationship with a man gains some of the privilege held by men, but in other ways, women in relationships with men may lose privilege.

In a system that deemed public discussion of contraception to be obscene, women in sexual relationships with men lost power over their own reproductive freedom. Until the 1970s, husbands in all states had the legal right to forced intercourse with their wives—behavior that is legally defined as rape today and is therefore criminal.[42] In comparison to the perils of a marriage with a man, a Boston marriage with another woman might have been appealing.

Aspects of privilege often remain elusive to groups that have been oppressed—such as queer individuals of all races and genders, people of color of all genders and sexualities, and women of all races and sexualities. A person's multiple identities intersect—some bringing privilege and others oppression. A white, heterosexual woman will be privileged based on her race and sexual identity, but heterosexual privilege often does not carry the same benefit for women as it does for men. When women enter relationships with men, they often are subjected to gender roles that reduce their power.

Men who identify as queer have also been denied the typical privilege associated with masculine gender. As noted in previous chapters, sodomy laws were legalized oppression of queer individuals that criminalized same-sex sexual behavior. The Stonewall Riots of June 1969 erupted as a response to enforcement of a New York law specifying that arrest was warranted for an individual who "loiters or remains in a public place for the purpose of engaging, or soliciting another person to engage, in oral sexual conduct, anal sexual conduct or other sexual behavior of a deviate nature."[43] Further, the statute specified that "being masked or in any manner disguised by unusual or unnatural attire" was illegal (except in the case of a masquerade party with prior permission from the police). Police applied this rule by arresting anyone wearing fewer than three pieces of clothing considered appropriate for the person's sex.[44] This is an example of binary thinking: the law assumed that biological sex always neatly falls into one of two categories (with gross ignorance of intersex individuals) and dictated that biological sex should correspond to gender as a man or a woman, with criminalization of trans individuals. Further, there is an assumption in the application of this law that queer gender expression indicates queer sexuality.

As noted in the case of Margaret Sanger being jailed for distributing material deemed to be obscene and in the law that forbade New Yorkers from dressing in clothing deemed inappropriate for their sex, rights to free expression have been curtailed when related to some matters of gender and sexuality. The Supreme Court has consistently ruled that First Amendment rights to free speech do not apply to the sale or distribution of material determined to be obscene.[45] The case of *Miller v. California* in 1973 set three criteria that continue to be used to judge obscenity.[46] First, "'the average person, applying contemporary community standards' would find that the work, taken as a whole, appeals to the prurient interest in sex." In other words, the material must be designed to arouse excessive lust and it must deviate from local norms. Second, a state law must be violated such that "the work depicts or describes, in a patently offensive way, sexual conduct specifically defined by the applicable state law." In words or images, the work must present sexual conduct that, when practiced, violates distinct laws. Third, "the work, taken as a whole, lacks serious literary, artistic, political, or scientific value." Works deemed to have merit as art, social commentary, or science will not be defined as obscene.

If one were to apply these criteria, often described as the *Miller Test* or the *Three Prong Obscenity Test*, to the publications of Alfred Charles Kinsey and colleagues on human sexuality (described in chapter 1), one would anticipate that a jury in 1973 or more recently would determine these books were not designed to arouse excessive sexual desire and therefore would not meet the first criterion. Although these works described sexual behavior that was illegal when the works were published, these descriptions were not presented in the books in an "offensive way" and hence do not meet the second criterion. The publications likely would be found to have scientific value and therefore would not meet the third criterion. All three criteria must be met for material to be illegal to sell or to distribute.[47]

While selling and distributing material determined to be obscene can be a criminal offense, private possession of pornography depicting adults cannot be criminalized, even for material that would be illegal to sell or distribute.[48] The Supreme Court determined this right to possession of pornography in 1969 in the case of *Stanley v. Georgia*. In contrast to possession of obscene material depicting adults, the 1990 Supreme Court decision of *Osborne v. Ohio* clarified that private possession of pornography depicting children can be a criminal offense.[49] Under current law, possession or distribution of sexual images of individuals under the age of eighteen is criminal.

Teen *sexting*—sending or receiving sexually explicit text messages, including sexual images of teens—did not exist when the Supreme Court set the current rule for child pornography. As of 2013, twenty states had enacted legislation to distinguish teen sexting from child pornography.[50] In states that do not distinguish sexting from child pornography, teens have been indicted for sharing sexually explicit videos among friends. Parents and activists have encouraged new laws that focus on educating teens rather than punishing them as child pornographers.[51]

RELIGIOUS RIGHTS

Religion often functions as a social institution that espouses injunctive norms. Within the United States, diverse religions are practiced with dramatically different expectations for appropriate gender roles and expressions of sexuality. As we noted in chapter 4, some religions of American Indian nations venerate individuals who identify as both masculine and feminine—sometimes translated into the term two-spirit.[52] As another example, across Protestant Christian denominations there are stark differences, and often passionate arguments, regarding the roles of men and women, marriage, and sexuality.

Individuals like Mithleya, who practice Islam and are queer, describe the importance of religion in all aspects of their lives, including their sexual lives. Mithleya writes in the *Huffington Post* that while she has "issues with the way [her] religion has been interpreted and practiced by many," she believes that "my relationship with God is what truly matters." Mithleya explains, "My space in Islam is established by virtue of my existence. I am Muslim, so Islam has a space for me. My relationship with God and my sexuality are not at odds with one another. As far as I am concerned, there is no conflict."[53]

We admire Mithleya's identification of her faith in her understanding of sexuality. Both of the authors of this text have connections to Judeo-Christian religious practice. Amy Eshleman's father dedicated his career to the Presbyterian Church (USA) as a pastor. She attended Hope College, an institution that maintains close ties to the Reformed Church in America, such that all but one of her college professors was openly Christian and religious beliefs were regularly applied to every topic of study. For Jean Halley, Catholicism was an important part of her early family life, including messages about appropriate roles for women and pressures against divorce, even in the case of abusive marriages. Halley has been involved with the long-standing leftist and activist tradition in the Catholic Church, including living in and working at a Catholic Worker community. Halley's master's degree in theology from Harvard University afforded her the opportunity to think critically about the roles religions play in the United States. Judeo-Christian perspectives on sexuality and appropriate gender roles will be our focus in this section because of the cultural and political power of Judeo-Christian perspectives in the United States, the privilege inequitably conferred on those who belong to these groups (especially in comparison to pervasive stereotyping and discrimination against schools of Islam and common prejudicial misunderstanding of other religions), and our personal connections to these perspectives that allow a critical analysis from an ingroup perspective.

Judeo-Christian pundits have justified denying rights to queer individuals based on interpretations of religious texts or claims of divine insight. Christian author and psychologist Dr. James Dobson, who has been highly respected among conservatives, has reached nearly two hundred million people worldwide on his radio show, "Focus on the Family." Dobson, who had no theological training, claims to be an interpreter of God's will for families in the United States. He started his career by writing and speaking on parenting, and as he addresses child-rearing, he also makes claims about "the destruction of the family by gays and lesbians."[54] Setting all contemporary scientific evidence aside, Dobson believes and argues that homosexuality is a disorder and one that can be cured with treatment, in particular, a treatment Dobson called "reparative therapy" (further discussed in chapter 7).[55] He regularly discusses his concerns about homosexuality, including one show on a completely unfounded description of prevention and treatment of homosexuality in boys. About homosexuality and its relationship to the institution of marriage, and prior to the implementation of marriage equality, Dobson warns his listeners of the peril he perceives in same-sex marriage: "If the definition of marriage should change, the family as we know it will die and with it will go everything else that sits on that foundation." Dobson argues that gays are comparable to Nazis and will destroy what he believes to be the Christian foundation of the United States.

People like Dobson influenced Mary Lou Wallner, a septuagenarian white woman, Christian, and mother interviewed in the 2007 documentary film *For the Bible Tells Me So*. Like many fundamentalist Christians,[56] Wallner expressed great confidence in having clarity and strength in her beliefs.[57]

Wallner explains that she raised her child Anna in, and with extensive involvement in, a conservative Christian church that assured her their way of interpreting and adhering to the Bible was the one right way. Wallner notes, "My earliest memory of Anna was that she could hum 'Jesus Loves Me' when she was ten months old." With a smile and small shake of her head, Wallner says, "She couldn't talk but she could hum the tune." In spite of their church's bias against queer individuals, as a child Anna gave Wallner many clues about Anna's lesbianism. Yet Wallner says she "did not want to know." Wallner continues, "I just dismissed it. It was like I blocked it completely." Wallner notes that when her daughter was young, Anna loved to sing and was in a lot of musicals in school. In her senior year in high school, Anna had been mentored by a lesbian drama teacher at her school.

After Anna went away to college in 1988, in her first year, she came out to her mother by writing a letter explaining that she was lesbian.[58] Anna wrote, "I guess I should've been honest with you . . . instead of saying it was all okay. I feel like I have been saying that all my life." Anna said that "she was never comfortable with men, but now she understood that she was comfortable with women." "I love women," Anna wrote. Wallner was stunned and literally sickened. She went to the bathroom to "become physically ill." Wallner explains that after Anna's letter she went "completely underground, not telling anyone, being ashamed and embarrassed." Wallner's voice breaks when she explains to the viewer that she responded by writing Anna and telling her "things in that letter that were not very loving," including that she would "never accept" Anna's lesbianism. Wallner reads a piece of her letter aloud, "I feel it's a terrible waste besides being spiritually and morally wrong. . . . For a reason I don't quite fathom, I have a harder time dealing with that issue than almost anything in the world." She told her daughter that homosexuality was forbidden by Christianity and not just a sin, "but the sin above all sins." Wallner says that she had harsh words for Anna "many times." At the time, Wallner believed that homo-sexuality was a choice, and she emphasized, that Anna needed to "get her act together and stop this!"

Waller recounts that Anna began to withdraw from her in early 1996. "There was no contact on Mother's Day, which was very painful for me," she says. "And finally in July, I wrote her a letter and just said, 'What have I done? Whatever it is, I'd like to make it right.'" Wallner continues, "And her letter back to me was maybe even more difficult than her first one." In this letter, Anna said that Wallner "had done colossal damage to her soul" with Wallner's "shaming words." Anna stated, Wallner was her mother "biologically only." Anna told her moth-er that she did "not want to and did not have to forgive" her and that she, Anna, "wanted nothing more to do with" Wallner.

Tragically, Wallner says, "So when the phone rang at nine or ten o'clock at night eight months later, there was a part of me that knew what had happened. Anna had committed suicide . . . in her closet." Fifteen hours passed before someone found her. Wallner says, "So that's the way it ended for Anna and me. She took her life before there was any reconciliation."

As this documentary explains, "Gay and lesbian people are three to seven times more likely to attempt suicide" than heterosexual people. "It's estimated that every five hours an LGBT teen takes his life. And for every teen that takes his or her own life, there are twenty more who try." Jorge Valencia, who works with suicidal queer teenagers at the Trevor Project Suicide Hotline, explains that one of the top five reasons that teenagers call his organization is for religious reasons. "They're feeling there isn't a place for them" to be with their God. The church, another speaker argues, shapes the thinking of children who are queer, making them feel alone, making them hate themselves. Valencia contin-ues, "They are afraid to talk to their parents. They are afraid to talk to their peers about what they are going through, and sadly they resort to that irreversible decision which is suicide. Closets are a place of death." Mary Lou Wallner concedes, "My daughter is dead because of the untruth I was taught by the church."

With her face stricken, gripped with sorrow years later, Mary Lou Wallner says, "It took her death to make me really research the topic of homosexuality and what the Bible *really* says about it. I did my own study of the scriptures and I prayed a lot. I can remember lots of times saying, 'God, are you *sure* this is what you want me to believe? Are you sure you want me to change my beliefs on this?'" Wallner continues, "The answer I always got was yes." Wallner explains, "The teaching I was taught by the church and in my home was not only that, not only was homosexuality an abomination, but that it was also a choice. It was a *lifestyle choice*." Wallner notes, "After researching extensively, I began to understand that it *isn't* a choice. I don't think that anybody in their right mind, especially a person who is a Christ follower, would choose something that would invite hatred and misunderstanding and death." Wallner says, "What I've learned is that instead of taking the Bible literally, I have to take it in the context and culture of the day in which it was written. I have come to believe differently than the way I was raised. And once you have made that transformation there is really no going back. And I get affirmation every single day that this is what God wants for me." Wallner is now an activist fighting prejudice against queer people in the Christian church. Wallner says about Anna, "I don't want her death to be in vain."

Religion has played a major role in slowing queer movements, yet religious groups and individuals, like Mary Lou Wallner today, have also supported queer rights. In 1972, the United Church of Christ became the first denomination to ordain an openly gay pastor.[59] In 1977, Reform Judaism "called for an end to discrimination of gays and lesbians."[60] As we noted at the start of this chapter, an Episcopal church adjacent to the campus of the University of Wisconsin–Madison provided a gay center that became the place that Pauline Park first came out. Yet it was still controversial in the Episcopal church in 2003 when an openly gay and admittedly sexually active man became a bishop.[61]

In the 1990s, some Protestant Christian churches welcomed lesbian and gay church leaders only if they chose to be celibate; individuals who identified as bisexual could be celibate or marry someone of the other sex. Decades of passionate debates regarding openly queer church leaders were fueled by a desire to follow Christ's teachings of acceptance conflicting with an intense fear that ordaining openly sexually active queer pastors might tear the denomination apart. Historic bias against queer individuals has been justified based on biblical interpretation, yet some religious scholars counter that Christ never directly spoke of queer issues and that many Bible verses identified as anti-queer have been misinterpreted or taken out of context.[62]

Jake Reitan considers himself fortunate. He came from a long line of Lutherans on both sides of his family. His mother and father met as undergraduate students at a Lutheran college in California. They raised their three boys and one girl in the Evangelical Lutheran Church in America. It was, as his mother put it, at the center of their lives. Reitan, the youngest of his siblings, laughs as he says, "We are like any other Minnesota family. We are like Garrison Keillor would portray us, Lutheran people who come from Scandinavia." He continues, "We went to church every Sunday. My father was president of our congregation and my mother was a Sunday school teacher. So we were a pretty involved family." Reitan says that he remembers when, as a child, he found out that most of the world was not Christian. He was shocked and wondered whether all of those people were "going to hell." He also remembers when his pastor preached about homosexuality "and it wasn't in the best of light." "But," Reitan continues, "I didn't want to question because I knew that the answers wouldn't be good."[63]

Reitan realized he was gay when he was in middle school in the 1990s, and came out to his sister when he was a sophomore in high school and fifteen years old. He explains, "About a year later I told my parents, when I was sixteen." His father, Phil Reitan, reflects:

> When Jake came out, I was home and he was crying and he told me that he was gay. It hit me so hard. I felt like I had just had a death, or like somebody had kicked me in the stomach. It just took all the wind out of me. And it didn't go away. It was that way for months. It was the type of thing that you couldn't have fifteen seconds of the day that you didn't think about. I had so many dreams for Jake. And somehow I think that they were instantly shattered in my mind.

Reitan's mother, Randi Reitan, agrees, "It was hard to hear. He told us that he had told Britta a year before and I just thought a whole year. He told somebody and he couldn't tell me. I am a stay-at-home mom. And I was always there for everybody. And I just felt like I had let him down."

About his parents, Reitan says, "They were scared, very scared. My mother was scared about AIDS. She talked about AIDS that night." He continues, "I also think there was a real present fear in my parents' minds about how the Reitans would be perceived by the community. You know, a lot of people knew us. I was the fourth of four kids. My dad had a good law practice in town. And I think a lot of family friends weren't necessarily accepting of gay and lesbian people."

Reitan's mother describes one hateful incident when someone wrote "fag" in large chalk letters on their driveway. She says, "I just stood there and I thought the kids must know that Jake is gay and it's already starting." She ran back to the house and got a bucket of water and scrubbed off the chalked driveway as fast as she could because she did not want her son to see it. Reitan says, "A lot of stuff happened. Dad had a brick thrown through his office window. My car window was smashed in." His mother says, "When the window was broken, I thought this is getting very bold. And I remember never being able to go to sleep until Jake got home at night."

Reitan's parents read about homosexuality, went to see professionals, including a psychiatrist, and tried to learn all they could about their child's sexuality. And after coming from an anti-queer perspective, his parents changed. Indeed, his mother led him and his father into activism protesting the bigoted position of much of the Lutheran and other Christian churches, starting in 2001.[64] In the same documentary discussed earlier, *For the Bible Tells Me So*, Reitan's mother says, "I just feel so sad for the Lutheran Church. They had a chance to make this bold statement that God loves everyone. And they blew it."

Based on the Reitans' dismay at the slow response of the Evangelical Lutheran Church in America, they left the denomination in 2005. Randi Reitan writes, "We were weary of the debate. We needed to hear the good news that God loves us all exactly as we were created. We needed to surround ourselves with people who rejoiced in that truth. We found many welcoming churches that embraced us as we worshiped in different denominations." Although they had lost confidence in the Lutheran Church, the Reitans rejoiced in 2009.[65] Following half a decade of ponderous consideration, the Evangelical Lutheran Church in America began ordaining openly queer individuals who are sexually active. Similarly, in 2011, the Presbyterian Church (USA) voted to welcome openly queer pastors.[66]

These decisions to ordain openly queer clergy were enacted by elected representatives at the level of the denomination. Queer ordination has been controversial within these faith groups, and a minority of congregations has chosen to end their affiliation.[67] Randi Reitan notes that the Evangelical Lutheran Church in America still has work to do to make queer individuals feel fully welcome. She is waiting "to hear from the leadership" of the Lutheran Church that the decision to ordain openly queer pastors "was a good step, an end to a terrible discrimination." She wants leaders within the church to rejoice "that the church had reached a place of understanding and truth about God's gay children." She urges the leadership of the Lutheran Church to boldly stand on the side of queer rights. She expresses concern that the church is trying "to embrace two different truths" in an attempt "to hold the church together."[68]

Religious groups comprise individuals with social connections that range from intimate to multiple degrees of separation. Diverse perspectives on sexuality and gender identity can be found even within religions with doctrine that is regularly interpreted as rejecting queer expressions. For example, queer rights activists in the Reformed Church in America have created the Room for All organization with a "commitment to the welcome and affirmation of lesbian, gay, bisexual and transgender people and their allies, while pursuing grace-filled dialogue with those who believe differently."[69] Current policy within the Catholic Church now allows congregations to explicitly welcome people of "all sexual orientations" to worship.[70]

Some Muslims perceive queer sexuality as sinful, unnatural, and contrary to the Quran—similar to the beliefs of some Christians regarding queer sexuality and the Bible. Other scholars of Islam argue "that there is no definitive basis in the Quran or other theological texts for the condemnation of gay, lesbian, and bisexual people." Organizations such as Muslims for Progressive Values and Al-Fatiha "seek to promote a theologically-sound framework for Islamic liberalism," including queer rights. Al-Fatiha "works to enlighten the Muslim and outside world that Islam is a religion of tolerance and not hate, and that Allah (God) loves His creations, no matter what their sexual orientations might be."[71] As Mithleya (discussed earlier) eloquently writes, "I know that Allah is with me and will guide me through my life and my relationships, regardless of the gender of my partner."[72]

EMPATHIC UNDERSTANDING

Individuals might seek the services of a mental health worker for reasons as diverse as posttraumatic stress following military service, griev-
ing state discrimination that might bar the formation of a family
through becoming a foster or adoptive parent, or reconciling one's sexual desire and experiences with religious interpretation. Training programs for therapists regularly prepare mental health professionals to
work with military veterans and individuals who have been marginalized
by the law. The United States Office of Veterans Affairs invests resources into internship experiences that help mental health workers to
understand how military experience interacts with mental health. Therapy is a career that often draws individuals who are dedicated to building empathy with people who lack privilege; many therapists seek to
understand another's perspective through intellectual effort and emotional connection.[73]

A therapist of an individual or family who strongly identifies with a
religion will be more successful in building an empathic therapeutic
relationship if the therapist develops an appreciation of the role religion
plays in the life of the client. Like a therapist who elects to develop
expertise in working with military veterans, therapists who seek to
understand people who identify with a religion might communicate
with leaders of that religion and work to intellectually understand the
religious belief, doctrine (injunctive norms), and common practice (descriptive norms).[74]

We encourage a focus on empathy. Developing empathy is one
route among many to a more just world. We encourage readers to
practice empathy by seeking to account for historical time, culture, and
religion when trying to understand another person's perspective on a
controversial issue. As noted in multiple examples in this chapter, rejection of and discrimination against people who seem different from the
norm have been all too common. Social institutions—including the military, laws that affect family structure and sexual criminality, and religion—have been used to conscript rights based on gender and sexuality.
Yet these social institutions have the potential to promote empathy. A
military or religious institution that openly welcomes individuals across
sexual and gender identities has the potential to create rich opportunities for developing empathic understanding. Laws that expand rights

can influence what citizens perceive as normal and healthy. In one's interpersonal interactions, especially when someone seems different from oneself, seeking to intellectually and emotionally understand another person's perspective can enhance communication.

DISCUSSION QUESTIONS

1. Select one of the ways heteronormativity has been historically institutionalized. Identify how policy, law, or practices worked to institutionalize heteronormativity. Describe any activism that has occurred to challenge this institutionalization of heteronormativity.

2. To what extent is the military fully integrated based on race, gender, sexual identity, and gender identity? To further explore issues addressed in this chapter, we invite readers to search for and evaluate relevant evidence to bring to a discussion. Please look for evidence of concerns that were expressed prior to military integration based on at least two of the following aspects: race, gender, sexual identity, and gender identity. How has historical time within a culture influenced these concerns?

3. Select a legal issue related to gender or sexuality, such as women's right to vote, contraception, abortion, sodomy laws, spousal rape, marriage, foster parenting, or adoption. For this issue, look for evidence within and beyond this chapter regarding who has been privileged by legislative and judicial action. How has this issue been differently understood during at least two points in time? Describe continued activist work related to this issue.

4. Contrast the marriage equality argument and the antimarriage argument. What rights are the goals of each argument? Determine which argument you find more compelling and explain why.

5. Does the state in which you live distinguish teen sexting from child pornography? What legal response to teen sexting would you consider to be ideal?

6. Select a religious group, such as a mosque, church, or temple, and research how its members understand the role of sexuality and gender identity within the religion they practice. What are the injunctive norms of the religion? What are the descriptive

norms of the religious group? For example, is the group affiliated with a sect that has published statements regarding sexuality and gender identity? Is sexuality or gender identity of central importance to the group's practice of religion? To what extent is there dissent or agreement regarding how to respond to queer people as potential members or religious leaders?

6

PRIVILEGED (POPULAR) CULTURE AND INTERNALIZED EXPECTATIONS

At the age of three, Isaiah sat on his mother's lap, gazed lovingly at her, and said sweetly and in all seriousness, "Mommy, you have a beautiful mustache." At age four, Isaiah's sister Lena expressed vocal admiration for her mother's "great, big hiney."

These children meant to give their mother sincere compliments on aspects of her appearance that they admired. At three and four, the children did not yet know that women in our mainstream culture are not meant to have facial hair or great, big hineys, and that indeed, the compliments were actually insults in the normative culture. Children have to learn these cultural norms. They are not born knowing them. These examples help us to see that our contemporary mainstream ideals for beauty in women are not "natural" but social and constructed. As noted in chapters 2 and 3, idealized females in our mainstream society are small, thin, and even frail. They have no body hair, no wrinkles, and no flab. They hold their body in a controlled manner that folds the body inward, legs pressed together or crossed, instead of spreading out their legs and arms and taking up more space. Girls and women learn to pick at their food and, especially in public, eat tiny amounts. Sex educator and body image activist Melissa A. Fabello identifies ways that thin women experience privilege, such as fashionable stores stocking clothing in their size and being able to enjoy a high-calorie treat in public without fear of open scoffing from bystanders.[1] Inspired by Peggy McIntosh's seminal work that identified unfair privileges that are awarded without merit to people socially understood to be white (described in chapter 2), Fabello similarly lists advantages afforded to thin women that are denied to fat women.

While women are expected to be thin, men are pressured to be muscular. It is okay in the mainstream, and even cute, for girls and women to cry, to not know how to throw a ball or land a punch. To achieve hegemonic masculinity (first mentioned in chapter 1), boys and men are encouraged to internalize expectations to act in ways opposite to female caretakers and girl peers. Indeed, many people refer to male and female as "opposite sexes," thereby promoting binary thinking. In contrast, like our fellow social constructionists, we argue that male and female sexes as well as masculine and feminine genders are not actually opposite, rather, social expectations work to produce seemingly opposing behavior. All of these norms for appropriate gender behavior are socially constructed. In other words, young children learn social assumptions as they grow up, and individuals interact across their lifespan within social contexts that expect everyone to conform to these norms. Girls and boys, men and women who do not learn these rules, or who choose to deviate from them, often suffer consequences, and those can be severe.[2]

At four years old, Lena expressed distress about one aspect of the children's books she loved to read. She asked her mother why so many characters were boys. For example, A. A. Milne's *Winnie-the-Pooh* series focuses on a human boy, a male bear, a male piglet, a male tiger, a male owl, a male rabbit, a male donkey, and a male baby kangaroo, who is carried by the only female character, his mother. While all the other characters have desires, goals, and adventures, Roo's mother, Kanga, exists only to care for her child. Female characters are far outnumbered in children's literature and other media and often appear only on the periphery of the action.[3]

As children age into adolescent and adult consumers, media images are often designed to generate insecurity and then profit off products advertised to address socially constructed deficits. Media images have been used to provoke fear and to maintain privilege of those in power. Idealized media images of men and women are often unrealistic or even impossible for actual people to emulate. Digital alteration is normative for photographs in magazines, creating unobtainable models of beauty.[4] On film, lighting, cosmetics, and body doubles are used to create untenable representations. Male actors are known to perform push-ups immediately before filming a shirtless scene to engorge their muscles with blood and fulfill cultural expectations of muscular appearance.[5] The body of a single female character might be portrayed on film by splicing images of one woman's thighs, another's buttocks, a third's breasts.[6]

Affluent, well-educated, white, heterosexual men have often appeared as the protagonist on film—the person whose desires are important and whose perspective is valuable. Heterosexual women are often treated as objects to be obtained. Fictionalized images in feature films regularly portray heterosexual male teens or adults as solely focused on pursuing sexual activity.[7]

INTERSECTIONALITY AND MEDIA MYTHS

As we consider socially constructed rules for appropriate behavior, it is valuable to explore how aspects of identity combine to make a whole person. The perspective of *intersectionality* focuses on how different parts of a person's identity interact, such as gender, sexuality, wealth, education, and race, in other words, how aspects of identity intersect. Sociologists Margaret L. Andersen and Patricia Hill Collins identify that a *matrix of domination* occurs when an individual is stigmatized on multiple levels.[8] As noted in chapter 2, Barbara Smith's definition of feminism acknowledges the intersections of race, socioeconomic class, disability, and sexual identity.[9]

Intersecting identities are explored in *This Bridge Called My Back*, edited by Cherríe Moraga and Gloria E. Anzaldúa, which presents critical pieces written by queer women of color about oppression and resistance.[10] Lesbian feminist scholars of color, such as Anzaldúa and Audre Lorde, explore embodying multiple stigmatized aspects of identity that form a matrix that may be used to dominate, to oppress. Lorde, a poet and essayist, addresses intersecting stigmatization in an essay comparing her experience as a Black lesbian feminist to the experience of Mary Daly, a white lesbian feminist. In "An Open Letter to Mary Daly," Lorde writes, "Within the community of women, racism is a reality force within my life as it is not within yours."[11] Daly faces sexism and heteronormativity; Lorde faces both of these plus racism. Black women who identify as heterosexual, or middle or upper class, do not face oppression on as many dimensions as does Lorde as a lesbian who grew up in poverty.[12]

Sociologist Michael Kimmel describes a moment when he became keenly aware of intersecting identities. Because of white privilege, people who identify as white are often able to think of themselves as "just human," of having the privilege of not thinking about their own racial identity. Privilege is often invisible for those who benefit from it. Kimmel recognized this during a seminar he attended in the early 1980s when an African American woman asked a white woman, "When you wake up in the morning and look in the mirror, what do you see?" The white woman responded, "I see a woman." "'That's precisely the problem,' responded the black woman. 'I see a *black* woman. To me, race is visible every day, because race is how I am *not* privileged in our culture. Race is invisible to you, because it's how you are privileged. It's why there will always be differences in our experience.'"

Kimmel realized that he is able to look in a mirror without focusing on his own race and gender. "When I look in the mirror, I see a human being." He saw himself as "universally generalizable." He noted that his perception at that time was that, "As a middle-class white man, I have no class, no race, no gender." He was surprised to realize that his belief had been "I'm the generic person!" This conversation made his privilege visible.

> Since then, I've begun to understand that race, class, and gender didn't refer only to other people, who were marginalized by race, class, or gender privilege. Those terms also described me. I enjoyed the privilege of invisibility. . . . What makes us marginal or powerless are the processes we see. Invisibility is a privilege in another sense— as a luxury. Only white people in our society have the luxury not to think about race every minute of their lives.[13]

Being a man does not always mean (or only mean) having privilege. Intersectionality helps us to understand that each person has multiple identities, some of which might carry privilege while others might bear the historical weight of oppression.

Heterosexual men who are African American experience racism, including profoundly racist stereotypes about their sexuality. A racist stereotype in normative United States culture is the idea that Black men are sexual predators of white women. Linked to this ugly idea is the ungrounded belief that Black men cannot control themselves and that they are dangerous and likely to sexually assault white women. Cultural materialists identify that the system of slavery in the United States produced and reproduced beliefs by whites that people of African descent were more animalistic and therefore better at physical than at intellectual activities. In this racist way of thinking, whites thought that Black people were stronger at physical labor, better dancers, and excessively sexual in comparison with those understood to be white.[14] Racist whites believed Black men to be out of control sexually and particularly out of control around the normative white symbol of purity, white womanhood.

This racist thinking culminated in white justification for violence, including lynching many African American men in the late nineteenth and early twentieth centuries in the United States.[15] Using cultural materialism, we see the way of living from which this racist thinking sprang; that is, whites were invested in the exploited labor of African Americans. Racism justified the exploitation. The racism was rationalized by whites through stereotypes about Blacks, including portrayals of Black men as sexual predators of white women. Violence by whites, including lynching as a white terrorist practice, was used to scare African Americans into accepting oppression.

The history of major motion pictures is linked to these racist depictions of Black men. D. W. Griffith's 1915 feature-length film, *Birth of a Nation*, is often cited as being transformative in terms of advancing the field of filmmaking. The film is a celebration of the Ku Klux Klan's potential for saving the United States from the menace of African American men's debauchery, based on Thomas Dixon's popular novel *The Clansman*. Scenes are meant to horrify white viewers of the terrors that would occur if Black men had power.

In one set of scenes, Griffith portrays an idealized white girl. She happily focuses on housework and caring for her family. The implication is that she is innocent of sexuality, pure, virginal. Her downfall is that she does not heed warnings of dangerous Black men in the nearby woods. Instead, she traipses out of the house to fetch a pail of water. A character portrayed as a Black man follows her into the woods. The actor is a European American man wearing makeup to indicate that he is playing an African American character. In a brief encounter, the man indicates that he wants to marry the girl. She is shown running away with a look of abject terror. The man runs after her. Griffith implies that the man is intent on committing stranger rape. In the novel, the girl is raped, but in the film, she jumps from a cliff to her death rather than be defiled.[16]

Africana studies scholar Tricia Rose traces this "long and entrenched history of associating black culture and black people with violence, law-lessness, and deviant sexuality" from early film to contemporary hip-hop videos.[17] She notes, "These associations have been fabricated to justify and maintain various forms of racialized and gendered oppres-sion and inequality of black people throughout U.S. history."[18] White male executives at the top of record companies have been the most recent group to profit from media images of predatory Black male sexuality.

AGENTS AND OBJECTS

Sexual agency focuses on an individual's choices that fulfill personal goals related to sexual desire. In contrast, *objectification* focuses on being treated as an aspect of someone else's desire, often in a way that does not acknowledge or respect the agency of the individual. Patriar-chal systems have traditionally objectified women, ignoring or rejecting women's potential for sexual agency.

To explore contemporary messages about sexual agency and objec-tification, we invite readers to watch a titillating music video with the sound muted. Whose desire is central? Who takes action? Who is re-spected? Communications scholar Sut Jhally challenges viewers to think critically about portrayals of race, gender, and sexuality in music videos. Across three installations of his *Dreamworlds* films, Jhally removes the original music and pairs images from the videos with critical analysis. Across decades and genres of music, videos frequently portray hetero-sexual male sexual desire as central, men as sexual agents, and women as sexual objects. Jhally argues that many videos appeal to a ridiculous heterosexual male fantasy that all young, beautiful women desire to be treated as men's sexual toys.

As noted above, in the profoundly racist film *Birth of a Nation*, D. W. Griffith presented a virginal white girl trying to escape a Black man's violent lust. Alternatively, many music videos of our current era depict girls and women who want a man to use them sexually. White girls and women are often presented in a false binary that implies they have two choices: to remain virtuous virgins until marriage to a nice man or to become vice-filled whores. In a racist society such as the United States, women of color historically have been relegated to the role of satisfying men's passions. Women's sexual agency—fulfilling their own desire—is often invisible in media that focus on men's desire. The *virgin/whore dichotomy* creates a false binary that suggests women can enjoy their sexuality, or they can be moral, but they cannot do both. This binary seeks to force women into strict, opposing categories of bad or good. Men are not bound by such a dichotomy.[19]

The 1996 film *Scream* explicitly explored the typical virgin/whore dichotomy in the moral lessons of horror films. Across many films in the slasher genre, a single honorable female virgin is tormented but manages to live to the end of the film (presumably to deal with a lifetime of posttraumatic stress). Any young woman with sexual experience is murdered in horrific fashion, with violent ends often occurring during a sexual act. These films suggest that sex is extremely dangerous for women. Women who enjoy sex in the slasher genre forfeit their lives.[20]

MEDIA REPRESENTATION OF QUEER INDIVIDUALS

Reflecting the arguments of cultural materialism (discussed in chapter 3), media studies scholar Stuart Ewen contends that the mass media exist as parts of our culture, not distinct and separate voices telling us fictional stories, for example, in television drama and factual truths in the news.[21] Instead, what the media portray as morally good and factually correct reflect our culture's ways of thinking, especially the normative culture, in a particular time and place. Like people of color in the United States, queer people historically have played very limited roles in the mass media if they are represented at all. When they are represented, it is often in very limited, stereotypical, and derogatory ways.

Film historian Vito Russo's *The Celluloid Closet* details representations of queer characters on film.[22] Across early decades of film, sometimes queer characters were presented as tragically flawed or sinister. Sometimes queer male characters were portrayed as stereotypical "sissies," who appeared in minor roles for comic effect. None were role

models. Historic film portrayals of queer men were often archetypal
characters who broke masculine gender norms, suggesting a conflation
of sexuality and expression of gender—as though evil behavior or
stereotypically feminine behavior of men revealed their sexual desire.

As Lena noticed, women and girls are outnumbered in the media.
Russo notes that lesbians and other queer women were not *just* outnumbered but were largely nonexistent in mass media representations.
In part, this lesbian invisibility has stemmed from the celebration of
hegemonic masculinity in our society and of compulsory heterosexuality
(as discussed in chapter 3). Comparing the sissy stereotype to that of
the lesbian "tomboy," Russo writes, "In celebrating maleness, the ren-
dering invisible of all else has caused lesbianism to disappear behind a
male vision of sex in general. The stigma of tomboy has been less than
that of sissy because lesbianism is never allowed to become a threatening reality any more than female sexuality of other kinds."[23]

From 1934 to 1962, no characters on film were openly gay. Roles
might subtly suggest queer identity, but the Production Code for motion pictures prevented direct discussion or outright portrayal of certain
types of sexuality. Prohibitions included "sex relationships between the
white and black races" and "sex perversion or any inference to it."[24]
Same-sex sexual desire was treated as perversion. Films based on plays
or novels with central queer characters, such as Tennessee Williams's
Cat on a Hot Tin Roof, were altered to meet production standards—
with new dialogue, altered scenes, and even changes to the outcome of
the story.[25]

Decades after the end of the Production Code, queer characters
could be openly represented, but they were often depicted in negative
ways. *The Crying Game*, a critically acclaimed 1992 British film that
played to wide audiences in the United States, challenged viewers to
confront racism and queer love. In the film, openly gay, biracial male
actor Jaye Davidson plays a trans woman named Dil. Stephen Rea plays
Fergus, a heterosexual, cisgender white man who is surprised to find
himself attracted to a woman of color. Dil assumes that Fergus is aware
that she is a trans woman, but Fergus only learns this shortly after they
have kissed. His initial response is violent revulsion. In a carefully kept
secret, the revelation of Dil as transgender was treated as a plot twist
intended to shock audiences. Dil prompts empathy, but also discom-

fort. The film demands that viewers consider the complexity of gender, but suggests that disgust is a natural response to queer desire. [26]

As the queer rights movement in the United States grew stronger and bigger, queer people struggled for change in the mass media. The 1990s saw queer people challenging derogatory queer representations and demanding that their existence, their lives and loves, be seen in the mass-mediated culture. Thus a particularly exciting moment was when Ellen DeGeneres's character, Ellen Morgan, in her network situation comedy, *Ellen*, came out as lesbian. Aired first in 1994 on the ABC network, *Ellen* was initially extremely popular, but its audience started to wane after a couple of years. An ABC executive thought that the character Ellen should adopt a puppy so as to give the show more focus. Instead, Ellen DeGeneres, who had been out in her personal life for nineteen years, suggested that her character come out of the closet. The corporate owner of ABC, the Walt Disney Company, worried about negative responses from both advertising and consumers. Eventually, however, the company decided to support the idea. [27]

Because of the ABC executive's unused suggestion, they called the coming-out show "The Puppy Episode." The show included a number of famous guest cameos, including Melissa Etheridge, k.d. lang, Billy Bob Thornton, and Oprah Winfrey. Ellen Morgan came out to a new friend at an airport. Inadvertently using an airport loudspeaker, she also came out to everyone waiting to board a flight. [28]

The show was "ABC's highest rated regular program of the entire season, and the critics loved it." About the response, Neil Miller writes, "Even Vice-President Al Gore noted in an October 17, 1997 Hollywood speech that, thanks to DeGeneres, 'millions of Americans were forced to look at sexual orientation in a more open light.'" Miller continues, "Still, the comedian was a little overwhelmed by it all. 'I never wanted to be "the lesbian actress,"' she told *Time*. 'I never wanted to be the spokesperson for the gay community. Ever. I did it for my own truth. . . . But let's get beyond this, and let me get back to what I do.'" [29]

DeGeneres was not the only critic. At the other end of the main-stream political spectrum, the Christian Right expressed dismay. Jerry Falwell called DeGeneres "Ellen DeGenerate." And a large Protestant denomination, the Southern Baptists, organized a (short-lived) boycott of Disney for its "anti-Christian and anti-family direction." [30]

Probably unrelated to the boycott, the show *Ellen* fizzled out, but Ellen was part of a movement that had started to depict queer individuals positively on television. In the opening year of *Ellen*, MTV's reality program *The Real World* cast Pedro Zamora, who became one of the first openly gay individuals to be featured on television.[31] Zamora, an activist for HIV/AIDS awareness, was commended by President Bill Clinton for educating audiences and inspiring the public to feel empathy.[32]

A growing interest in gay programming yielded *Will & Grace*, premiering in 1998, and *Queer as Folk* in 2002. Openly gay men played important roles in other shows, including Richard Hatch in 2000 on the popular reality show *Survivor*.[33]

Initially airing in 2013, *Orange Is the New Black* explores race, gender, and sexuality in a prison for women. Sexual connection between women is portrayed as a positive in the lives of the characters. Women who love women within the prison include Lorna, who dreams of marrying the man she adores and living as a straight woman when she finishes her sentence, Piper, who is torn between her attraction to her ex-girlfriend and her affection for her male fiancé, and Nicky, who celebrates her ability to please women sexually. Gender presentation is diverse across characters such as Big Boo, who affects a butch persona, Red, who seeks to be feminine and fierce, and Sophia, who constructs a glamorous feminine appearance with carefully coiffed long hair and flattering cosmetics. Both the character of Sophia and Laverne Cox, who plays her, are trans women. All of the characters are flawed human beings, but queer sexuality and personalized expressions of gender are depicted as sources of strength rather than weakness. Unlike historical representations of queer people in the media, there is nothing sinister or tragic about queer identity in this series. Alternatively, the anti-lesbian bigotry of Corrections Officer Healy is presented as a tragic flaw.

IMAGES OF QUEER FAMILIES IN THE MEDIA

In 1989, author and editor Lesléa Newman self-published *Heather Has Two Mommies*. This children's book describes an idyllic family with two lesbian parents who are presented as best friends. The following year, the publisher Alyson created the series Alyson Wonderland, dedicated to "books for and about the children of lesbian and gay parents." In 1990, Alyson Wonderland rereleased *Heather Has Two Mommies* and published artist and writer Michael Willhoite's *Daddy's Roommate*. Narrated from the perspective of a young boy, Willhoite's children's book describes a child processing the divorce of his parents and his father's new relationship with a man named Frank. Within the book, children learn that the word gay represents "just one more kind of love."

Children's books focusing on queer families have been strongly supported by some educators, who found the picture books to be valuable ways to start conversations about diversity. Anti-queer activists have perceived these books to be factious. Gender studies scholar Alyson Miller notes that in 2006, *Heather Has Two Mommies* prompted "a clear demonstration of the ways in which controversial literature acts as a mechanism through which existing cultural anxieties can be expressed. The right-wing American political columnist Alisa Craddock, for example, uses the book as a launching point for a series of homophobic arguments, claiming that if homosexual unions were legalized in the United States, 'the crumbling vestiges of our culture would not be able to withstand it.'"[34]

As discussed in chapter 5, the queer movement against marriage is a form of resistance against assimilation into heteronormative culture by working to redefine what family means. Educational policy scholar Jennifer Esposito has raised concerns that children's literature that describes families with lesbian mothers has focused too much on fitting heteronormative culture and not enough on acknowledging the discrimination faced by lesbian mothers and their children. She argues that picture books have focused on how similar queer families are to straight families, rather than challenging the notion that families must be headed by a romantic dyad. Children's literature could be used to acknowledge the love that occurs across diverse combinations of caregiving, care-receiving pairs. Children's literature can be used to raise awareness of unfairness. Picture books focusing on queer families could explain how privileged, heteronormative assumptions are damaging to many families.[35]

When large corporations create images of families, they often portray heteronormative values. When corporations have chosen to feature queer families in their advertisements, they have often faced anti-queer backlash and then harnessed their creative teams for clever responses. When JC Penney featured a family with two lesbian mothers in a 2012 Mother's Day promotion, it faced a boycott from One Million Moms, a conservative advocacy group that promises "to stand against the immorality, violence, vulgarity and profanity the entertainment media is throwing at . . . children."[36] JC Penney responded with a Father's Day advertisement featuring a family with two gay fathers.[37] In 2014, a television commercial advertising Honey Maid's snack products, titled "This Is Wholesome," presented families with same-gender parents and interracial parents. Honey Maid's response to hateful messages was a second advertisement in which they printed each vitriolic social media post, rolled it into a tube, and used it like a pixel in a three-dimensional art project spelling the word "Love."[38]

MORE ALTERNATIVES TO THE HETERONORMATIVE

During the rise of the sexual revolution, researchers explored choices that provided an alternative to traditional, heteronormative nuclear families consisting of a married mother and father with their children. Family studies scholar Roger H. Rubin notes, "The late 1960s and early 1970s was a period of intense reexamination of interpersonal relationships, marriage, and family life."[39] At a time when heterosexual marriage was expected and divorce was stigmatized, "the term *alternative lifestyles* included a variety of nontraditional family forms and personal living arrangements including singlehood, non-marital heterosexual cohabitation, single-parent family, stepfamilies, dual career/work families, gay and lesbian relationships, open marriages and multiple relationships, and communes."[40] Research on many of these topics flourished over the following decades, but scholarly work on open marriages, multiple relationships, and communes quickly declined.

In 1972, anthropologists Nena O'Neill and George O'Neill published *Open Marriage*, an argument for marital companionship focused on realistic expectations, honest communication, equality, and trust. O'Neill and O'Neill contend that sexual fidelity is not an essential component of a strong relationship, and they encourage couples to work together to establish and abide by guidelines if they choose to be open to sexual experiences beyond the relationship.[41] They acknowledge that extramarital sexual activity could occur within a healthy marriage, but an "open marriage," as they define it, is not synonymous with sexual swinging.[42]

Swinging is pursuit of sexual activity with multiple individuals for the purpose of sexual pleasure. Swingers in committed romantic relationships have the consent of their partner for sexual activity with additional people.[43] They maintain a sense of commitment to their romantic partner and do not seek emotional attachment beyond the dyad of their committed relationship.[44] Swinging is distinct from *polyamory*, in which individuals seek multiple partners for "long-term, emotionally intimate relationships" with the "focus on honesty and (ideally) full disclosure of the network of relationships to all who participate in or are affected by them."[45] *Group marriages* are a form of polyamory in which three or more individuals share housing, economic resources, and child care.[46]

Sociologist Elisabeth Sheff addresses the relative lack of research on polyamory with an impressive program of ongoing study. One of Sheff's approaches has been to compare polyamorous families to families led by a dyad of same-gender parents. She challenges heteronormative assumptions that suggest that heterosexual, nuclear families are the appropriate comparison for all other family structures. Sheff does not use the term queer for polyamorous families, but she notes that polyamorous families might benefit from recent civil rights work focused on families led by same-gender parents and that both types of families face stigma. Another point of comparison is that conservatives often argue "against same-sex marriage as leading to a 'slippery slope' that inevitably sanctions multiple-partner marriage, bestiality, and incest."[47]

We invite readers to continue to develop their definition of sexuality and to continue to consider what desires or behaviors might be included within queer sexuality. If three people enjoy consensual sexual activity as a group, two women and a man, under what circumstances would you apply different labels to the sexuality of the women, such as heterosexual or queer? If two men and a woman had group sex, would you see the situation as parallel or as different? Sheff has found that the majority of men in polyamorous relationships identify as heterosexual, while most of the women identify as bisexual.[48] In your definition of sexuality, to what extent would you respect the way individuals identify themselves, and to what extent would you want to impose your own interpretation of sexual desire and sexual behavior?

COMMUNICATING CONSENT

Fraternity culture often offers its own interpretation of "normal" sexual desire and behavior. In 2014, Texas Tech University's Phi Delta Theta fraternity was sanctioned after displaying a banner at a party that read NO MEANS YES, YES MEANS ANAL.[49] While this complete disregard for sexual consent is horrifying, many institutions such as schools, workplaces, and religious congregations have struggled with how to promote empathic understanding of consent. Many colleges and universities are moving from a policy that "no means no" to *affirmative consent*, in which a person initiating sexual action is responsible for obtaining ongoing consent throughout a sexual experience.[50] In both of these policies, consent can be withdrawn at any time within a sexual encounter—previous consent does not imply continued consent. A major distinction is that affirmative consent places the responsibility on the person initiating an action to look for or ask for consent prior to that action, while "no means no" places the burden of responsibility on the person who would like to stop an action—possibly after an unwanted action has been initiated.

Some readers might find it surprising that one community known for thoughtful communication about consent comprises individuals who practice bondage and discipline, domination and submission, or sadism and masochism (BDSM). Although human applications of models of consent will be imperfect, people in the BDSM community often communicate explicitly prior to a sexual experience about desires, boundaries, and how to clearly read signs of consent. For example, a specific safety word or a tune hummed might be agreed on to indicate that consent has been withdrawn. A symbol of consent might be used such as holding onto an object as long as consent continues and dropping it if consent concludes at any point.[51]

FEMINIST PERSPECTIVES ON PORNOGRAPHY

Rich diversity among feminist thinkers often leads to differing perspectives on how to promote the status of women. Evaluation of pornography is an issue where branches of feminism have heated debates. Some feminists lead campaigns against pornography based on the prevalence of pornographic material that portrays women as sexual objects for consumption, rather than as sexual agents.[52] And some of these antipornography (and other) feminists argue that all forms of female sex work exploit the sex workers and objectify and abuse all women. For example, feminists involved with the National Organization for Women (NOW)—cofounded in part by the author of *The Feminine Mystique*, Betty Friedan—have historically argued that nearly all forms of sex work harm women.[53] Sex workers challenge these feminists (who sometimes identify themselves as radical feminists). In sharp contrast to the anti–sex work position, sex workers, many of whom identify as feminist, argue that sex work can be liberating for women. Sex as work includes the potential of allowing and celebrating women's sexuality. This potential celebration of women as sexual beings—including the celebration of women as beings who can, do, and deserve to enjoy their sexuality on their own terms—offers a challenge to the virgin (good)/whore (bad) dichotomy. In other words, women can be sexual and still be "good."[54]

Some pro-pornography feminists promote forms of pornography that portray women as consenting sexual agents. Pornography, like other products of sex work, offers the possibility of greater enjoyment of sexuality and therefore can be a form of enacting a politics of celebrating sexuality. Artists have playfully created sexually explicit images, designed both to appeal to prurient interests and to challenge viewers to see women as powerful and valuable.[55] Feminist reviews of pornographic films and other materials are widely available for those who wish to select images that present women in a positive light.

DISCUSSION QUESTIONS

1. Analyze a music video, film, or television series in terms of the messages it provides about men's and women's sexuality. Is this piece of media heteronormative? Does it acknowledge or cele-

brate queer sexuality? To what extent are women and men sexual agents (individuals making their own choices to fulfill personal goals), and to what extent are they sexual objects (acted on by others)?

2. Consider intersectionality within the piece of media chosen for the previous question—how race, social class, gender, and sexual identity intersect. Who is privileged based on aspects of identity? What identities interact in a matrix of domination?

3. Analyze an animated film or picture book that was a favorite in your childhood. Are male and female characters equally represented? Are they equally involved in the action? Do they have similar goals and desires? Are there subtle (or not-so-subtle) messages about appropriate gender roles?

4. What effects might result from presentations of families with same-gender parents in children's literature? What might be the outcome of family-focused media campaigns that show happy queer people?

5. Before reading this chapter, how would you have defined an "open marriage"? After reading about the goals of Nena O'Neill and George O'Neill in promoting open marriage, in what ways, if any, has your perspective changed?

6. What are the laws in the state in which you live regarding consent for sexual activity? Does your school or workplace have a policy regarding consent for sexual activity? In laws and policies that affect you, to what extent is consent described as an ongoing and active process? What would you consider to be an ideal consent law or policy?

7. Can pornography serve as an effective challenge to the virgin/whore dichotomy? Are sex workers typically seen as sexual agents or sexual objects? How would feminist pornography look?

7

VIOLENCE, AGGRESSION, AND PRIVILEGE

Isaiah and Lena each experienced bullying that is typical for their gender. When Isaiah was four, other boys told him that pink should not be his favorite color and directly verbally insulted him in ways that were intended to hurt. Lena experienced indirect aggression when she was eight, which came in the form of a peer trying to end her friendship with her favorite classmate through acts such as preventing Lena from eating lunch with her friend and the peer. Boys who bullied Isaiah tried to directly demean him, while girls who bullied Lena sought to socially exclude her. When the authors of this book were children, bullying tended to be defined as direct physical aggression such as pushing or punching, but understanding has grown of the psychological distress caused by direct and indirect verbal aggression. Social scientific research in recent decades has widened the range of behaviors recognized as bullying.[1]

Intentional and unintentional harm comes in many forms. Although casual uses of the word "aggressive" are often synonymous with "assertive," social scientists use *aggression* for behaviors that cause harm, ranging from unintentional insults and invalidation to intentional violence. Microaggression (discussed in chapter 3) occurs on a continuum from unexamined privilege causing inadvertent insults to insensitivity causing subtle, but purposeful, psychological injury. For example, a person might unintentionally hurt the feelings of another by assuming heteronormativity in a way that excludes a queer individual. In contrast, one might intentionally, but subtly, cause psychological distress by using a pejorative term while pretending to be confused about polite phrasing. For instance, a speaker might understand that either "trans" or "transgender" would be respectful terms, but intentionally offend someone by using "transsexual," while maintaining plausible deniability that it was an simply a naïve error.[2]

Children tend to perform intentional aggression in gendered ways. Social norms often encourage boys who are in conflict with each other to directly fight with words or fists, whereas norms deter girls from overt acts of verbal or physical harm against other girls.[3] Girls are likely to use *indirect aggression*—subtle intentional harm, such as *relational aggression*, which focuses on damaging a target's social relationships through indirect means such as spreading rumors or telling embarrassing secrets (also called *social aggression*).[4]

The American Psychological Association defines violence as an extreme form of aggression.[5] The World Health Organization defines *violence* as "the intentional use of physical force or power, threatened or actual, against oneself, another person, or against a group or community, that either results in or has a high likelihood of resulting in injury, death, psychological harm, maldevelopment, or deprivation."[6] In other words, violence requires an intention to harm. This harm can be caused by actual or threatened physical force or by use of power. Violence can be directed at oneself, another, or others. In addition to an intention to cause physical injury or death, violence also includes intended psychological damage, disruption of healthy development, or preventing access to basic necessities.

This chapter focuses on developing understanding of violence related to gender and sexuality, including tragic and infuriating examples that range from intimate attacks to mass murder. Solutions—some of which will be explored in chapter 8—are often successful when they develop from a critical understanding of the problem.

MEAN GIRLS: A CASE OF VIOLENCE IN THE MEDIA

At a time when the significance of damage caused by common forms of girls' aggression toward one another was often overlooked, and rarely labeled as bullying, comedic writer and actor Tina Fey was inspired to write the screenplay for the film *Mean Girls* after reading parenting educator Rosalind Wiseman's description of relational aggression, *Queen Bees and Wannabees.* Fey's goals were to reveal that indirect aggression is an important problem and to generate thoughtful discussion.[7] She sought to inspire empathy that would help viewers consider the perspectives of victims, survivors, bystanders, and perpetrators of relational aggression.

Unfortunately, uncritical viewing of violence in the media often prompts aggression rather than compassion.[8] Although Fey hoped to reduce violence by making *Mean Girls*, psychologist Sarah M. Coyne and colleagues found that viewing relational aggression in the film increased both relational aggression and physical aggression in comparison to viewing a nonviolent film clip. In a laboratory study of female college students, each woman watched one of three video clips before interacting with a female experimenter who intentionally acted in an antagonizing way. Women who had just watched a piece of *Mean Girls* seized opportunities to physically aggress against the antagonist and to relationally aggress against her.[9]

Social psychologists regularly examine behavior in a controlled setting to see the effects of one situation in comparison to others. Before exposing any people to procedures, proposed studies must pass an ethics review board that determines, among other considerations, that the anticipated benefits of the research outweigh the predicted costs of the study. Deception should be employed only when the research question would not be accurately explored if research participants were aware of the true goals of the study.

In the first part of this experiment, Coyne and colleagues asked each woman to watch one of the following three film scenes: relational aggression in *Mean Girls*, a graphic physical fight from Quentin Tarantino's *Kill Bill*, or a nonviolent scene of a séance in *What Lies Beneath*, directed by Robert Zemeckis. After watching the film clip, each woman met with a new experimenter, purportedly for a completely different study. To increase the likelihood that participants would want to hurt the experimenter, she followed a script concocted by the researchers. She acted impatiently while the participant worked on a difficult task and then expressed a concern that the participant's difficulty with the task was "really going to screw things up!"[10]

Following the frustrating interaction with the experimenter, each woman had the opportunity to physically aggress against her. The participant was led to believe that she and the experimenter were competing to see who could react faster. The task was repeated twenty-five times, and each time the participant set the loudness and the length of a blast of noise that would be played through the experimenter's headphones if the experimenter lost. The volume and the duration of the blast were measures of physical aggression. (The experimenter did not actually endure the noise blasts.) Finally, participants were given an opportunity to relationally aggress against the experimenter by rating her performance, ostensibly for consideration in a hiring decision.[11]

Viewing relational aggression in *Mean Girls* prompted both physical aggression and relational aggression at levels similar to viewing physical aggression in *Kill Bill* and greater than watching the nonviolent clip.[12] Beyond controlled studies such as the work of Coyne and colleagues, we wonder how many girls learned new techniques for harming their peers from watching *Mean Girls* and then applied them. A quick Internet search reveals step-by-step instructions for creating a "burn book" as depicted in the film, including warnings about potential harm that might befall anyone caught writing insults about peers.

Indirect relational aggression is more likely to be committed among girls than among boys,[13] but by adulthood, social expectations increasingly discourage men from overt acts of violence. On average, men become more likely than boys to use indirect forms of aggression. Women continue to use indirect rather than direct aggression. Studies reveal that gender differences in indirect aggression decrease in adulthood as men increase their use of these techniques and women continue to use them.[14]

In contrast to gender similarity in adulthood for indirect aggression, gender difference continues for direct aggression. Girls and women use direct aggression much less than boys or men. In comparison to boys, men are less likely to use direct aggression, but in comparison to women, men perpetrate many more acts of direct violence.[15]

MISOGYNY AND MISANDRY

Misogyny—hating women—has been a focus of much feminist analysis. Across diverse perspectives within feminism, work to make everyday misogyny visible has been a critical task. Misogyny is often prevalent in popular culture, with dehumanizing and degrading portrayals of women in films,[16] music lyrics and videos,[17] and video games.[18] Misogyny is frequently communicated through the use of degrading terms such as bitch and slut.[19]

The acronym *thot* has been described as an abbreviation for "that ho over there" or similar phrases, such as "thirsty hoes out there," that present women as whores. While thot is often used interchangeably with slut in casual conversation, analysis of its initial use in music lyrics indicates that the term was applied primarily to African American women seeking to present themselves as belonging to a higher social class than would be suggested by their current wealth. For example, Kevin Lavell's "Love No Thot" refers to a woman borrowing her best friend's clothes, with the implication that she is trying to create an appearance of being more sophisticated than her own wardrobe would allow. Uses of thot play on the virgin/whore dichotomy (discussed in chapter 6) in ways that degrade African American women for enjoying being sexual and for presenting themselves as elegant. In four letters, it manages to degrade based on gender, race, and social class.[20]

Given that language evolves quickly, especially for slang terms, thot might follow ratchet as a term whose meaning shifts over time. Like thot, the word *ratchet* was initially used to express disapproval of African Americans, especially women, who were seen as failing to meet societal expectations for people in the middle class. Some African American women and men sought to reclaim ratchet as a complimentary term, using it to suggest that someone is authentic and fierce. We urge caution when tempted to use terms that others might interpret as pejorative. As discussed in chapter 3, members of a privileged outgroup will often come across as insensitive or offensive if they attempt to use a term that would never be targeted at them.[21]

Critical examinations of misogyny have a long and rich history. In comparison, interrogation of *misandry*—hating men—has been much more sparse. Recent observations regarding misandry include a disturbing intersectionality of race and gender for African American men, who are unfairly stereotyped as potential troublemakers. Ethnic studies scholar William A. Smith and colleagues define *Black misandry* as "an exaggerated pathological aversion toward Black men created and reinforced in societal, institutional, and individual ideologies, practices, and behaviors."[22] Race and gender intersect in Black misandry to create unfair problems for African American men, who are too often stereotyped by police. Black men who are college students report being uncomfortably aware of careful surveillance of their actions on and off campus.[23] (We discuss intersectionality and a related stereotype about African American men in chapter 6.)[24]

The term misandry is also used within men's rights movements, a controversial, loose collective, predominantly of white men, who are preoccupied by a perception that men have been losing their traditional power. Men's rights activists tend to ignore intersectionality of social class and race and to idealize an archetype of a powerful male breadwinner. Men's rights activists are particularly concerned that men have lost power relative to women. As an example of this thinking, the mission statement of one men's rights organization expresses concern that "the noble idea of freedom and equity between the sexes has been corrupted. It has become a malignancy on our social consciousness. What used to be cooperation between the sexes is now gynocentric parasitism that inhabits every level of men's existence, from cradle to coffin. The efforts to enhance the rights of women have become toxic efforts to undermine the rights of men."[25]

Frankly, the authors of this book are confused by the arguments of men's rights activists. Although we seek to understand a multitude of perspectives on gender issues, we do not grasp how someone can rationalize claiming gynocentrism in the United States. This term seems to be a play on androcentrism (defined in chapter 3 as a system that makes masculine experience central, disregarding or devaluing others). Men's rights activists' claim of "gynocentric parasitism" is an argument that societal systems have swung far past androcentrism to being centered on feminine experience.

As feminists, we seek gender fairness, and we are heartened to see progress toward more equitable leadership in the United States, which is less androcentric than it has ever been. Yet the United States is still far from reaching parity. We certainly do not see evidence to support gynocentrism. As of 2016, a major political party had nominated only one woman for President, and women leaders at the rank of the Cabinet had never exceeded 41 percent (which was achieved in President Clinton's second administration in 1997). Women have never held more than a third of the nine seats on the Supreme Court. Women's representation is remarkably low in Congress, with women constituting merely 20 percent of the members of the Senate, 20.2 percent of the members of the House of Representatives, and less than 3 percent of the historical membership of Congress. In terms of income, women on average earn less than men. In 2016, the average woman earned seventy-nine cents for every dollar earned by a man.[26] If historic patterns continue in the gender pay gap, women's average incomes will not achieve parity with men's until the year 2059.[27] In the early part of the twenty-first century, a woman in the middle of the distribution of women's incomes (from lowest income to highest) earned an annual $10,876 less than a man in the middle of the distribution of men's incomes.[28] (Extreme numbers strongly influence the average; therefore, it is customary to report the median score—the score in the middle of a distribution—when there are extreme scores.) Women are often encouraged to work in fields that are less lucrative, while men who work in fields that are associated with women—such as teaching young children or nursing—are often encouraged to become supervisors of women.[29] At the time of this writing, women continue to be significantly more likely than men to live in poverty.[30]

Men's rights activists express concern that men are unfairly treated in court cases that decide disputes between a man and a woman.[31] On one website, the self-named Men's Human Rights Movement argues that men should not be made to support biological children that result from casual sexual interactions and that child support following divorce should be applied only in exceptional cases. The group argues that alimony should be granted after a divorce only if it was included in a prenuptial agreement. The members call for an end to *rape shield laws* that prohibit introducing a victim's sexual history into evidence to support a defendant's case that rape did not occur.[32]

A particularly disturbing example of men's rights activism came from Paul Elam, who wrote a "deliberately provocative" piece on rape "to get attention and challenge people to think." After insulting women like the authors of this book by referring to feminist experts on rape as "pinheads" and "morons," Elam builds to an argument that reveals his utter lack of respect for women's control over their own bodies and over their expression of sexuality. He asks whether women ask to be raped: "What I mean is, do women who act provocatively; who taunt men sexually, toying with their libidos for personal power and gain, etc., have the same type of responsibility for what happens to them as, say, someone who parks their car in a bad neighborhood with the keys in the ignition and leaves it unlocked with the motor running?" Elam suggests that some women have "sinister" motives for sexually provoking men. He continues: "I have ideas about women who spend evenings in bars hustling men for drinks, playing on their sexual desires so they can get shitfaced on the beta dole; paying their bar tab with the pussy pass. And the women who drink and make out, doing everything short of sex with men all evening, and then go to his apartment at 2:00 a.m. Sometimes both of these women end up being the 'victims' of rape." Elam asks, "But are these women asking to be raped?" He answers, "In the most severe and emphatic terms possible the answer is NO, THEY ARE NOT ASKING TO GET RAPED." And then he emphasizes, "They are freaking *begging* for it." He goes on to claim that "women get pummeled and pumped because they are stupid (and often arrogant) enough to walk through life with the equivalent of a I'M A STUPID, CONNIVING BITCH—PLEASE RAPE ME neon sign glowing above their empty little narcissistic heads."[33]

Disturbingly, men's rights activism includes excusing violence against women. Many men's rights activists have a confused understanding of feminism that mistakes feminism's focus on women's rights for hatred of men.[34] Working toward greater rights for women need not harm men.[35] As discussed later in this chapter, communicating clearly about sexual consent benefits everyone regardless of gender or sexual identity.

GAY BASHING

The brutal beating of Matthew Shepard on October 6, 1998, causing his death six days later at the age of twenty-one, helped to spark renewed outrage and passion for justice in the queer rights movement. *Gay bashing*, violence against individuals who are queer or are perceived to be queer, is a form of hate crime that happens far too often in the United States. The brutal murder of forty-nine people who were dancing at a queer nightclub in Orlando, Florida, early in the morning on June 12, 2016, set a stunning record as the highest mortality rate from a mass shooting.

Violence against queer people is widespread enough that even young children may know something about it. As noted in chapter 5, when Lena was a preschooler, she often talked with her parents about her daydreams of growing up to marry one or another of the girls she knew. With a nod to Adrienne Rich, Lena seemed to have a girl-identified consciousness, but she openly challenged her own consciousness by telling her mother on a walk home from kindergarten that she was not going to be a "lezbun" after all. When her mother asked why, Lena said, tragically, because it is too scary.

It took some questioning to figure out that Lena had heard conversations about prejudice and bigotry against queer people on a number of occasions. Her scholarly and queer-friendly family openly discussed this entrenched social problem. Frightened by the hatefulness in the larger world, Lena at age five opted for perceived safety even if it infringed on her young dreams.

Lena's young awareness of gay bashing lies in stark contrast to evidence that gay bashing has often gone unnoticed. In particular, violence against queer people of color remains relatively unseen.[36] Brilliant filmmaker Arthur Dong, a gay man who was attacked by gay bashers in 1977, made *Licensed to Kill* (1997). In the documentary, Dong interviews seven convicted murderers to discover why they brutally killed gay men. Film expert Gary Morris notes that Dong "explores 'laws'— sometimes written, sometimes simply understood—against homosexuality and the men who take it upon themselves to rid the world of what they've been trained to think of as a weak, disposable group—gay men. In this graphic look at a loose subculture of murderers of gays, Dong exposes not simply a group of rampaging sociopaths but, more importantly, a society that carefully creates them."[37] In other words, the deeply homophobic and prejudiced society in the United States gave these gay bashers an implied "license to kill" queer people.[38]

While the culture of the United States promotes violence against all queer people, transgender individuals are especially vulnerable to violence and abuse. The federal government's Office for Victims of Crime states, "One in two transgender individuals are sexually abused or assaulted at some point in their lives." Further, "Some reports estimate that transgender survivors may experience rates of sexual assault up to 66 percent, often coupled with physical assaults or abuse." Transgender people who are also members of other oppressed groups, such as people of color and people living in poverty, experience even higher rates of violence, including at the hands of those meant to be helping. "Fifteen percent of transgender individuals report being sexually assaulted while in police custody or jail, which more than doubles (32 percent) for African-American transgender people."[39]

Attackers beat Shepard with the handle of a gun and left him tied to a fence on a bitterly cold night outside of Laramie, Wyoming; but attacks can also take the form of words, as happens in relational aggression. Social media offers avenues for such bullying. Electronic bullies can stay relatively safe and anonymous while doing immense harm to their victims. Outing or threatening to out queer individuals is a tactic commonly used and one that led to the death in 2010 of Tyler Clementi, an eighteen-year-old gay man in his first year of college at Rutgers University. The Tyler Clementi Foundation describes this tragedy:

> At college Tyler became a victim of cyber-bullying. His privacy was invaded when his college roommate set up a webcam to spy on him. The roommate viewed him in an intimate act, and invited others to view this online. Tyler discovered what his abuser had done and that he was planning a second attempt. Viewing his roommate's Twitter feed, Tyler learned he had widely become a topic of ridicule in his new social environment. He ended his life several days later by jumping off the George Washington Bridge. Tyler was eighteen years old.[40]

Based on concerns about online bullying, social psychologists Angela J. Bahns and Nyla R. Branscombe conducted a controlled study to examine whether a simple intervention could discourage gay bashing. Bahns and Branscombe asked heterosexual male college students to read a list of examples of heterosexual privilege (as mentioned in a discussion question in chapter 2). Half the men were then exposed to an endorsement of the importance of understanding discrimination against gay people while the other half read comments that negated the issue. The men who read about the importance of understanding discrimination were less likely to engage in online gay bashing during a computer-based interaction with a discussion partner, regardless of whether the partner was described as gay or heterosexual. The researchers were able to reduce gay bashing by educating people about heterosexual privilege and emphasizing the importance of the issue.[41]

INTIMATE PARTNER VIOLENCE

The Centers for Disease Control and Prevention define *intimate relationships* as those with "emotional connectedness, regular contact, ongoing physical contact and sexual behavior, identity as a couple," and "familiarity and knowledge about each other's lives." *Intimate partner violence* encompasses all forms of abuse that occur in intimate relationships. This term acknowledges abuse across different types of intimate relationships and therefore has replaced "domestic violence," which focuses only on the subset of intimate partners who share a home. Intimate partner violence can take many forms, including physical abuse, sexual abuse, stalking, and psychological abuse (such as emotional abuse, abusive control of finances, social control over friendships and relationships with family, mind games, and exploitation of vulnerabilities).[42]

The Department of Justice reports rates of intimate partner violence based on carefully constructed surveys. Within a given year, women are victimized at a rate that is more than five times higher than the rate experienced by men. Women are targeted by aggravated assault from an intimate partner at two and three-quarters the rate experienced by men, and by simple assault at five times the rate experienced by men. Women report nearly all cases of sexual assault and robbery committed by an intimate partner. Girls and women ages sixteen to thirty-four are the population at greatest risk for intimate partner violence. Data available from the Federal Bureau of Investigation indicate that women are two and a half times more likely to be murdered by an intimate partner.[43]

Survey respondents reported to the Centers for Disease Control and Prevention that 24.3 percent of women and 13.8 percent of men "have experienced severe physical violence by an intimate partner (e.g., hit with a fist or something hard, beaten, slammed against something) at some point in their lifetime."[44] Women were much more likely to report being stalked by an intimate partner: 10.7 percent of women and 2.1 percent of men experienced "stalking victimization at some point during their lifetime in which they felt very fearful or believed that they or someone close to them would be harmed or killed."[45] Unfortunately, but not surprising, given the research noted earlier on relational aggression, rates of psychological aggression were alarmingly high and practically identical: "Nearly half of all women and men in the United States have experienced psychological aggression by an intimate partner in their lifetime (48.4 percent and 48.8 percent, respectively).[46]

As we first noted in chapter 2, privilege is often invisible until critical analysis reveals it. When one carefully examines the language often used to describe intimate partner violence, male privilege becomes apparent. Men's acts of physical violence against women are frequently described in ways that focus solely on the harm to the woman, with no reference to the man who caused the injury, as though it happened without any person taking intentional action. Nursing scholars Debby Phillips and Dorothy Henderson identified the shockingly passive language that regularly describes male violence against women, titling their work with a classic example—"Patient Was Hit in the Face by a Fist." In their review of descriptions of intimate partner violence, Phillips and Henderson found that male perpetrators are rarely mentioned. The researchers note that the effect of victimization of women is often described, but no one is identified as causing the violence.[47]

In contrast to the typical description of male violence against women, second-wave radical feminist Adrienne Rich directly argues that men oppress women as a group. This oppression works to maintain women's relative powerlessness in a society ruled by men who benefit economically, psychologically, and socially by women's oppression. The radical feminist argument critiques both the intimate, personal ways women are oppressed and the larger capitalist oppression of women. Women's labor—often unpaid, and widely underpaid—helps to reproduce our capitalist economic system and the position of elite males who rule, and benefit by, it. Not only does women's labor reproduce capitalism, but as illuminated by cultural materialists, the ideas that come from this economic system work to reproduce the system. (Rich is first introduced in chapter 2, and cultural materialism is explored in chapter 3.) As noted by Rich, Barbara Ehrenreich and Deirdre English argue that "the advice given American women by male health professionals, particularly in the areas of marital sex, maternity and child care, has echoed the dictates of the economic marketplace."[48] Health professionals have shaped and continue to shape an understanding of women's work as a labor of love and effort that women should invest in, without expectation of economic reward. Women's unpaid work has helped to produce and reproduce our capitalist economy.

For most radical feminists, violence is the fundamental way in which the oppression of women is reproduced. This violence includes intimate partner violence and sexual violence such as rape, incest and child sexual abuse, and sexual harassment. Rich adds the new and important idea that compulsory heterosexuality also forms a layer of women's oppression. Rich argues that "women's choice of women as passionate comrades . . . life partners, co-workers, lovers . . . has been crushed, invalidated" and that there is a "virtual or total neglect of lesbian existence in a wide range of writings, including feminist scholarship."[49] Rich offers a challenge to the idea that women are naturally and normally heterosexual. She claims that instead of heterosexuality being the natural choice of women, it is compulsory. Indeed, Rich argues that "compulsory heterosexuality" is a kind of "political institution" that we must study as such to advance feminism and social justice.[50]

Intimate partner violence is a use of power (such as physical or emotional power) to control another person. Ironically, abusers frequently claim that they abuse a partner because they cannot control their fury when someone upsets them. Attorneys Ian Harris and Manar Waheed work with forensic social worker Claire McCue to support victims and survivors of intimate partner violence. They identify clear evidence that abusers can indeed control themselves. In court, a judge will often confront an abuser in ways that would prompt the abuser to fly into a rage if the abuser were in a position of greater power than the judge. Yet Harris, Waheed, and McCue consistently observe the abuser maintain control with the judge. If the abuser is able to maintain control when someone has greater power, the abuser is capable of maintaining control—and not abusing others—at home.

SEXUAL AGGRESSION

In our discussion of sexual aggression, we focus on moral decisions in addition to legal definitions. Regardless of whether the law recognizes certain forms of sexual aggression as criminal, all sexual aggression is harmful. *Sexual aggression* is any sexual act that occurs under coercion or without consent. Like other forms of aggression, sexual aggression can occur in unintentional forms, based on unexamined privilege and problematic gender norms that frame sexual activity as something one person scores off another, as though one is playing a sport with an offensive side trying to reach goals despite the defenses of an opposing side.[51] *Sexual violence*, also called *sexual victimization*, constitutes any sexual act obtained by force or use of power.

To understand sexual aggression, it is critical to determine what constitutes communication of consent. Definitions of consent must consider whether consent can be clearly communicated through the body language of nonverbal actions, or whether a person who desires to initiate a sexual act should always seek verbal consent. As noted in chapter 6, consent can be removed at any point during a sexual encounter. Another consideration is for an initiator to determine whether a potential partner's state of consciousness makes consent valid. When using alcohol or other drugs that alter consciousness, an initiator must make judgments regarding level of intoxication and whether a potential partner has the ability to consent. If a person initially consents and then becomes too intoxicated to be able to withdraw consent, we, along with many scholars, educators, and legislators, argue this should be treated as though the person is unable to consent.[52]

There is wide agreement that use of direct physical force or overt threat of force would constitute sexual violence. Clinical psychologists Charlene L. Muehlenhard and Zoë D. Peterson note that some forms of coercion are more ambiguous. A person might feel coerced to comply if an initiator of a sexual act teases that the secret of their sexual activity will be kept only if the sexual relationship continues. Coercion could occur if an initiator of a sexual act does not realize that another person fears that force might be used if compliance is not given.[53] Unintended coercion can be avoided by communicating clearly regarding consent. We urge readers to thoughtfully develop a personal moral code to avoid coercion and to clarify that a partner is consenting.

Regardless of one's own gender or the gender of those one sexually desires, individuals should invest effort to respect consent and avoid unintentional coercion. Legal scholars Lara Stemple and Ilan Meyer identify obstacles to understanding sexual victimization of boys and men, including gender stereotypes that unfairly present men as constantly receptive to sexual activity. Unfortunately, "jokes about prison rape, the notion that 'real men' can protect themselves, and the fallacy that gay male victims likely 'asked for it,' pose obstacles for males coping with victimization."[54]

In 2010, the Centers for Disease Control and Prevention conducted a national survey of households, asking respondents whether they had experienced sexual aggression at any point in their lifetime. Among women, 18.3 percent reported being raped by indicating that they had "any completed or attempted unwanted vaginal (for women), oral, or anal penetration through use of physical force (such as being pinned or held down, or by the use of violence) or threats to physically harm, and includes times when the victim was drunk, high, drugged, or passed out and unable to consent." Thirteen percent reported coercion ("unwanted sexual penetration after being pressured in a nonphysical way"), and 27.2 percent reported unwanted sexual contact ("unwanted sexual experiences involving touch but not sexual penetration"). Among men, 1.4 percent reported being raped, 4.8 percent reported being forced to penetrate another person, 6 percent reported sexual coercion, and 11.7 percent reported unwanted sexual contact.[55]

The vast majority of the perpetrators of sexual violence were men: 98.1 percent of the women and 93.3 percent of the men who were raped reported male rapists. For women, 92.5 percent of other forms of sexual victimization were committed by men, whereas men were more likely to be victimized by women for certain types of sexual victimization: "being made to penetrate (79.2 percent), sexual coercion (83.6 percent), and unwanted sexual contact (53.1 percent)."[56] Given the high rates of incarceration of men in the United States, who would not be available to respond to this survey of households, sexual aggression in which men victimize men in prison was likely underreported in these statistics.[57]

In her work to understand men who rape, sociologist Diana Scully invites readers to critically reflect on the influence of gender norms and stereotypes on understandings of aggression and violence. Scully and her colleague interviewed men serving prison sentences for rape. She recognizes that most rapists are never reported to the criminal justice system for possible prosecution, or convicted, but she chose to focus on men who had been convicted to avoid the ethical problem of "the researcher [becoming] an accomplice by protecting the identity of men actively engaged in rape."[58]

Like other feminist scholars, Scully shifts the focus from seeing rape as a problem of women being victimized—with the perpetrators invisible—to revealing that rape is a problem caused by men who rape. Her work focuses on those with privilege and centers on understanding why perpetrators commit sexual violence. After critiquing two perspectives on rape that fail to match the evidence, she offers a model drawing on feminist and sociocultural theory to understand why men rape. First, Scully is not convinced by an argument that men rape because of an evolutionary drive to spread their genetic material. Even if males experienced a deep-seated desire to spread their genes any way they could, humans can practice control over their own behaviors (as noted earlier in the example of abusers' ability to control their rage when facing a hostile judge). Further evidence against the evolutionary explanation of rape includes that male rapists target girls who are too young and women who are too old to conceive, as well as boys and men. Second, Scully refutes "the prevailing assumption that sexual violence is the result of an individual, idiosyncratic disease."[59] Scully notes that rape is too widespread to be a problem of unusual individuals who have an illness, and expresses concern that conceiving of each rapist as a sick, singular person "removes the necessity of investigating or changing those elements within a society that may precipitate sexual violence against women."[60] Rather than treating rape like an individual psychological problem, she combines feminist and sociocultural explanations of rape.

Scully develops the *feminist/sociocultural model of rape*, which explains sexual violence as an expression of power that is normative in a culture of imbalanced power, one that privileges men above women. As identified in the World Health Organization's definition, violence can be an expression of power used to keep a group at a lower status. "In feminist theory rape is viewed as a singularly male form of sexual coercion—an act of violence and social control that functions to 'keep women in their place.'"[61] Rather than being abnormal, Scully argues that "rape is the logical extension of a male dominant-female submissive gender role stereotyped culture."[62] In other words, in a patriarchal society, rape is normative rather than abnormal. Scully draws on anthropology, which "suggests that sexual violence is related to cultural attitudes, the power relationship between women and men, the social and economic status of women relative to the men of their group, and the amount of other forms of violence in society."[63] Rape is more likely in violent societies where men dominate women.

Scully draws on *rape culture*—feminist Dianne F. Herman's explanation of rape that focuses on how culture both creates attitudes and encourages behavior that increase the likelihood of men committing sexual violence.

> American culture produces rapists when it encourages the socialization of men to subscribe to values of control and dominance, callousness and competitiveness, and anger and aggression, and when it discourages the expression by men of vulnerability, sharing, and cooperation. . . . To end rape, people must be able to envision a relationship between the sexes that involves sharing, warmth, and equality, and to bring about a social system in which those values are fostered.[64]

Herman does not claim that men cannot control their violence because of an evolutionary drive to dominate or spread their genes. She does not focus on rape as a problem of individual men who are mentally ill. Neither of those explanations would prompt optimism about reducing rape. Little could be done if it was in the very nature of men to rape. Scant progress would be likely if those seeking to reduce rape had to try to identify sick individuals and prevent them from raping. Herman's focus on culture offers reason to hope that the prevalence of rape can be addressed. Although a cultural shift is not a simple issue, changing the culture is a possibility.

To change the culture for the better, we must first examine current problems in the United States. Men face social pressures to uphold hegemonic masculinity, traditional roles of being in control and dominant. *Rape myths* are erroneous beliefs about rape, such as stereotypical thinking that victims tend to be virtuous beauties and that rapists tend to be unable to control themselves. Psychologist Diana L. Payne and colleagues identify examples of rape myths, including that women lie about rape ("Many so-called rape victims are actually women who had sex and 'changed their minds' afterwards") or were asking for it ("If a woman is raped while she is drunk, she is at least somewhat responsible for letting things get out of control"; Elam's rant, presented earlier, is an example of this rape myth). Rape myths claim that rape is a small problem ("Women tend to exaggerate how much rape affects them") that does not happen to good people ("Usually, it is only women who do things like hang out in bars and sleep around that are raped").[65]

Contrary to the myth that rape is overreported, empirical evidence reveals that only a minority of cases are reported to the criminal justice system.[66] Scully notes that women were more likely to report rape for possible criminal prosecution when it was

> a sudden, violent attack by a stranger in a public place or a house that was broken into, involving the use of a weapon and resulting in injuries in addition to rape. For a number of reasons—fear of retaliation from the rapist, fear of not being believed or the stigma of trial, self-blame, or the desire to protect friends and families—reported rape underrepresents assaults between people who are acquaintances, friends, or relatives; that occur in social situations such as dates; and where verbal threats, rather than more direct forms of violence, are used to make the victim comply.[67]

Clinical psychologists David Lisak and Paul M. Miller corroborate Scully's argument: "By attacking victims within their social networks . . . and by refraining from the kind of violence likely to produce physical injuries in their victims, these rapists create 'cases' that victims are least likely to report, and that prosecutors are less likely to prosecute."[68] The Centers for Disease Control and Prevention confirm that most women and men who experience sexual assault are victimized by someone they know.

> More than half of female victims of rape (51.1%) reported that at least one perpetrator was a current or former intimate partner. . . . Four out of 10 female victims (40.8%) reported being raped by an acquaintance. Approximately 1 in 8 female victims (12.5%) reported being raped by a family member, and 2.5% by a person in a position of authority. About 1 in 7 female victims (13.8%) reported being raped by a stranger [similar to] 1 in 7 male victims (15.1%) . . . raped by a stranger.[69]

This evidence of sexual violence within social networks discredits the common rape myth that imagines perpetrators of sexual violence as strangers hiding in the bushes.

As noted above, Scully's interest in in-depth interviews led her to the ethical conclusion that she should focus only on rapists who had been convicted of their crimes. In contrast, Lisak and Miller provide an ethical justification for asking men who are not incarcerated about sexually violent behavior.[70] Across multiple samples at an urban university of moderate size that serves commuter students, Lisak and Miller surveyed 1,882 men and found that 6.4 percent reported behavior that could be legally defined as rape or attempted rape. Among these 120 admitted rapists, "80.8% reported committing rapes of women who were incapacitated because of drugs or alcohol; 17.5% reported using threats or overt force in attempted rapes; 9.2% reported using threats or overt force to coerce sexual intercourse; and 10% reported using threats or overt force to coerce oral sex."[71] The majority of these 120 rapists, 63.3 percent (76 men) "reported committing repeat rapes, either against multiple victims, or more than once against the same victim. In total, the 120 rapists admitted to 483 rapes. . . . Since 44 of the 120 rapists admitted to only a single rape, the 76 repeat rapists actually accounted for 439 of the rapes."[72] Eleven rapists reported responsibility for nine or more rapes. The median was three rapes per repeat rapist.

"The evidence that a relatively small proportion of men are responsible for a large number of rapes and other interpersonal crimes may provide at least a partial answer to an oft-noted paradox: namely, that while victimization surveys have established that a substantial proportion of women are sexually victimized, relatively small percentages of men report committing acts of sexual violence."[73] When rape is reported for criminal investigation, Lisak and Miller suggest examination of the social network of the accused. Rapists are likely to have multiple victims.[74]

STATE-SPONSORED VIOLENCE

Before and during World War II, Nazis persecuted gay men along with Jews, people with disability, people of color, and political dissidents such as communists. The Nazis embraced eugenics, a movement that was popularized in Britain and the United States (briefly defined in chapter 5). In this racist and classist philosophy, individuals with traits that were valued were encouraged to breed to improve the human race, while others were prohibited from having children. In the United States and its territories, eugenics justified forced sterilization imposed on women.[75]

Drawing from the eugenics movement, the Nazis saw the groups they persecuted as threats to the purity of the Aryan race. Interestingly, for the most part, the Nazis did not pursue lesbians in the same way as gay men. Like Jews, men that the Nazis identified as gay were harassed, beaten, rounded up, and sent to concentration camps. In the camps, gay men were forced to wear a pink triangle to quickly and visually identify them as homosexual. German writer and gay concentration camp survivor Heinz Heger detailed the experiences of one of the few gay men who survived Nazi incarceration in an Austrian prison and then concentration camps from 1939 to the end of World War II in 1945.[76] Drawing from Heger and the work of German refugee Richard Plant in *The Pink Triangle*, journalist and historian Neil Miller notes that gay men were among the most abused and least supported in the camps.

> They were often given the worst jobs, were usually rejected by other concentration camp inmates, and were denied the protection that capos (camp middlemen who headed work brigades) provided other prisoners. They had little contact with the outside world; very few families were willing to stand by them, and friends on the outside were fearful that "guilt by association" might land them in a camp as well.[77]

Along with extensive physical abuse, gay men were often forced to do the harshest labor because some Nazis believed it would turn them into heterosexuals. Indeed, unlike the Nazi agenda that people who were Jewish could not be integrated into society, Nazis claimed to work for the "reeducation" of homosexuals. Yet death rates for gay men were extremely high compared with other groups interned for the purported purpose of "reeducation." Miller writes, "Fifty-three percent of homosexual prisoners died, as opposed to 40 percent among political prisoners."[78] Some estimate that five thousand to fifteen thousand men marked with a pink triangle died in the camps, but those estimates are likely to be low.[79]

The men who survived to leave the camps then faced antigay bigotry and hatred in the world at large. Many did not even have caring families or communities to return to after the camps. Indeed, the very law Nazis used to arrest gay men had been enacted in 1871 in Germany; Paragraph 175 that made "male homosexual acts" illegal still existed post–World War II. Some jurists from the United States and England decided that a concentration camp was not a prison; so if a gay man was sentenced to six years for violating Paragraph 175 and had spent two years in prison and four in a concentration camp, he would have to spend four more years in prison to complete the six.[80] About this, Miller notes, "It is not known how many people, if any, were reincarcerated for this reason." Miller writes that we do know that "men who were put in camps for being homosexual were not able to take advantage of the financial restitution which the West German government offered to Jews, political prisoners, and other groups that survived the camps."[81]

THE HARM OF CONVERSION THERAPY

As noted previously, in 1973, the American Psychiatric Association removed "homosexuality" from its classification of mental disorders, thereby officially recognizing that psychologically healthy people may be lesbian, gay, or bisexual. The organization took several more decades to remove "gender identity disorder" from its list of mental disorders, but with that removal in 2013, the organization clarified that trans people can be psychologically healthy. Therefore, queer sexuality or gender identity cannot be classified as disordered. Indeed, the American Psychological Association specifies, "The longstanding consensus of the behavioral and social sciences and the health and mental health professions is that homosexuality per se is a normal and positive variation of human sexual orientation."[82] Yet *conversion therapy*—use of religious or psychological techniques in an attempt to convert people to heterosexual or cisgender identity—continued well after there was no justification for trying to change sexual identity or gender identity.

Conversion therapy has also been called "reparative therapy" (the preferred term of James Dobson, discussed in chapter 5). Examination of this term reveals the privilege inherent in being perceived as heterosexual and cisgender. Rather than accepting queer identity as normal and positive, this term suggests that queer people are broken and must be repaired. As noted in chapter 5, some religious groups are particularly likely to stigmatize queer people. Certain interpretations of religion have encouraged adults to seek conversion therapy, or parents to enroll their children in conversion therapy.

Based on a thorough analysis, the American Psychological Association found no compelling evidence that conversion therapy is effective in its goals. In other words, neither prayer nor therapy can change queer people to heterosexual or cisgender. More importantly, there is concern that conversion therapy can be harmful. People who have participated in conversion therapy have reported "anger, anxiety, confusion, depression, grief, guilt, hopelessness, deteriorated relationships with family, loss of social support, loss of faith, poor self-image, social isolation, intimacy difficulties, intrusive imagery, suicidal ideation, self-hatred, and sexual dysfunction."[83] *Suicidal ideation*—thoughts of committing suicide—is a particularly disturbing effect of conversion therapy, in a list of alarming harms.

In 2009, the American Psychological Association issued recommendations for therapists. When parents seek conversion therapy for their children or adults request conversion therapy for themselves, therapists are urged to redirect the focus to work with a client to "recognize the negative impact of social stigma on sexual minorities."[84] Rather than working to change sexual or gender identity, therapists are encouraged to focus on addressing true problems, such as the problems caused by stigma. Therapists are urged to be sensitive to the concerns of their clients and to practice cultural competence in a way that seeks to understand how religion, gender identity, sexual identity, social class, race, and ethnicity intersect for each client. While being sensitive to the client's concerns, therapists should be steadfast in the conclusion that queer sexuality and queer gender identity are normal and positive. Therapy should not attempt to change sexual identity or gender identity. Rather, therapy should focus where it is likely to be both helpful and effective. In contrast to the ineffectiveness of conversion therapy, therapists can be successful in addressing the harmful effects of stigma by helping clients to improve self-esteem, to reduce depression and thoughts of suicide, and to develop relationship skills that might improve interactions with family members and others who continue to stigmatize them.

Tragically, Leelah Alcorn was subjected to conversion therapy after she came out to her parents as a trans girl. In 2014, the seventeen-year-old wrote a suicide note and timed it to be posted on Tumblr. She then committed suicide by walking into traffic. Alcorn's suicide note is a powerful condemnation of conversion therapy:

> If you are reading this, it means that I have committed suicide and obviously failed to delete this post from my queue.
>
> Please don't be sad, it's for the better. The life I would've lived isn't worth living in . . . because I'm transgender. I could go into

detail explaining why I feel that way, but this note is probably going to be lengthy enough as it is. To put it simply, I feel like a girl trapped in a boy's body, and I've felt that way ever since I was 4. I never knew there was a word for that feeling, nor was it possible for a boy to become a girl, so I never told anyone and I just continued to do traditionally "boyish" things to try to fit in.

When I was 14, I learned what transgender meant and cried of happiness. After 10 years of confusion I finally understood who I was. I immediately told my mom, and she reacted extremely negatively, telling me that it was a phase, that I would never truly be a girl, that God doesn't make mistakes, that I am wrong. If you are reading this, parents, please don't tell this to your kids. Even if you are Christian or are against transgender people don't ever say that to someone, especially your kid. That won't do anything but make them hate them self. That's exactly what it did to me.

My mom started taking me to a therapist, but would only take me to Christian therapists, (who were all very biased) so I never actually got the therapy I needed to cure me of my depression. I only got more Christians telling me that I was selfish and wrong and that I should look to God for help.

When I was 16 I realized that my parents would never come around, and that I would have to wait until I was 18 to start any sort of transitioning treatment, which absolutely broke my heart. The longer you wait, the harder it is to transition. I felt hopeless, that I was just going to look like a man in drag for the rest of my life. On my 16th birthday, when I didn't receive consent from my parents to start transitioning, I cried myself to sleep.

I formed a sort of a "fuck you" attitude towards my parents and came out as gay at school, thinking that maybe if I eased into coming out as trans it would be less of a shock. Although the reaction from my friends was positive, my parents were pissed. They felt like I was attacking their image, and that I was an embarrassment to them. They wanted me to be their perfect little straight Christian boy, and that's obviously not what I wanted.

So they took me out of public school, took away my laptop and phone, and forbid me of getting on any sort of social media, completely isolating me from my friends. This was probably the part of my life when I was the most depressed, and I'm surprised I didn't kill myself. I was completely alone for 5 months. No friends, no support, no love. Just my parent's disappointment and the cruelty of loneliness.

At the end of the school year, my parents finally came around and gave me my phone and let me back on social media. I was excited, I finally had my friends back. They were extremely excited to see me and talk to me, but only at first. Eventually they realized they didn't actually give a shit about me, and I felt even lonelier than I did before. The only friends I thought I had only liked me because they saw me five times a week.

After a summer of having almost no friends plus the weight of having to think about college, save money for moving out, keep my grades up, go to church each week and feel like shit because everyone there is against everything I live for, I have decided I've had enough. I'm never going to transition successfully, even when I move out. I'm never going to be happy with the way I look or sound. I'm never going to have enough friends to satisfy me. I'm never going to have enough love to satisfy me. I'm never going to find a man who loves me. I'm never going to be happy. Either I live the rest of my life as a lonely man who wishes he were a woman or I live my life as a lonelier woman who hates herself. There's no winning. There's no way out. I'm sad enough already, I don't need my life to get any worse. People say "it gets better" but that isn't true in my case. It gets worse. Each day I get worse.

That's the gist of it, that's why I feel like killing myself. Sorry if that's not a good enough reason for you, it's good enough for me. As for my will, I want 100% of the things that I legally own to be sold and the money (plus my money in the bank) to be given to trans civil rights movements and support groups, I don't give a shit which one. The only way I will rest in peace is if one day transgender people aren't treated the way I was, they're treated like humans, with valid feelings and human rights. Gender needs to be taught about in schools, the earlier the better. My death needs to mean something. My death needs to be counted in the number of transgender people who commit suicide this year. I want someone to look at that number and say "that's fucked up" and fix it. Fix society. Please.
Goodbye,
(Leelah) Josh Alcorn[85]

If Alcorn's therapists had followed guidelines, they would have worked with her to create a therapeutic bond that addressed her feelings of isolation. They would have helped her to address the stigma she felt. They might have worked with her parents to better understand her. Deplorably, they failed her.

Alcorn's death prompted a petition signed by over 120,000 people to call for an end to conversion therapy in the United States.[86] As of September 2016, five states, Washington, DC, and the city of Cincinnati have banned the practice of conversion therapy on individuals under the age of eighteen. In May 2015, Representative Ted Lieu of California proposed a bill to the United States House of Representatives. The Therapeutic Fraud Prevention Act would make conversion therapy an illegal practice across the United States for minors and adults. The bill clarifies that conversion therapy is both ineffective and harmful. In line with the American Psychological Association's discounting of the practice, Lieu argues continued use of conversion therapy is fraudulent.[87]

LOOKING FORWARD

We have empathy toward our readers; examining violence is painful. This discomfort can be valuable when used to inspire personal commitment to address aggression and to form connections with others—often across privilege and identity. Our final chapter seeks to inspire such solutions.

DISCUSSION QUESTIONS

1. Uncritical viewing of media depictions of both direct and indirect violence have been shown to prompt aggressive behavior. As noted in the discussion of *Mean Girls*, some media depictions of violence are created to prompt viewers to empathize with victims of violence or to understand and address why people commit violence. How might encouraging empathy with a victim, showing the aftermath of violence, or other techniques in a film prompt critical thinking and reduction of aggressive behavior?
2. Explore relational aggression in gender-based insults. What messages about normatively appropriate sexuality, the value of women, and social power are communicated in misogynist terms, such as "slut" or "bitch"? Do gender-based insults against men, such as "cock," communicate misandry? What message is conveyed when

a man is targeted with a misogynist term, such as telling him not to "act like a bitch"?

3. What does gay bashing reveal about heterosexual privilege?

4. Explore intimate partner violence as gendered behavior. How do the sorts of aggression committed and the victimization of each gender connect to normative gender roles?

5. Responding to the arguments and evidence in this chapter, how will you personally define your ethic of sexual consent?

6. How can unintentional sexual coercion be combated by ensuring sexual consent?

7. Evaluate conversion therapy in terms of the harm it causes. Explain whether you perceive this harm as generally caused by unintentional microaggression, intentional aggression, or violence.

8

IT'S GETTING BETTER

Queer Hope, Queer Courage

In the 2015 New York City queer Pride March, an eight-year-old boy in a rainbow-colored tutu "dazzled everyone with his fierce and fabulous strut,"[1] wrote journalist Dan Avery. He quotes the child's mother:

> He has always been very gender fluid when it came to toys and his development. He preferred fashion dolls to action figures. I looked at both in the store and figured that the action figure was as much a doll as a Barbie, so if he wanted the one marketed to girls, that was fine with me.
>
> He is a shy boy who is self-conscious about his missing teeth when he smiles and very intelligent. He doesn't like school because he gets bullied, but he does well academically. We do our best to stop the bullying and involve the LGBT services at his school. We keep him involved in the LGBT community because we believe that by speaking to other people who were like him when they were his age reinforces that he is of value and that his life as he wants to live it is okay.
>
> He is 8 years old and is starting to get crushes on boys. That is pretty much the extent of what he knows about sexuality. . . . He is old enough and smart enough to know he would be marching in the Pride parade in front of thousands of people and did all of it willingly. In fact, I thought he would stop after 10 blocks of walking, but he felt so good about being dressed up and being who he is that he vogued and danced the entire two miles.[2]

When this child was born in 2007, Massachusetts was the only state that allowed lesbian and gay couples to legally marry. The Defense of Marriage Act was in effect, which meant that the marriage of a lesbian couple from Massachusetts was not recognized at the federal level, and the couple's rights of marriage could be denied if they visited or moved to other states. Since the child's birth, national polls show increasing acceptance of queer people,[3] including support for marriage equality.[4] This child danced in the parade just two days after queer people gained marriage equality throughout the United States.

Only four years before this child was born, gay couples in fourteen states could have been charged with criminal offenses for consensual sexual acts—a critical civil rights issue that was openly fought from the riots at the Stonewall Inn in 1969 through the Supreme Court's 2003 decision in *Lawrence and Garner v. Texas*. The Stonewall Inn (briefly discussed in chapter 5) has been named a New York City landmark, the first site named because of its importance in queer history.

Until this boy was four years old, Don't Ask, Don't Tell was in effect. Throughout his early years, members of the military could face dismissal simply for expressing a queer sexual identity. As the boy participated in the 2015 parade, regulations of the military continued to call for dismissal of transgender people, but an announcement just a few weeks after the parade heralded the policy change, implemented in 2016, that allows trans service members to openly celebrate their identity. In this boy's lifetime, we have witnessed unprecedented gains in civil rights for queer people.

Early in the book (chapter 2), we asked readers to think about prom. We imagine that prom will continue to change with shifts in culture over time. When we compare Isaiah's parents' experiences in adolescence to his own experiences, the contrast is dramatic. In school, his parents regularly witnessed blatant bigotry regarding queer people. In 2015, Isaiah's high school elected two boys to be prom king and queen. Positive social change can and does happen.

THE QUEER CIVIL RIGHTS MOVEMENT IS ONGOING

For each gain in queer civil rights, conservative leaders have initially expressed distress. As we note in previous chapters, conservatives often use religious justifications to predict dire consequences if heteronormativity is challenged. For example, Ken Paxton, the Attorney General of Texas, issued a response on the day the Supreme Court ruled in favor of marriage equality, "Far from a victory for anyone, this is instead a dilution of marriage as a societal institution. . . . The truth is that the debate over the issue of marriage has increasingly devolved into personal and economic aggression against people of faith who have sought to live their lives consistent with their sincerely-held religious beliefs about marriage."[5]

Two days later, Paxton argued, "The United States Supreme Court again ignored the text and spirit of the Constitution to manufacture a right that simply does not exist. In so doing, the Court weakened itself and weakened the rule of law, but did nothing to weaken our resolve to protect religious liberty and return to democratic self-government in the face of judicial activists attempting to tell us how to live." Paxton focused on the "religious freedoms" of county clerks, justices of the peace, and judges who might object to issuing marriage licenses or conducting wedding ceremonies for gay and lesbian couples. He acknowledged that "any clerk who wishes to defend their religious objections and who chooses not to issue licenses may well face litigation and/or a fine. But, numerous lawyers stand ready to assist clerks defending their religious beliefs, in many cases on a pro-bono basis, and I will do everything I can from this office to be a public voice for those standing in defense of their rights."[6]

In contrast to Paxton's perspective, Dana DeBeauvoir, the clerk of Travis County, Texas, was one of many to begin issuing marriage licenses for gay and lesbian couples on the day of the Supreme Court ruling. She noted, "We are public servants in a secular role to uphold the law of the land." Further, "We have separation of church and state. We need to remember that."[7]

PAULINE PARK AND THE FIGHT FOR DIGNITY

With anti-queer conservatives such as Paxton doing their best to slow or reverse queer social movements, we are thankful to have powerful activists such as Pauline Park accomplishing gains. As we conclude our book, we explore several stories of hope and queer courage—stories of social change; stories about people like Park. Park's connections to queer communities grew as she spent two years in London as a young adult—her final year in college and a second year to earn her master's degree. There she began to explore her identity as a trans woman:

> I actually started going out dressed as a woman, cross-dressing. . . . It was an amazing experience. For the first time I was going out . . . in a gender presentation . . . that reflected my own sense of self. I didn't do this all the time. I did it probably once a week. I joined a little support group. . . . They didn't call it transgender. I mean this was 1982 or '83. The word transgender did not really come into general use until around 1990. So the terminology at the time would have been transvestites and transsexuals, both of which are somewhat problematic terms. [8]

Park described connecting with others through support groups that met at locations as disparate as a small house in need of repair and a hotel that offered a pleasant garden. In the mid 1990s, after earning her doctorate in political science at the University of Illinois, Park moved to New York City and came out as an openly transgender woman.

Since then, in her ongoing work as an activist, Park is a role model who has greatly expanded opportunities for others to be themselves. Her remarkable accomplishments span the past two decades, and throughout she has lived at the forefront of queer social movements. Indeed, Park envisioned and helped negotiate and write transgender inclusion into the historic Dignity for All Students bill. Signed into law in New York State in 2010, this bill plays an important role in the education of so many children, including Lena, as it protects them from bullying.

INSTITUTIONAL SUPPORT OF QUEER CIVIL RIGHTS

We have seen the effects of Dignity for All Students in Lena's school, Central Park East II, an East Harlem school in New York City. When Lena was in second grade, the school developed gender diversity workshops, first for teachers and staff and then for the adult caregivers of students in the school.

Jean Malpas of the Ackerman Institute has offered help and guidance in this process as Lena's school works to support all of its students across the gender spectrum. Malpas directs the Gender & Family Project (GFP) at the Ackerman Institute. The GFP helps children and young people, families, and communities by offering "gender affirmative services, training and research. GFP promotes gender inclusivity as a form of social justice in all the systems involved in the life of the family."[9] In a podcast interview, Malpas describes gender variance, or differences across gender identity and expression, in children and clarifies that there is nothing wrong with gender nonconforming children. Gender nonconformity is not a limitation of a child. Rather, lack of acceptance is our society's limitation.[10]

Officially, the public school system in New York State is committed to protecting gender nonconforming students from bullying and discrimination, yet it is struggling to achieve this goal. Journalist Emma Whitford writes about a recent New York Civil Liberties Union report, "Public schools across New York state continue to demonstrate a fundamental ineptitude when it comes to addressing the needs of transgender and gender nonconforming students."[11] A parent of a New York City first-grader said, "My daughter was kicked and stepped on, and her hair was pulled, all while students shouted at her that she was a boy. . . . People knock over her tray during lunch." Because of the brutal bullying her child faces, this parent made "repeated attempts to file bullying reports with the school's administration" to no avail.

While there is still significant work to do, the public school system of New York City has made the important step of mandating, at least on paper, that schools support queer students. For example:

> It is the policy of the New York City Department of Education to maintain a safe and supportive learning and educational environment that is free from harassment, intimidation, and/or bullying and free from discrimination on account of actual or perceived race, color, creed, ethnicity, national origin, citizenship/immigration status, religion, gender, gender identity, gender expression, sexual orientation, disability, or weight.[12]

New York City specifies that the schools respond to and take seriously "complaints alleging discrimination or harassment based on a person's actual or perceived transgender status or gender nonconformity."

Offering hope and exhibiting courage, one child, nine-year-old Q Daily, has just completed his first year as a boy at the Brooklyn New School, a public school in New York City. Journalist Yasmeen Kahn highlighted Q's experience of transitioning from a girl to a boy in a series of news pieces that describe the support he has experienced from his parents as well as adults and peers at his school. "Really," Q explains to Kahn, "it's everything: 'It feels like—instead of a dead flower—a growing flower.'"[13] Kahn acknowledges that Q's peers might not fully understand what it means to him to be able to express himself as a boy. Yet remarkably, these schoolchildren do not seem to mind that their friend has transitioned. Their friend Q is still their friend Q. With support from his family and the friendship of his peers, Q is thriving.

A PERSON OF COURAGE

The authors of this text are fortunate to work closely with students like Georgia Brooke Guinan. Jean Halley first met Guinan in a college course that critically explored families in the United States. For Halley, watching Guinan blossom into an out trans woman in the Fire Department of New York City has been an honor.

Guinan has struggled against our society's oppressive demands to be "normal" for much of her life. She has come out multiple times, and each time coming out has meant challenging privileged, conventional ideas of what it means to be a person. Journalist Irene Chidinma Nwoye writes about Guinan, whom she interviewed for the *Village Voice*, "As early as second grade, Brooke discovered how some peers react to an effeminate boy who prefers to play with girls: A bully slammed her head against a window in the school bus. Over the next several years, she would be shoved into lockers and called names, forced to live in constant fear of being beaten up."[14]

When she was eleven years old, Guinan came out as a gay boy to those closest to her. Nwoye writes,

> After three years of wrestling with self-loathing and consulting with a school guidance counselor, George Guinan VI came out as gay, announcing in a typed two-page letter, titled "Decisions," that "I'm not the manliest man of all."

The letter continued: "I have been questioning my sexuality for about three years now. I have, and still do sit up crying until the morning comes. I can't feel bad any longer.

"I think I am gay and love you so much. I have dealt with this and I need to know where you stand on this because I love you and I don't want to do this journey without you."[15]

As a child, she continued to bravely widen the circle of people she told that she was gay. In college, she came to understand herself as, and came out as, genderqueer. She and her best friend, Shayne Zaslow, explored their genderqueer identities together, while leading the Wagner College gay-straight alliance, majoring in sociology, and completing their senior-year research by examining the effectiveness of a queer diversity workshop that they developed and gave to classes of first-year students. At this time, Brooke called herself George Brooke and supported Shayne as he transitioned from identification as a lesbian woman to trans man.

Shortly after graduating college and while working as a firefighter for the city of New York, she came out as transgender. Guinan is the first out trans person in the Fire Department of New York. "The FDNY employs more than 10,400, only 44 of whom are women, and Guinan is the only member who has served the department as both a man and a woman."[16]

Firefighting runs in Guinan's family. "In fact, she's third-generation. Her father, George William Guinan V, is an FDNY lieutenant; her grandfather George IV retired as a captain."[17] About Guinan, Nwoye writes, "Growing up, she heard stories about the escapades of her forebears—both of whom are heterosexual and, as she puts it, masculine and athletic. 'There's such an attitude in society that firefighting is for straight, masculine men,' Guinan says."

Although she has grown accustomed to feeling separate from the norm, she admits it took years of burning under society's intolerant glare for her to emerge stronger, certain of who she is and her place in the world. . . . "I had to get to a point where it didn't matter if the world didn't accept me as a woman, because I identify as one. I don't care who believes it. This is me. This is my truth. This is my identity."[18]

Her brave coming out, and working openly as trans in the male-dominated environment of the FDNY, has given the fire department the opportunity to change, to examine privilege, and to challenge sexism and prejudice against trans people that ranges from microaggression to bigotry.

SLUTWALKS OFFER HOPE AND CHALLENGE SEXIST PRIVILEGE

In January 2011, a police officer in Toronto, Ontario, Canada, announced to students of York University "that if women want to avoid rape, they shouldn't dress like 'sluts.'" Student Heather Jarvis and her peers were livid that this authority figure was propagating a rape myth. "We were fed up and pissed off, and we wanted to do something other than just be angry." Jarvis and four friends organized a march, hoping for one hundred or more participants. Over three thousand joined the SlutWalk, in which women and men protested to challenge rape myths and rape culture.[19] Similar protests have been inspired in diverse cities throughout the world,[20] in which women are encouraged to dress however they choose, with the understanding that no outfit is an excuse for sexual violence.

As noted in previous chapters, feminists have diverse perspectives. Journalist and social justice activist Harsha Walia explores feminist critiques of SlutWalks, including whether this movement started by white college students recognizes the impact of sexism against women in poverty and women of color. Walia identifies ways that institutionalized sexism disproportionately harms women who lack privilege based on income or race, "from lack of access to childcare and denial of reproductive justice to stratification in precarious low-wage work and disproportionate criminalization." In particular, she notes that the term slut "disproportionately impacts women of colour and poor women to reinforce their status as inherently dirty and second-class, and hence more rape-able. The history of genocide against indigenous women, the enslavement of black women, and the forced sterilization of poor women goes beyond their attire. It is a means of gender control that is embedded within the intersecting processes of racism and colonialism."[21]

After weighing these concerns and questioning whether reclaiming the term slut should be a goal, Walia chose to join the SlutWalk local to her in Vancouver. "I attended for the simple reason that I am committed to ending victim blaming." She argues that photographers covering the event sought "sensationalist images" of women in "bras and fish nets," but she describes that the actual event was surprisingly diverse. "There was no attempt to recruit everyone into one uniform vision of femininity, nor was there an overarching romanticizing of 'sluttiness.'" Walia was heartened to see many teenage girls demand their right to be free of sexual violence. [22]

Women across the world have been inspired by SlutWalks to adapt the concept to their local culture. For example, in Delhi, India, organizers prepared the city by staging street plays to raise awareness of sexual harassment. Women were encouraged to wear their typical street clothes to raise awareness of the problem of sexual assault regardless of what women wear. SlutWalks continue to inspire feminist debate and activism. [23]

THE PERSONAL IS POLITICAL: MASTURBATION AS FEMINISM

One of the themes within SlutWalks is to acknowledge women's ownership of their own sexuality. A colleague who teaches college courses on gender studies shared her accidental discovery that owning her sexuality was normal and healthy. As an adolescent, she regularly heard boys joke and brag about masturbation, but she assumed she was a freak to be a girl who masturbated. Other girls never acknowledged that they masturbated, and friends would quickly change the subject if she tried to joke like the boys did. She concluded that she must not be normal. Yet one day, flipping through her seventh-grade science textbook, looking for an answer to a homework question, the page fell to the section on sexual education. When she read that masturbation was normal for girls and for boys, she was so relieved.

Reflecting decades later, she understands that the words that reassured her were based on research inspired by the work of Alfred Charles Kinsey to understand sexual behavior. She also realizes that invisibility of girls' and women's masturbation relates to the virgin/

whore dichotomy as well as compulsory heterosexuality. In both the virgin/whore dichotomy (discussed in chapter 6) and compulsory heterosexuality (first discussed in chapter 2), girls are expected to wait to use their sexuality only to serve the interests of a husband. Journalist Amy Shaw adds that silence about girls' and women's masturbation is rooted in patriarchal thinking that suggests women's sexuality should merely be a tool for producing sons for husbands.[24]

With growing popularity of television and movie comedies focusing on the lives of women, we are hopeful that equality of masturbation humor may come.

POTENTIAL FOR ACTIVISM AND COMMUNITY THROUGH SOCIAL MEDIA

If the Internet had existed when our colleague was questioning whether a normal girl would enjoy masturbation, she could have quickly found answers and support through an online search. Although bullies can use social media to spread the impact of relational aggression (see chapter 7), the tools of social media can also be used for activism and to create a sense of community, especially for queer individuals who might otherwise feel alone. For example, queer activists Dan Savage and Terry Miller created the It Gets Better Project in 2010 as a response to reports of students committing suicide after bullying, often bullying based on assumptions that the target was queer. Over fifty thousand videos have been created and viewed many million times, assuring young people who are considering suicide that "it gets better." Any person is welcome to create a video message for the project. Politicians such as President Barack Obama and Secretary of State Hillary Clinton and celebrities such as Anne Hathaway, Colin Farrell, Ellen DeGeneres, Adam Lambert, and Ke$ha, have contributed to the project.[25]

ECONOMIC JUSTICE AND HOPE

Ultimately, there can be no justice without economic justice.[26] Queer people, like all people, have economic needs. Because of profound hate of and bigotry against queer people, for many—particularly queer people of color and trans people—meeting one's economic needs can be extremely difficult.[27] Homeless youth are far too likely to be queer and "thrown away" by their families.[28] Rather than being a choice, sex work has been historically a default career for queer people and women in general.[29] Trans people often struggle to afford medical care.[30] Queer people, as with others who face gender or race oppression, are also more vulnerable to economic oppression and poverty.[31]

As in our book *Seeing White: An Introduction to White Privilege and Race*, we ask readers to critically examine justice as it relates to intersecting identities. We urge readers to consider how discrimination might affect access to basic human rights. If a child is bullied at school because of expression of gender or sexuality, how might access to fundamental education be disrupted? If the parents of a queer adolescent throw their child from their home based on sexuality or gender expression, how is that person to survive?

Based on executive orders from President Obama, federal employees have been protected since 2014 from discrimination on the basis of gender identity or sexual orientation, and employees of federal contractors have been protected since 2015.[32] Yet employment discrimination based on sexual orientation or gender identity continues to be legal in many states at the time of this writing. Even where discrimination is banned, a heteronormative workplace might justify turning down a job applicant or firing an employee by finding an excuse that is legal, thereby hiding discrimination.

As we argued in *Seeing White*, at a minimum, "all humans, young and old, children and adults, have the right to basic nutrition, adequate shelter, and literacy education."[33] To gain justice for queer people—and for all people—economic justice is essential. For a more thorough development, we encourage readers to examine the arguments and evidence in *Seeing White*. The goal of greater economic justice for all includes public education that provides a welcoming environment in which individuals may build critical skills. Justice requires access to health care—for queer individuals in particular, medical professionals should understand that sex, gender, and sexuality are not binary.

In *Seeing White*, we reveal employment discrimination ranging from overt bigotry to subtle microaggressions and challenge justifications that hide inequality in employment. Paying employees a living wage would provide an adequate standard of living for all workers. Further, a guaranteed income—government funding to each and every person regardless of wealth or work—would prevent anyone from experiencing extreme poverty.

For readers unfamiliar with the concept of a guaranteed income, we encourage a comparison to the publicly funded education system in the United States. Through that system, everyone is guaranteed access to an education. Similar to people choosing to invest in a private education when a public education is available, within a guaranteed income system, many people will choose to work for pay because of attraction to opportunities through that work. With a guaranteed income, no queer person would be homeless or resort to undesired sex work to get by. We encourage readers to learn more about the guaranteed income and other programs to bring about greater economic justice.

HOPE, COURAGE, PRIDE

We began this final chapter by celebrating the experience of an eight-year-old boy at a pride parade. As we conclude this book, we are hopeful for the opportunities of today's queer youth. Although we anticipate ongoing challenges for queer movements and feminism, our optimism is bolstered by this boy's story. He has a family that supports him. Services for queer students available in his school will benefit all children regardless of gender or sexual identity. As he grows, we hope that queer and gender movements continue to expand opportunities for employment, legal protection, medical understanding, and institutional recognition and support of families. We applaud what this child's mother wrote about her dancing son and all queer children: "This was his Pride today. He felt it. He loved it. He was it." We join this courageous parent in urging "love, respect, and acceptance."[34]

DISCUSSION QUESTIONS

1. How can institutions, such as schools and workplaces, support queer lives and gender equality?
2. Evaluate SlutWalks as social activism. What messages are conveyed? How is rape culture addressed?

3. Despite use of social media for bullying, explore its potential for offering support and being a place of activism.

4. Select a recent queer civil rights issue and analyze the basis of conservative backlash. For example, has your city debated or enacted equal rights legislation to ensure queer civil rights, or has your state considered or passed laws that might allow queer discrimination based on religious justification?

5. Please explore the multiple ways diversity happens within queer communities. How does privileged status on one dimension intersect with stigmatized status on another dimension? How might race, ethnicity, social class, and culture impact the experiences and identities of queer people?

NOTES

1. PRIVILEGED THINKING

1. R. W. Connell and James W. Messerschmidt, "Hegemonic Masculinity: Rethinking the Concept," *Gender and Society* 19, no. 6 (2005): 829–59.

2. Michael Kimmel, *The Gendered Society*, 5th ed. (New York: Oxford University Press, 2012).

3. Social theorist Judith Butler contributed to queer theory by referring to these assumed links as important components of the *heterosexual matrix*, to be discussed in chapter 3.

4. *GLAAD Media Reference Guide*, 9th ed. (2014), identifies *transgender* as an inclusive term. We respect some writers' choice to use an asterisk, *trans**, to remind readers that this term encompasses many identities. The asterisk directly acknowledges that a term can continue in any of multiple ways, such as trans woman or trans man. Please see http://www.glaad.org/reference and http://www.pdxqcenter.org/bridging-the-gap-trans-what-does-the-asterisk-mean-and-why-is-it-used/.

5. Julia R. Johnson, "Cisgender Privilege, Intersectionality, and the Criminalization of CeCe McDonald: Why Intercultural Communication Needs Transgender Studies," *Journal of International and Intercultural Communication* 6, no. 2 (2013): 135–44.

6. Kathleen Stassen Berger, *The Developing Person through the Life Span*, 8th ed. (New York: Worth, 2012).

7. Sandra Lipsitz Bem, *An Unconventional Family* (New Haven, CT: Yale University Press, 1998), 109.

8. Janice D. Yoder, *Women and Gender: Transforming Psychology* (Upper Saddle River, NJ: Prentice Hall, 1999), 70.

9. Anne Fausto-Sterling, "The Five Sexes, Revisited," *Sciences* 40, no. 4 (2010): 18–23.

10. US National Library of Medicine, "Turner Syndrome," *Genetics Home Reference*, http://ghr.nlm.nih.gov/condition/turner-syndrome.

11. Fausto-Sterling, "The Five Sexes," 20.

12. As in our earlier book, *Seeing White: An Introduction to White Privilege and Race*, we emulate thinkers such as Audre Lorde (*Sister Outsider: Essays and Speeches* [Freedom, CA: Crossing, 1984]) in intentionally choosing not to capitalize "western."

13. In her seminal text, *Gender Trouble: Feminism and the Subversion of Identity* (New York: Routledge, 1990), Judith Butler argues that we perform our gender. Our bodies are the instruments of that performance, and gender is produced and reproduced in the performance.

14. Ursula Kuhnle and Wolfgang Krahl, "The Impact of Culture on Sex Assignment and Gender Development in Intersex Patients," *Perspectives in Biology and Medicine* 45, no. 1 (2002): 85–103.

15. Paul L. Vasey and Nancy H. Bartlett, "What Can the Samoan 'Fa'afafine' Teach Us about the Western Concept of Gender Identity Disorder in Childhood?," *Perspectives in Biology and Medicine* 50, no. 4 (2007): 481–90.

16. Mrinalini Purandare, "Transgender: A Psychosocial Profile," *Journal of Psychosocial Research* 8, no. 1 (2013): 61–69.

17. Margaret Mead, *Sex and Temperament in Three Primitive Societies* (New York: William Morrow, 1935; reprint 1963).

18. Kimmel, *The Gendered Society*.

19. Emily W. Kane, "'No Way My Boys Are Going to Be Like That!' Parents' Responses to Children's Gender Nonconformity," *Gender & Society* 20, no. 2 (2006): 149–76.

20. Kane, "'No Way My Boys Are Going to Be Like That!'"

21. Connell and Messerschmidt, "Hegemonic Masculinity."

22. David Shneer and Caryn Aviv, *American Queer: Then and Now* (Boulder, CO: Paradigm, 2006).

23. Gregory M. Herek, "On Heterosexual Masculinity: Some Psychical Consequences of the Social Construction of Gender and Sexuality," *American Behavioral Scientist* 29, no. 5 (1986): 563–77.

24. Kimmel, *The Gendered Society*.

25. Jackson Katz, "Reconstructing Masculinity in the Locker Room: The Mentors in Violence Prevention Project," *Harvard Educational Review* 65, no. 2 (1995): 163–74.

26. BBC Science, "Dr Money and the Boy with No Penis," *BBC Science*, September 2005, http://www.bbc.co.uk/sn/tvradio/programmes/horizon/dr_money_prog_summary.shtml. See also BBC News Health, "Health Check:

The Boy Who Was Raised a Girl," *BBC News Health*, November 23, 2010, http://www.bbc.co.uk/news/health-11814300.

27. Charlene L. Muehlenhard and Zoë D. Peterson, "Distinguishing between *Sex* and *Gender*: History, Current Conceptualizations, and Implications," *Sex Roles* 64, no. 11/12 (2011): 791–803.

28. Rhoda K. Unger, "Toward a Redefinition of Sex and Gender," *American Psychologist* 34, no. 11 (1979): 1084–94.

29. Fausto-Sterling, "The Five Sexes," 20.

30. We are prompted to wonder whether David Reimer came to deeply regret consenting to allow John Colapinto to publish his identity.

31. Fausto-Sterling, "The Five Sexes," 21.

32. Shneer and Aviv, *American Queer*, ix–x.

33. Arthur B. Shostak, "Oral Sex: New Standard of Intimacy and Old Index of Troubled Sexuality," *Deviant Behavior* 2, no. 2 (1981): 127–44.

34. Jami S. Leichliter et al., "Prevalence and Correlates of Heterosexual Anal and Oral Sex in Adolescents and Adults in the United States," *Journal of Infectious Diseases* 196, no. 12 (2007): 1852–59.

35. Shneer and Aviv, *American Queer*, 31.

36. Gary Goldbaum, Thomas Perdue, and Donna Higgins, "Non-Gay-Identifying Men Who Have Sex with Men: Formative Research Results from Seattle, Washington," *Public Health Reports* 111, Suppl. 1 (1996): 36–40.

37. Neil Miller, *Out of the Past: Gay and Lesbian History from 1869 to the Present* (New York: Alyson, 2006), xvi.

38. Miller, *Out of the Past*, xvi.

39. John Boswell, *Christianity, Social Tolerance, and Homosexuality* (Chicago: University of Chicago Press, 1980).

40. Miller, *Out of the Past*, xvi.

41. Michel Foucault, *The History of Sexuality: An Introduction*, vol. 1 (New York: Vintage, 1978), 18.

42. Foucault, *The History of Sexuality*, 22.

43. Foucault, *The History of Sexuality*, 23.

44. Miller, *Out of the Past*, 14.

45. Indiemcemopants, "Thomas Jefferson Wasn't a Homophobe," *Daily Kos* (blog), August 15, 2010, http://www.dailykos.com/story/2010/08/15/893304/-Thomas-Jefferson-wasn-t-a-homophobe#.

46. Miller, *Out of the Past*, 4.

47. Michigan Legislative website, Penal Code section 750.338, section 750.338a, section 750.338b, http://www.legislature.mi.gov.

48. Miller, *Out of the Past*, 198.

49. Foucault, *The History of Sexuality*, 43.

50. Shneer and Aviv, *American Queer*, 2.

51. Miller, *Out of the Past*, 166.

52. Radclyffe Hall, *The Well of Loneliness* (New York: Covici Friede, 1930).

53. Miller, *Out of the Past*, 166.

54. Miller, *Out of the Past*, 17.

55. Miller, *Out of the Past*, 17.

56. Havelock Ellis and John Addington Symonds, *Sexual Inversion* (London: Wilson and Macmillan, 1897). Symonds was deceased at the time of the publication. The publisher required Ellis to be listed as the sole author in subsequent editions of the work.

57. Miller, *Out of the Past*, 17.

58. Peter Gay, *The Tender Passion: The Bourgeois Experience*, vol. 2 (New York: Oxford University Press, 1986), 231.

59. Miller, *Out of the Past*, 19.

60. Miller, *Out of the Past*, 19.

61. Even *Wikipedia* notes that "few critics rate *The Well* highly as a work of literature." *Wikipedia*, s.v. "*The Well of Loneliness*," accessed July 6, 2016, http://en.wikipedia.org/wiki/The_Well_of_Loneliness.

62. Sigmund Freud, "Three Essays on Sexuality," in *On Sexuality*, Pelican Freud Library, vol. 7, ed. James Strachey (Harmondsworth: Penguin Books, 1977/1905), 33–170, quoted in Nikki Sullivan, *A Critical Introduction to Queer Theory* (New York: New York University Press, 2003), 14.

63. Sullivan, *Critical Introduction*, 14.

64. Sigmund Freud, quoted in Sullivan, *Critical Introduction*, 14.

65. Wardell B. Pomeroy, *Dr. Kinsey and the Institute for Sex Research* (New York: Harper & Row, 1972), 4.

66. Alfred C. Kinsey et al., *Sexual Behavior in the Human Male* (Philadelphia: Saunders, 1948); Alfred C. Kinsey et al., *Sexual Behavior in the Human Female* (Philadelphia: Saunders, 1953).

67. Pomeroy, *Dr. Kinsey and the Institute for Sex Research*, 16.

68. Pomeroy, *Dr. Kinsey and the Institute for Sex Research*, 4.

69. Miller, *Out of the Past*, 226.

70. Miller, *Out of the Past*, 226–27.

71. Pomeroy, *Dr. Kinsey and the Institute for Sex Research*, 139.

72. Miller, *Out of the Past*, 228.

73. Kinsey et al., *Sexual Behavior in the Human Female*, 471.

74. Kinsey et al., *Sexual Behavior in the Human Female*, 477.

75. Kinsey et al., *Sexual Behavior in the Human Female*, 477.

76. Kimmel, *The Gendered Society*.

77. Philip Blumstein and Pepper Schwartz, "The Creation of Sexuality," in *Homosexuality/Heterosexuality: Concepts of Sexual Orientation*, ed. D. P.

Whirter, S. A. Sanders, and J. M. Reinisch (New York: Oxford University Press, 1990), 307–20.

78. Phillip L. Hammack, "The Life Course Development of Human Sexual Orientation: An Integrative Paradigm," *Human Development* 48 (2005): 267–90.

79. Letitia Anne Peplau and Linda D. Garnets, "A New Paradigm for Understanding Women's Sexuality and Sexual Orientation," *Journal of Social Issues* 56, no. 2 (2000): 329–50.

80. Hammack, "Life Course Development."

81. Jean Halley, Amy Eshleman, and Ramya Mahadevan Vijaya, *Seeing White: An Introduction to White Privilege and Race* (Lanham, MD: Rowman & Littlefield, 2011).

2. PRIVILEGED ASSUMPTIONS

1. Markie L. C. Blumer and Megan J. Murphy, "Alaskan Gay Males' Couple Experiences of Societal Non-support: Coping through Families of Choice and Therapeutic Means," *Contemporary Family Therapy* 33, no. 3 (2011): 276.

2. Martha Nussbaum, "A Right to Marry? Same-Sex Marriage and Constitutional Law," *Dissent: A Quarterly of Politics and Culture* (Summer 2009): 43–55.

3. Nussbaum, "A Right to Marry?"

4. Muzafer Sherif, *The Psychology of Social Norms* (Oxford: Harper, 1936).

5. John C. Turner, *Social Influence* (Pacific Grove, CA: Brooks/Cole, 1991).

6. Robert B. Cialdini, Raymond R. Reno, and Carl A. Kallgren, "A Focus Theory of Normative Conduct: Recycling the Concept of Norms to Reduce Littering in Public Places," *Journal of Personality and Social Psychology* 58, no. 6 (1990): 1015–26.

7. Turner, *Social Influence*.

8. James M. Henslin, *Sociology: A Down-to-Earth Approach*, 12th ed. (New York: Pearson, 2013).

9. Martha Finnemore and Kathryn Sikkink, "International Norm Dynamics and Political Change," *International Organization* 52, no. 4 (1998): 891.

10. James G. March and Johan P. Olsen, "The Institutional Dynamics of International Political Orders," *International Organization* 52, no. 4 (1998): 948.

11. March and Olsen, "Institutional Dynamics," 948.

12. Jennifer Hewlett, "Same-Sex Couple Barred from Lexington Catholic Prom," *Lexington Herald-Leader*, May 13, 2012, http://www.kentucky.com/2012/05/13/2186828/same-sex-couple-denied-entrance.html.

13. Kayla Webley, "Indiana High Schoolers Push to Ban Gay Classmates from 'Traditional' Prom," *Time*, February 11, 2013, http://newsfeed.time.com/2013/02/11/indiana-high-schoolers-push-to-ban-gay-classmates-from-traditional-prom/.

14. Christian S. Crandall, Amy Eshleman, and Laurie T. O'Brien, "Social Norms and the Expression and Suppression of Prejudice: The Struggle for Internalization," *Journal of Personality and Social Psychology* 82, no. 3 (2002): 359–78.

15. Robert B. Cialdini, "Crafting Normative Messages to Protect the Environment," *Current Directions in Psychological Science* 12, no. 4 (2003): 105–9.

16. Stanley Schachter, "Deviation, Rejection, and Communication," *Journal of Abnormal and Social Psychology* 46, no. 2 (1951): 190–207.

17. Samuel L. Gaertner and John F. Dovidio, "The Aversive Form of Racism," in *Prejudice, Discrimination, and Racism*, ed. John F. Dovidio and Samuel L. Gaertner (Orlando, FL: Academic, 1986), 61–89.

18. Robert B. Cialdini and Noah J. Goldstein, "Social Influence: Compliance and Conformity," *Annual Review of Psychology* 55 (2004): 591–621.

19. Gregory M. Herek, "Beyond 'Homophobia': Thinking about Sexual Prejudice and Stigma in the Twenty-First Century," *Sexuality Research & Social Policy* 1, no. 2 (2004): 6–24.

20. Jean Halley, Amy Eshleman, and Ramya Mahadevan Vijaya, *Seeing White: An Introduction to White Privilege and Race* (Lanham, MD: Rowman & Littlefield, 2011).

21. Peggy McIntosh, "White Privilege: Unpacking the Invisible Knapsack," in *Race, Class, & Gender: An Anthology*, 6th ed., ed. Margaret L. Andersen and Patricia Hill Collins (Belmont, CA: Wadsworth, 2007), 98–102.

22. Barbara Smith, "Racism and Women's Studies," *Frontiers: A Journal of Women's Studies* 5, no. 1 (Spring 1980): 48.

23. For a smart and engaging exploration of this debate, sometimes called the "sex wars," please see Lynn S. Chancer, *Reconcilable Differences: Confronting Beauty, Pornography, and the Future of Feminism* (Berkeley: University of California Press, 1998).

24. Earlham College, "Unpacking the Invisible Knapsack II: Daily Effects of Straight Privilege," http://www.cs.earlham.edu/~hyrax/personal/files/student_res/straightprivilege.htm.

25. See Jonathan Ned Katz, *The Invention of Heterosexuality* (Chicago: University of Chicago Press, 1995) for a historical analysis of the normalization of the term heterosexuality.

26. Michael S. Kimmel, *The Gendered Society*, 5th ed. (New York: Oxford University Press, 2012).

27. James Michael Nichols, "Arin Andrews and Katie Rain Hill, Transgender Teens, Discuss New Memoirs," *Huffington Post*, October 23, 2014, http://www.huffingtonpost.com/2014/10/23/trans-couple-memoirs_n_6035238.html.

28. Cavan Sieczkowski, "Arin Andrews and Katie Hill, Transgender Teenage Couple, Transition Together," *Huffington Post*, July 23, 2013, http://www.huffingtonpost.com/2013/07/23/transgender-teenage-couple-arin-andrews-katie-hill_n_3639220.html.

29. Lisa M. Diamond, "What Does Sexual Orientation Orient? A Biobehavioral Model Distinguishing Romantic Love and Sexual Desire," *Psychological Review* 110, no. 1 (2003): 176.

30. Diamond, "What Does Sexual Orientation Orient?," 176.

31. Neil Miller, *Out of the Past: Gay and Lesbian History from 1869 to the Present* (New York: Alyson, 2006), 53.

32. Louise Brackett, quoted in Miller, *Out of the Past*, 54.

33. Susan B. Anthony, quoted in Miller, *Out of the Past*, 54.

34. Miller, *Out of the Past*, 58.

35. Miller, *Out of the Past*, 58.

36. Miller, *Out of the Past*, 61–63.

37. Miller, *Out of the Past*, 63.

38. Nara Schoenberg, "Outing Jane Addams," *Chicago Tribune*, February 6, 2007, http://articles.chicagotribune.com/2007-02-06/features/0702060273_1_hull-house-mary-rozet-smith-lesbian.

39. Adrienne Rich, "Compulsory Heterosexuality and Lesbian Existence," *Signs: Journal of Women in Culture and Society* 5, no. 4 (1980): 631–60.

40. Rich, "Compulsory Heterosexuality," 648–49.

41. Phillip L. Hammack, "The Life Course Development of Human Sexual Orientation: An Integrative Paradigm," *Human Development* 48 (2005): 267–90.

42. Margaret Rosario, Eric W. Schrimshaw, and Joyce Hunter, "Ethnic/Racial Differences in the Coming-Out Process of Lesbian, Gay, and Bisexual Youths: A Comparison of Sexual Identity Development over Time," *Cultural Diversity and Ethnic Minority Psychology* 10, no. 3 (2004): 215–28.

43. D. Perry, K. Walder, T. Hendler, and S. G. Shamay-Tsoory, "The Gender You Are and the Gender You Like: Sexual Preference and Empathic Neural Responses," *Brain Research* 1534 (2013): 66–75.

44. Committee on Lesbian and Gay Concerns, "Avoiding Heterosexual Bias in Language," American Psychological Association, September 1991, http://www.apa.org/pi/lgbt/resources/language.aspx.

45. Sometimes the Q is used only to represent questioning.

46. Kimberley McLeod, "Sticks, Stones and Slurs: Does 'Reclaiming' Words Work?" *Ebony*, March 14, 2012, http://www.ebony.com/news-views/sticks-stones-and-slurs.

47. Justin Schuiletti and Sarah Sheffer, "Facebook Launches 50 New Gender Options for Users," *PBS Newshour*, February 13, 2014, http://www.pbs.org/newshour/rundown/facebook-launches-50-new-gender-options-users/.

48. Facebook also allows users to identify the gender pronouns they prefer.

49. Office of the Ombudsperson, "Preferred Gender Pronouns," Oberlin College, http://www.oberlin.edu/ombudsperson/news.htm.

50. In a blog entry at *The Stranger*, http://slog.thestranger.com/slog/archives/2013/07/10/pgp-wise-in-theory-but-obnoxious-in-practice, Dan Savage shared a link to J. Bryan Lowder's "What Is 'Preferred Gender Pronoun,' and Is It Always Obnoxious?," *Slate*, May 10, 2013, http://www.slate.com/blogs/xx_factor/2013/07/10/preferred_gender_pronouns_what_are_they_and_is_the_practice_of_pgps_always.html.

51. See also Margot Adler, "Young People Push Back against Gender Categories," National Public Radio, *All Things Considered*, July 16, 2013, http://www.npr.org/templates/story/story.php?storyId=202729367.

52. "GLAAD History and Highlights, 1985–Present," GLAAD, http://www.glaad.org/about/history.

53. GLAAD home page, http://www.glaad.org/.

54. Seth Adam and Nick Adams, "GLAAD Responds to ABC News Interview with Bruce Jenner, Releases Tip Sheet for Journalists," news release, April 24, 2015, http://www.glaad.org/releases/glaad-responds-abc-news-interview-bruce-jenner-releases-tip-sheet-journalists.

55. GLAAD, *GLAAD Media Reference* Guide, 9th ed., August 2014, http://www.glaad.org/reference/.

56. *Last Week Tonight with John Oliver*, episode 43 (June 28, 2015), provides a compelling montage of transgender people being asked inappropriate questions about their genitals and breasts by nationally known journalists of the United States. Oliver identifies that such questions would seem outrageous if asked by these journalists of cisgender people.

57. New York City Commission on Human Rights, "Guidelines Regarding 'Gender Identity' Discrimination, a Form of Gender Discrimination Prohibited by the New York City Human Rights Law" (New York: New York City Commission on Human Rights, 2004).

58. Melinda D. Kane, "Timing Matters: Shifts in the Causal Determinants of Sodomy Law Decriminalization, 1961–1998," *Social Problems* 54, no. 2 (2007): 211–39.

59. David Carter, *Stonewall: The Riots That Sparked the Gay Revolution* (New York: St. Martin's, 2004).

60. Kane, "Timing Matters."

61. Herek, "Beyond 'Homophobia.'"

62. For more information, please see Kathleen Ja Sook Berquist, M. Elizabeth Vonk, Dong Soo Kim, and Marvin D. Feit, *International Korean Adoption: A Fifty-Year History of Policy and Practice* (New York: Haworth, 2007); and Hosu Kim, "Television Mothers: Korean Birthmothers Lost and Found in the Search-and-Reunion Narratives," *Cultural Studies/Critical Methodologies* 12, no. 5 (October 2012): 438–49.

63. Pauline Park, "Homeward Bound: The Journey of a Transgendered Korean Adoptee," in *Homelands: Women's Journeys across Race, Place, and Time*, ed. Patricia Justine Tumang and Jenesha de Rivera (Emoryville, CA: Seal, 2006), 127.

64. Park, "Homeward Bound," 126.

65. Pauline Park, interview by the author, New York City, December 9, 2013.

66. Park, "Homeward Bound," 127.

67. Park, "Homeward Bound," 127.

68. "In Her Own Image: Transgender Activist Pauline Park," *The Gully*, July 2, 2002, http://www.thegully.com/essays/gaymundo/020702_transgender_p_park.html.

69. For more information on busing to racially integrate schools in Milwaukee, Wisconsin, please see Daryl Webb, "Race and Education: The Integration of Milwaukee Public Schools, 1960s–1980s," Children in Urban America Project, http://www.mu.edu/cgi-bin/cuap/db.cgi?uid=default&ID=4914&view=Search&mh=1.

70. Much of this section comes from Park, interview by the author, New York City, December 9, 2013.

3. PRIVILEGED POWER, HATE, AND HETERONORMATIVITY

1. Ryan T. Anderson, *Truth Overruled: The Future of Marriage and Religious Freedom* (Washington, DC: Regnery, 2015).

2. Jean O'Malley Halley, *Boundaries of Touch: Parenting and Adult-Child Intimacy* (Chicago: University of Illinois Press, 2007), 143.

3. George Gilder, *Men and Marriage* (Gretna, LA: Pelican, 1986), 12. For recent evidence of the influence of Gilder's work, important conservative Rich Lowry refers to Gilder's "classic book," *Men and Marriage*, to support his argument in "The Wages of Polygamy," *National Review*, April 22, 2008, http://www.nationalreview.com/article/224262/big-trouble-rich-lowry. And in Dennis Prager's "Four Legacies of Feminism: They Have Made Life—and Life for

Women—Worse," *National Review*, November 1, 2011, http://www.nationalreview.com/article/281795/four-legacies-feminism-dennis-prager, popular conservative Dennis Prager notes that Gilder's "classic book on single men" supports Prager's argument about feminism.

4. Barbara J. Risman, *Gender Vertigo: American Families in Transition* (New Haven, CT: Yale University Press, 1998), 70.

5. Adrienne Rich, "Compulsory Heterosexuality and Lesbian Existence," *Signs: Journal of Women in Culture and Society* 5, no. 4 (1980): 643.

6. Rich, "Compulsory Heterosexuality," 644.

7. Rich, "Compulsory Heterosexuality."

8. Gayle Rubin, "The Traffic in Women: Notes on the 'Political Economy' of Sex," in *Toward an Anthropology of Women*, ed. Rayna Reiter (New York: Monthly Review Press, 1975), 159.

9. Rubin, "The Traffic in Women," 178.

10. Rubin, "The Traffic in Women," 179.

11. Eric Cameron, "APA to Remove 'Gender Identity Disorder' from *DSM-5*," *Human Rights Campaign* (blog), December 4, 2012, http://www.hrc.org/blog/entry/apa-to-remove-gender-identity-disorder-from-dsm-5.

12. Kenneth J. Zucker and Peggy T. Cohen-Kettenis, "Gender Identity Disorder in Children and Adolescents," in *Handbook of Sexual and Gender Identity Disorders*, ed. David L. Rowland and Luca Incrocci (Hoboken, NJ: Wiley, 2008), 380–422.

13. Wynne Parry, "Gender Dysphoria: DSM-5 Reflects Shift in Perspective on Gender Identity," *Huffington Post*, June 4, 2013, http://www.huffingtonpost.com/2013/06/04/gender-dysphoria-dsm-5_n_3385287.html.

14. Daphne Scholinski, *The Last Time I Wore a Dress: A Memoir*, with Jane Meredith Adams (New York: Riverhead, 1997), xi.

15. Scholinski, *The Last Time I Wore a Dress*, 15.

16. Scholinski, *The Last Time I Wore a Dress*, ix.

17. Scholinski, *The Last Time I Wore a Dress*, x.

18. Scholinski, *The Last Time I Wore a Dress*, x.

19. Scholinski, *The Last Time I Wore a Dress*, x.

20. Scholinski, *The Last Time I Wore a Dress*, x.

21. Adam Mazmanian, "The Artistic Treatment," *Washington City Paper*, September 9, 2005, http://www.washingtoncitypaper.com/articles/31265/the-artistic-treatment.

22. Gregory M. Herek, "Beyond 'Homophobia': Thinking about Sexual Prejudice and Stigma in the Twenty-First Century," *Sexuality Research & Social Policy* 1, no. 2 (2004): 6–24.

23. Melinda D. Kane, "Timing Matters: Shifts in the Causal Determinants of Sodomy Law Decriminalization, 1961–1998," *Social Problems* 54, no. 2 (2007): 211–39.

24. George Weinberg, "Homophobia: Don't Ban the Word—Put It in the Index of Mental Disorders," *Huffington Post*, December 6, 2012, http://www.huffingtonpost.com/george-weinberg/homophobia-dont-ban-the-w_b_2253328.html.

25. Herek, "Beyond 'Homophobia,'" 8.

26. Herek, "Beyond 'Homophobia,'" 7.

27. Herek, "Beyond 'Homophobia.'"

28. Barry D. Adam, "Theorizing Homophobia," *Sexualities* 1, no. 4 (1998): 388.

29. Dylan Byers, "AP Nixes 'Homophobia,' 'Ethnic Cleansing,'" *Politico*, November 26, 2012, http://www.politico.com/blogs/media/2012/11/ap-nixes-homophobia-ethnic-cleansing-150315.html.

30. Herek, "Beyond 'Homophobia,'" 12.

31. Adam, "Theorizing Homophobia," 388.

32. Herek, "Beyond 'Homophobia,'" 15.

33. Herek, "Beyond 'Homophobia,'" 15.

34. Herek, "Beyond 'Homophobia,'" 15.

35. Herek, "Beyond 'Homophobia,'" 16–17.

36. Derald Wing Sue, *Microaggressions in Everyday Life: Race, Gender, and Sexual Orientation* (Hoboken, NJ: Wiley, 2010).

37. Sue, *Microaggressions in Everyday Life*.

38. Kevin L. Nadal, *That's So Gay! Microaggressions and the Lesbian, Gay, Bisexual, and Transgender Community* (Washington, DC: American Psychological Association, 2013).

39. Sue, *Microaggressions in Everyday Life*, 14.

40. Quoted in Michel Foucault, *Discipline and Punish: The Birth of the Prison* (New York: Vintage, 1977), 151.

41. Foucault, *Discipline and Punish*, 151.

42. Foucault, *Discipline and Punish*, 151.

43. Foucault, *Discipline and Punish*, 137–38.

44. Sandra Lee Bartky, *Femininity and Domination: Studies in the Phenomenology of Oppression* (New York: Routledge, 1990), 63–82.

45. Jean O'Malley Halley, *The Parallel Lives of Women and Cows: Meat Markets* (New York: Palgrave Macmillan, 2012), 10.

46. Candace West and Don H. Zimmerman, "Doing Gender," *Gender & Society* 1, no. 2 (June 1987): 125–51.

47. Jeanne Maglaty, "When Did Girls Start Wearing Pink?" Smithsonian.com, April 7, 2011, http://www.smithsonianmag.com/arts-culture/when-did-girls-start-wearing-pink-1370097/?no-ist.

48. Judith Butler, *Gender Trouble: Feminism and the Subversion of Identity* (New York: Routledge, 1990), 139. For an accessible and clarifying exploration of Butler, please see Nikki Sullivan's *A Critical Introduction to Queer Theory* (New York: New York University Press, 2003).

49. See Jean Halley, Amy Eshleman, and Ramya Mahadevan Vijaya, *Seeing White: An Introduction to White Privilege and Race* (Lanham, MD: Rowman & Littlefield, 2011), chap. 2.

50. Shelly Lundberg and Robert A. Pollack, "The Evolving Role of Marriage: 1950–2010," *Future of Children* 25, no. 2 (August 2015): 29–50.

51. Diana B. Elliott and Tavia Simmons, *Marital Events of Americans: 2009* (Washington, DC: United States Census Bureau, 2011).

52. Michael Warner, "Fear of a Queer Planet," *Social Text*, no. 29 (1991): 3–17.

53. Judith Lorber, "Believing Is Seeing: Biology as Ideology," *Gender and Society* 7, no. 4 (December 1993): 569.

54. Butler, *Gender Trouble*, 136.

55. Warner, "Fear of a Queer Planet," 6.

56. Warner, "Fear of a Queer Planet," 6.

57. Warner, "Fear of a Queer Planet," 16.

58. Halley, *Boundaries of Touch*, 7.

59. Lorber, "Believing Is Seeing," 569, quoted in Halley, *Boundaries of Touch*, 7.

60. Halley, *Boundaries of Touch*, 7.

61. A tragic story of stigmatization is powerfully portrayed by director Kimberley Peirce in the 1999 film *Boys Don't Cry*, based on the 1993 rape and murder of trans man Brandon Teena.

62. Erving Goffman, *Stigma: Notes on the Management of Spoiled Identity* (Englewood Cliffs, NJ: Prentice Hall, 1963), 74.

63. Goffman, *Stigma*, 74.

64. Mattilda (a.k.a. Matt) Bernstein Sycamore, ed., *Nobody Passes: Rejecting the Rules of Gender and Conformity* (Emeryville, CA: Seal Press, 2006).

65. Scholinski, *The Last Time I Wore a Dress*, x, 15.

66. Goffman, *Stigma*.

67. Kenji Yoshino, "The Pressure to Cover," *New York Times Magazine*, January 15, 2006, http://www.nytimes.com/2006/01/15/magazine/15gays.html?pagewanted=all.

68. Goffman, *Stigma*, 74.

69. Sycamore, *Nobody Passes*.

70. Goffman, *Stigma*.

71. Pauline Park, interview by the author, New York City, December 9, 2013.

4. FIFTY WAYS TO BE NORMAL AND OTHER CHALLENGES TO PRIVILEGE

1. When Facebook broke the gender binary and began allowing users to customize their gender identity, initial news reports indicated that fifty-some options were available. Today, users can choose the automatic categories of male or female, or they can customize their own gender identity. See Debby Herbenick and Aleta Baldwin, "What Each of Facebook's 51 New Gender Options Means," *Daily Beast*, February 15, 2014, http://www.thedailybeast.com/articles/2014/02/15/the-complete-glossary-of-facebook-s-51-gender-options.html. Also see Peter Weber, "Confused by All the New Facebook Genders? Here's What They Mean," *Slate*, February 21, 2014, http://www.slate.com/blogs/lexicon_valley/2014/02/21/gender_facebook_now_has_56_categories_to_choose_from_including_cisgender.html.

2. Sandra Lipsitz Bem advised parents to share the responsibility of driving as a way of reducing gender stereotypes. Sandra Lipsitz Bem, "Gender Schema Theory and Its Implications for Child Development: Raising Gender-Aschematic Children in a Gender-Schematic Society," *Signs* 8, no. 4 (1983): 598–616.

3. Gail Crombie et al., "Students' Perceptions of Their Classroom Participation and Instructor as a Function of Gender and Context," *Journal of Higher Education* 74, no. 1 (2003): 51–76.

4. Judith Butler, *Gender Trouble: Feminism and the Subversion of Identity* (New York: Routledge, 1990), 140.

5. Julianne Escobedo Shepherd, "RuPaul Runs the World," *Spin*, April 1, 2013, http://www.spin.com/2013/04/rupaul-runs-the-world-drag-race-supermodel/.

6. Butler, *Gender Trouble*, 137.

7. Nikki Sullivan, *A Critical Introduction to Queer Theory* (New York: New York University Press, 2003), 86.

8. Leonore Davidoff, "Gender and the 'Great Divide': Public and Private in British Gender History," *Journal of Women's History* 15, no. 1 (2003): 11–27.

9. Wendy Hollway, "V. Beyond Sex Differences: A Project for Feminist Psychology," *Feminism & Psychology* 4, no. 4 (1994): 538–46.

10. Eleanor E. Maccoby and Carol N. Jacklin, *The Psychology of Sex Differences* (Stanford, CA: Stanford University Press, 1974).

11. Janet Shibley Hyde, "Gender Similarities and Differences," *Annual Review of Psychology* 65 (2014): 373–98.

12. Janet Shibley Hyde, "The Gender Similarities Hypothesis," *American Psychologist* 60, no. 6 (2005): 581–92.

13. William Pollack, *Real Boys: Rescuing Our Sons from the Myths of Boyhood* (New York: Henry Holt, 1998), 185.

14. Pollack, *Real Boys*, 185–86.

15. Pollack, *Real Boys*, 186.

16. Transgender, butch lesbian activist and author Leslie Feinberg's novel *Stone Butch Blues* (Ann Arbor, MI: Firebrand, 1993) offers a rich portrayal of butch/femme culture in the mid-twentieth century United States and of the extensive police and other violence faced by butch/femme lesbians and other members of the queer community. *Stone Butch Blues* won the Stonewall Book Award in 1994 and is a seminal piece of queer literature.

17. Alison Eves, "Queer Theory, Butch/Femme Identities and Lesbian Space," *Sexualities* 7, no. 4 (2004): 481.

18. Eves, "Queer Theory, Butch/Femme," 482.

19. Joan Nestle, "A Fem's Feminist History," in *The Feminist Memoir Project: Voices from Women's Liberation*, ed. Rachel Blau DuPlessis and Ann Snitow (New York: Three Rivers, 1998), 339.

20. Nestle, "A Fem's Feminist History," 339.

21. Of the many wonderful queer centers in the United States, the Fenway Institute's National LGBT Health Education Center is an excellent example of a center working to "optimize quality, cost-effective health care" for queer people. http://www.lgbthealtheducation.org/.

22. Jeremiah Jurkiewicz, interview by the author, LGBTQ Resource Center of the College of Staten Island of the City University of New York, June 12, 2014.

23. Much of the above section comes from Jurkiewicz, interview by the author, LGBTQ Resource Center of the College of Staten Island of the City University of New York, June 12, 2014.

24. Since 2004, activists have been hosting an international event called Israeli Apartheid Week (IAW) to raise awareness about the Israeli occupation and Palestinian struggle. The IAW website (http://apartheidweek.org/about/) states that their aim "is to contribute to this chorus of international opposition to Israeli apartheid and to bolster support for the BDS campaign." They demand "full equality for Arab-Palestinian citizens of Israel, an end to the occupation and colonization of all Arab lands—including the Golan Heights, the Occupied West Bank with East Jerusalem and the Gaza Strip—and disman-

tling the Wall, and the protection of Palestinian refugees' right to return to their homes and properties as stipulated in U.N. resolution 194. In previous years IAW has played an important role in raising awareness and disseminating information about Zionism, the Palestinian liberation struggle and its similarities with the indigenous sovereignty struggle in North America and the South African anti-apartheid movement."

25. Advocate.com Editors, "LGBT Center Cancels Israeli Apartheid Event," *Advocate*, February 22, 2011, http://www.advocate.com/news/daily-news/2011/02/22/michael-lucas-boycott-lgbt-center.

26. Much of the above eight paragraphs comes from Park, interview by the author, New York City, December 9, 2013.

27. "Stop US Aid to 'Israeli' Occupation," *No Tax Dollars to Israel* (blog), April 15, 2014, http://www.notaxdollarstoisrael.com/2014/02/15/stop-us-aid-to-israeli-occupation/.

28. Danielle Lucchese, "Female or Not? Relational Aggression, Mixed Gender Messages and Disability Limitations," *Wagner College Forum for Undergraduate Research* 11, no. 2 (2013): 79.

29. Lucchese, "Female or Not?," 79.

30. Robert McRuer, "Compulsory Able-Bodiedness and Queer/Disabled Existence," in *The Disability Studies Reader*, 4th ed., ed. Lennard J. Davis (New York: Routledge, 2013), 369–79.

31. McRuer, "Compulsory Able-Bodiedness."

32. Eunjung Kim, "Asexuality in Disability Narratives," *Sexualities* 14, no. 4 (2011): 479–93.

33. Kim, "Asexuality in Disability Narratives," 483.

34. Andrew Morrison-Gurza, "Why Sex with Someone with a Disability Is the Best Sex You Could Be Having!," *Huffington Post*, May 13, 2014, http://www.huffingtonpost.com/andrew-morrisongurza/sex-disability_b_4950460.html.

35. Morrison-Gurza, "Why Sex with Someone with a Disability."

36. Kim, "Asexuality in Disability Narratives."

37. Dominique Mosbergen, "What Is Asexuality? A Community's Coming of Age," *Huffington Post*, June 17, 2013, http://www.huffingtonpost.com/2013/06/17/what-is-asexuality_n_3360424.html?1371784133.

38. Dominique Mosbergen, "LGBT, Asexual Communities Clash over Ace Inclusion," *Huffington Post*, June 21, 2013, http://www.huffingtonpost.com/2013/06/21/lgbt-asexual_n_3385530.html.

39. Mosbergen, "LGBT, Asexual Communities Clash."

40. Brynn Tannehill, "Why 'LGB' and 'T' Belong Together," *Huffington Post*, February 25, 2013, http://www.huffingtonpost.com/brynn-tannehill/why-lgb-and-t-belong-together_b_2746616.html.

41. Megan Davidson, "Seeking Refuge under the Umbrella: Inclusion, Exclusion, and Organizing within the Category *Transgender*," *Sexuality Research & Social Policy* 4, no. 4 (December 2007): 61.

42. Kimberly Balsam et al., "Culture, Trauma, and Wellness: A Comparison of Heterosexual and Lesbian, Gay, Bisexual, and Two-Spirit Native Americans," *Cultural Diversity and Ethnic Minority Psychology* 10, no. 3 (2004): 287–301.

43. Peter Gamache and Katherine J. Lazear, *Asset-Based Approaches for Lesbian, Gay, Bisexual, Transgender, Questioning, Intersex, and Two-Spirit (LGBTQI2-S)*, FMHI pub. no. 252 (Tampa, FL: University of South Florida, College of Behavioral and Community Sciences, Louis de la Parte Florida Mental Health Institute, Research and Training Center for Children's Mental Health, 2009).

44. Gamache and Lazear, *Asset-Based Approaches*.

45. Balsam et al., "Culture, Trauma, and Wellness."

46. Wendy Chapkis, *Live Sex Acts: Women Performing Erotic Labor* (New York: Routledge, 1997), 96.

47. Chapkis, *Live Sex Acts*, 88.

48. Carol Leigh, a.k.a. Scarlot Harlot, "Inventing Sex Work," in *Whores and Other Feminists*, ed. Jill Nagle (New York: Routledge, 1997), 227–228.

49. Hima B., *Straight for the Money: Interviews with Queer Sex Workers* (1994), DVD.

50. Melissa Hope Ditmore, interview by the author, New York City, January 16, 2014.

51. NCAA Office of Inclusion, "NCAA Inclusion of Transgender Student-Athletes" (2011), ii, https://www.ncaa.org/sites/default/files/Transgender_Handbook_2011_Final.pdf.

52. Louis J. Elsas et al., "Gender Verification of Female Athletes," *Genetics in Medicine* 2, no. 4 (2000): 249–54.

53. Elsas et al., "Gender Verification."

54. NCAA Office of Inclusion, "NCAA Inclusion," 8.

5. INSTITUTIONALIZED HETERONORMATIVITY

1. Pauline Park, interview by the author, New York City, December 9, 2013.

2. Pauline Park, interview by the author, New York City, December 9, 2013.

3. US Naval Institute, "Key Dates in U.S. Policy on Gay Men and Women in Military Service," http://www.usni.org/news-and-features/dont-ask-dont-tell/timeline.

4. See also Randy Shilts, *Conduct Unbecoming: Gays & Lesbians in the U.S. Military* (New York: St. Martin's, 1993); Matthew K. Brown, "Constitutional Law: First Amendment and Congress's Spending Clause Power: The Supreme Court Supports Military Recruiters and the United States Military's Discrimination against Homosexuals despite Law Schools' Protests. Rumsfeld v. Forum for Academic & Institutional Rights," *University of Arkansas at Little Rock Law Review* 29, no. 2 (Winter 2007): 345–78.

5. John C. Fitzpatrick, ed., *The Writings of George Washington* (Washington, DC: United States Government Printing Office, 1934), available through Washington Resources at the University of Virginia Library, http://etext.virginia.edu/washington.

6. Brown, "Constitutional Law."

7. Ted Morgan, "The Newport Scandal," in *Gay Warriors: A Documentary History from the Ancient World to the Present*, ed. B. R. Burg (New York: New York University Press, 2002), 193.

8. Alan Bérubé, *Coming Out under Fire: The History of Gay Men and Women in World War II* (New York: Simon & Schuster, 1990). See also Naoko Wake, "The Military, Psychiatry, and 'Unfit' Soldiers, 1939–1942," *Journal of the History of Medicine and Allied Sciences* 62, no. 4 (October 2007): 461–94.

9. Fred L. Borch III, "The History of 'Don't Ask, Don't Tell' in the Army: How We Got to It and Why It Is What It Is," *Military Law Review* 203 (Spring 2010): 189–206.

10. David W. Dunlap, "Perry Watkins, 48, Gay Sergeant Won Court Battle with Army," *New York Times*, March 21, 1996, http://www.nytimes.com/1996/03/21/nyregion/perry-watkins-48-gay-sergeant-won-court-battle-with-army.html.

11. Shilts, *Conduct Unbecoming*.

12. A then-classified report had indeed found no increase in security risk for lesbian, gay, and bisexual military members. *The Crittenden Report:* Report of the Board Appointed to Prepare and Submit Recommendations to the Secretary of the Navy for the Revision of Policies, Procedures and Directives Dealing with Homosexuals (March 15, 1957).

13. United States General Accounting Office, "Defense Force Management DOD's Policy on Homosexuality: Report to Congressional Requesters" (Washington, DC: US General Accounting Office, June 1992).

14. William N. Eskridge Jr., "Gaylegal Narratives," *Stanford Law Review* 46, no. 3 (February 1994): 612.

15. Bruce W. Buchanan, "Lesbian Struggles to Serve in Army," *New York Times Archives*, August 10, 1989, http://www.nytimes.com/1989/08/10/us/lesbian-struggles-to-serve-in-army.html.

16. Open Jurist, *Ben-Shalom v. Marsh, United States Court of Appeals, Seventh Circuit*, http://openjurist.org/881/f2d/454/ben-shalom-v-o-marsh.

17. Buchanan, "Lesbian Struggles to Serve in Army."

18. Shilts, *Conduct Unbecoming*.

19. Burt A. Folkart, "Gay Activist Leonard Matlovich, 44, Dies," *Los Angeles Times*, June 24, 1988, http://articles.latimes.com/1988-06-24/news/mn-5916_1_leonard-matlovich.

20. See David F. Burrelli, "An Overview of the Debate on Homosexuals in the U.S. Military," in *Gays and Lesbians in the Military: Issues, Concerns, and Contrasts*, ed. Wilbur J. Scott and Sandra Carson Stanley (Hawthorne, NY: Aldine de Gruyter, 1994), 19.

21. Dunlap, "Perry Watkins."

22. Gisela Caldwell, "The Seventh Circuit in *Ben-Shalom v. Marsh*: Equating Speech with Conduct," *Loyola of Los Angeles Law Review* 24, no. 2 (January 1991): 421–65.

23. Linda Greenhouse, "Supreme Court Roundup; Justices Refuse to Hear Challenge to Military Ban on Homosexuals," *New York Times Archives*, February 27, 1990, http://www.nytimes.com/1990/02/27/us/supreme-court-roundup-justices-refuse-hear-challenge-military-ban-homosexuals.html.

24. Eric Schmitt, "The Inauguration; Clinton Set to End Ban on Gay Troops," *New York Times Archives*, January 21, 1993, http://www.nytimes.com/1993/01/21/us/the-inauguration-clinton-set-to-end-ban-on-gay-troops.html.

25. Ron Elving, "Ending 'Don't Ask' Lets Obama Fulfill Another Clinton Promise," *It's All Politics: Political News from National Public Radio* (blog), December 18, 2010, http://www.npr.org/blogs/itsallpolitics/2010/12/20/132163478/ending-militarys-gay-ban-lets-obama-fulfill-another-clinton-promise.

26. Editorial Board, "The Military Steps Up for Transgender Service Members," *Washington Post*, July 16, 2015, https://www.washingtonpost.com/opinions/the-military-steps-up-for-transgender-service-members/2015/07/16/e676c25a-2a4c-11e5-a5ea-cf74396e59ec_story.html.

27. Human Rights Campaign, "An Overview of Federal Rights and Protections Granted to Married Couples," http://www.hrc.org/resources/entry/an-overview-of-federal-rights-and-protections-granted-to-married-couples.

28. Martha Nussbaum, "A Right to Marry? Same-Sex Marriage and Constitutional Law," *Dissent: A Quarterly of Politics and Culture* (Summer 2009): 43–55.

29. Mildred Jeter Loving, quoted in Eric Nygren, "Happy Loving Day!" (blog), American Civil Liberties Union of Washington State, June 13, 2001, https://aclu-wa.org/blog/happy-loving-day.

30. Martha Albertson Fineman, *The Neutered Mother, the Sexual Family and Other Twentieth Century Tragedies* (New York: Routledge, 1995).

31. Kath Weston, *Families We Choose: Lesbians, Gays, Kinship* (New York: Columbia University Press, 1991).

32. American Civil Liberties Union, "Missouri Judge Rules That Lesbian Can Be Foster Parent," February 17, 2006, https://www.aclu.org/lgbt-rights_hiv-aids/missouri-judge-rules-lesbian-can-be-foster-parent.

33. American Civil Liberties Union, "Stewart and Stewart v. Heineman— Client Profiles," August 23, 2013, https://www.aclu.org/lgbt-rights/stewart-and-stewart-v-heineman-client-profiles.

34. Martha Stoddard, "Without Fanfare, Nebraska Lifts Ban on Gay People Being Foster Parents," *Omaha World-Herald*, March 2, 2015, http://www.omaha.com/news/nebraska/without-fanfare-nebraska-lifts-ban-on-gay-people-being-foster/article_742579c4-06da-5a69-8e3a-8f7a46e5bb2c.html.

35. "Mississippi's Gay Adoption Ban Is Dead," *Clarion-Ledger*, May 3, 2016, http://www.clarionledger.com/story/news/2016/05/03/mississippis-gay-adoption-ban-dead/83884788/.

36. The story of Sadie Sachs might have been a composite of multiple women rather than a historical account of one woman's experience. Michelle Goldberg, "Awakenings: On Margaret Sanger," *Nation*, February 27, 2012, http://www.thenation.com/article/166121/awakenings-margaret-sanger#.

37. Goldberg, "Awakenings"; Gloria Feldt, "Margaret Sanger's Obscenity," *New York Times*, October 15, 2006, http://www.nytimes.com/2006/10/15/opinion/nyregionopinions/15CIfeldt.html.

38. Goldberg, "Awakenings"; Feldt, "Margaret Sanger's Obscenity."

39. Obituary, "Margaret Sanger Is Dead at 82; Led Campaign for Birth Control," *New York Times*, September 7, 1966, http://www.nytimes.com/learning/general/onthisday/bday/0914.html.

40. Goldberg, "Awakenings."

41. Goldberg, "Awakenings."

42. Jennifer McMahon-Howard, Jody Clay-Warner, and Linda Renzulli, "Criminalizing Spousal Rape: The Diffusion of Legal Reforms," *Sociological Perspectives* 52, no. 4 (Winter 2009): 505–31.

43. New York Penal Code 240.35, Loitering.

44. David Carter, *Stonewall: The Riots That Sparked the Gay Revolution* (New York: St. Martin's, 2004).

45. Mark Huppin and Neil Malamuth, "The Obscenity Conundrum, Contingent Harms, and Constitutional Consistency," *Stanford Law & Policy Review* 23, no. 1 (2012): 65–100.

46. Miller v. California, 413 U.S. 15 (1973).

47. In the 1940s and 1950s, Kinsey sought to import erotic material for use as research material. He contacted customs agents and the federal government to explain his scientific interest and that the material was not to be used for prurient purposes. Until the Kinsey Institute won a test case in court, customs agents acted inconsistently—sometimes seizing Kinsey's imports and sometimes allowing them for scientific purposes. Kenneth R. Stevens, "*United States v. 31 Photographs*: Dr. Alfred C. Kinsey and Obscenity Law," *Indiana Magazine of History* 71, no. 4 (1975): 299–318.

48. Stanley v. Georgia, 394 U.S. 557 (1969).

49. Osborne v. Ohio, 495 U.S. 103 (1990).

50. National Conference of State Legislatures, "Sexting Legislation in 2013," October 30, 2013, http://www.ncsl.org/research/telecommunications-and-information-technology/2013-sexting-legislation.aspx.

51. Justin Jouvenal, "Teen 'Sexting' Case Goes to Trial in Fairfax County," *Washington Post*, April 17, 2013, http://www.washingtonpost.com/local/teen-sexting-case-goes-to-trial-in-fairfax-county/2013/04/17/4936b768-a6b7-11e2-b029-8fb7e977ef71_story.html.

52. Peter Gamache and Katherine J. Lazear, *Asset-Based Approaches for Lesbian, Gay, Bisexual, Transgender, Questioning, Intersex, and Two-Spirit (LGBTQI2-S)*, FMHI pub. no. 252 (Tampa, FL: University of South Florida, College of Behavioral and Community Sciences, Louis de la Parte Florida Mental Health Institute, Research and Training Center for Children's Mental Health, 2009).

53. Mithleya, "Coming of Faith: Queer and Muslim," *Huffington Post*, January 26, 2015, http://www.huffingtonpost.com/coming-of-faith/queer-and-muslim_b_6543878.html.

54. Daniel G. Karslake, *For the Bible Tells Me So* (2007; First Run Features), DVD.

55. In 2012, California passed legislation that bans reparative therapy (also called conversion therapy) for individuals under the age of eighteen. New Jersey followed in 2013; Oregon in 2015. The American Psychological Association notes that people who have undergone attempts to convert them from queer to heterosexual or to cisgender have a higher risk of psychological problems. Aaron Blake, "Christie Signs Bill That Bans Gay Conversion Therapy," *Washington Post*, August 19, 2013, http://www.washingtonpost.com/blogs/post-politics/wp/2013/08/19/christie-will-sign-bill-that-bans-gay-conversion-therapy/; Katy Steinmetz, "Oregon Becomes Third State to Ban Conversion

Therapy on Minors," *Time*, May 19, 2015, http://time.com/3889687/oregon-conversion-therapy-ban/.

56. Mark I. Wallace, "Postmodern Biblicism: The Challenge of René Girard for Contemporary Theology," *Modern Theology* 5, no. 4 (1989): 309–25.

57. Karslake, *For the Bible Tells Me So*.

58. Teach Ministries website, http://www.teach-ministries.org/.

59. S. Donald Fortson III, "The Road to Gay Ordination in the Presbyterian Church (U.S.A.)," *Christianity Today*, May 12, 2011, http://www.christianitytoday.com/ct/2011/mayweb-only/gayordinationpcusa.html?paging=off.

60. Human Rights Campaign, "Stances of Faiths on LGBT Issues: Judaism," http://www.hrc.org/resources/entry/stances-of-faiths-on-lgbt-issues-judaism.

61. Fortson, "Road to Gay Ordination."

62. Fortson, "Road to Gay Ordination."

63. Karslake, *For the Bible Tells Me So*.

64. Randi Reitan, "Lutherans Should Rejoice over Policy Change toward Gays," *Minnesota Public Radio News*, December 11, 2009, http://www.mprnews.org/story/2009/12/11/reitan.

65. Reitan, "Lutherans Should Rejoice."

66. Fortson, "Road to Gay Ordination."

67. Fortson, "Road to Gay Ordination."

68. Reitan, "Lutherans Should Rejoice."

69. Room for All, http://www.roomforall.com.

70. Thomas Gumbleton, "All Races, Sexual Orientations Welcome at Christ's Table," *Catholic Reporter*, January 6, 2011, http://ncronline.org/blogs/peace-pulpit/all-races-sexual-orientations-welcome-christs-table.

71. Human Rights Campaign, "Stances of Faiths on LGBT Issues: Islam," http://www.hrc.org/resources/entry/stances-of-faiths-on-lgbt-issues-islam.

72. Mithleya, "Coming of Faith."

73. Lawrence Dyche and Luis H. Zayas, "Cross-Cultural Empathy and Training the Contemporary Psychotherapist," *Clinical Social Work Journal* 29, no. 3 (2001): 245–58.

74. Simon Dein, "Working with Patients with Religious Beliefs," *Advances in Psychiatric Treatment* 10 (2004): 287–94.

6. PRIVILEGED (POPULAR) CULTURE AND
INTERNALIZED EXPECTATIONS

1. Melissa A. Fabello, "Let's Talk about Thin Privilege," *Everyday Feminism Magazine*, October 23, 2013, http://everydayfeminism.com/2013/10/lets-talk-about-thin-privilege/?upw.

2. Michael S. Kimmel, *The Gendered Society*, 5th ed. (New York: Oxford University Press, 2012).

3. Janice McCabe et al., "Gender in Twentieth-Century Children's Books: Patterns of Disparity in Titles and Central Characters," *Gender & Society* 25, no. 2 (April 2011): 197–226.

4. Susan Bordo, "The Empire of Images in Our World of Bodies," *Chronicle of Higher Education* 50, no. 17 (December 19, 2003).

5. Logan Hill, "Building a Bigger Action Hero," *Men's Journal Magazine*, May 2014, http://www.mensjournal.com/magazine/print-view/building-a-bigger-action-hero-20140418.

6. Hilary Radner, "Pretty Is as Pretty Does: Free Enterprise and the Marriage Plot," in *Film Theory Goes to the Movies: Cultural Analysis of Contemporary Film*, ed. Jim Collins, Ava Preacher Collins, and Hilary Radner (New York: Routledge, 1993), 56–76.

7. Daniel G. Linz, Edward Donnerstein, and Steven Penrod, "Effects of Long-Term Exposure to Violent and Sexually Degrading Depictions of Women," *Journal of Personality and Social Psychology* 55, no. 5 (1988): 758–88.

8. Margaret L. Andersen and Patricia Hill Collins, *Race, Class and Gender: An Anthology*, 7th ed. (Belmont, CA: Wadsworth, 2010), 7–8.

9. Barbara Smith, "Racism and Women's Studies," *Frontiers: A Journal of Women's Studies* 5, no. 1 (Spring 1980): 48.

10. Cherríe Moraga and Gloria E. Anzaldúa, eds., *This Bridge Called My Back: Writings by Radical Women of Color* (Lanthan, NY: Kitchen Table: Women of Color Press, 1981; reprint 1983).

11. Audre Lorde, "An Open Letter to Mary Daly," in *This Bridge Called My Back: Writings by Radical Women of Color*, ed. Cherríe Moraga and Gloria Anzaldúa (Latham, NY: Kitchen Table: Women of Color Press, 1981; reprint 1983), 94–97.

12. Audre Lorde, "The Master's Tools Will Never Dismantle the Master's House," in *This Bridge Called My Back: Writings by Radical Women of Color*, ed. Cherríe Moraga and Gloria Anzaldúa (Latham, NY: Kitchen Table: Women of Color Press, 1981; reprint 1983), 99.

13. Kimmel, *The Gendered Society*, 7.

14. Stuart Ewen and Elizabeth Ewen, *Typecasting: On the Arts and Sciences of Human Inequality* (New York: Seven Stories Press, 2006).

15. For examples of this brutal white social practice, please see Douglas A. Blackmon, *Slavery by Another Name: The Re-Enslavement of Black Americans from the Civil War to World War II* (New York: Anchor, 2008).

16. In the film, Griffith's presentation of choosing death over rape hearkens to early laws regarding rape. Feminist journalist Susan Brownmiller notes that girls and women were once the property of men—belonging first to the patriarch of their family of birth, and then possibly to a husband if the woman seemed valuable enough for a husband to take on the expense of being responsible for her. Rape was a property crime against the patriarch or husband because rape of a girl or a woman harmed his material interest. Within such a system, choosing death over rape would be preferable for the owner—he would no longer have to support damaged goods. See Susan Brownmiller, *Against Our Will: Men, Women and Rape* (New York: Ballantine, 1993). For discussion of *The Birth of a Nation*, see Michael Rogin, "'The Sword Became a Flashing Vision': D. W. Griffith's *The Birth of a Nation*," *Representations* 9 (Winter 1985): 150–95.

17. Tricia Rose, *The Hip Hop Wars: What We Talk about When We Talk about Hip Hop—and Why It Matters* (New York: Basic Civitas, 2008), 97.

18. Rose, *Hip Hop Wars*, 97.

19. Leah M. Wyman and George N. Dionisopoulos, "Transcending the Virgin/Whore Dichotomy: Telling Mina's Story in *Bram Stoker's Dracula*," *Women's Studies in Communication* 23, no. 2 (2000): 209–37.

20. Kim Newman, *Nightmare Movies: A Critical History of the Horror Film, 1968–88*, new ed. (London: Bloomsbury, 1988), 147.

21. For example, see Stuart Ewen, *Captains of Consciousness: Advertising and the Social Roots of the Consumer Culture* (New York: McGraw-Hill, 1976) and *All Consuming Images: The Politics of Style in Contemporary Culture* (New York: Basic, 1989).

22. We recommend both Russo's book and the accompanying film of the same name. Vito Russo, *The Celluloid Closet: Homosexuality in the Movies*, rev. ed. (New York: Harper & Row, 1987).

23. Russo, *The Celluloid Closet*, 5.

24. Kenneth Kammeyer, *The Hypersexual Society: Sexual Discourse, Erotica, and Pornography in America Today* (New York: Palgrave Macmillan, 2008), 143.

25. Chon Noriega, "'Something's Missing Here!': Homosexuality and Film Reviews during the Production Code Era, 1934–1962," *Cinema Journal* 30, no. 1 (Autumn 1990): 20–41.

26. Jeff Giles, "The Open Secret—in a Rare Interview, Jaye Davidson Leaves Nothing to the Imagination When Discussing the Oscar-Nominated

Film, 'The Crying Game,'" *Seattle Times*, March 22, 1993, http://community. seattletimes.nwsource.com/archive/?date=19930322&slug=1691795.

27. Neil Miller, *Out of the Past: Gay and Lesbian History from 1869 to the Present* (New York: Alyson, 2006), 556.

28. Mark Driscoll et al., "The Puppy Episode," *Ellen*, season 4, episodes 22 and 23, directed by Gil Junger, aired on ABC April 30, 1997 (New York: A&E Home Video, 2006), DVD.

29. Miller, *Out of the Past*, 557–58.

30. Miller, *Out of the Past*, 557.

31. Choire Sicha, "Pedro Zamora: From 'Real World' to Real Legend," *Los Angeles Times*, March 31, 2009, http://www.latimes.com/entertainment/la-et-pedro31-2009mar31-story.html#page=1.

32. William J. Clinton, "Statement on the Death of Pedro Zamora," *The American Presidency Project*, ed. Gerhard Peters and John T. Woolley, November 11, 1994, http://www.presidency.ucsb.edu/ws/?pid=49482.

33. Miller, *Out of the Past*, 588–89.

34. Alyson Miller, "Unsuited to Age Group: The Scandals of Children's Literature," *College Literature* 41, no. 2 (2014): 120–40.

35. Jennifer Esposito, "We're Here, We're Queer, but We're Just Like Heterosexuals: A Cultural Studies Analysis of Lesbian Themed Children's Books," *Educational Foundations* 23, no. 3–4 (Summer–Fall 2009): 61–78.

36. One Million Moms, http://onemillionmoms.com/about-us/.

37. Abby Ellin, "JC Penney Raises Ire with Another Gay-Friendly Ad," *ABC News*, June 1, 2012, http://abcnews.go.com/blogs/business/2012/06/jc-penney-comes-out-with-another-gay-friendly-ad/.

38. Paula Fairs, "Honey Maid Counters Same-Sex Ad Backlash with Unapologetic Sequel," *ABC News*, April 7, 2014, http://abcnews.go.com/blogs/business/2014/04/honey-maid-counters-same-sex-ad-backlash-with-unapologetic-sequel/.

39. Roger H. Rubin, "Alternative Lifestyles Revisited, or Whatever Happened to Swingers, Group Marriages, and Communes?" *Journal of Family Studies* 22, no. 6 (2001), 711.

40. Rubin, "Alternative Lifestyles," 711, emphasis in original.

41. Nena O'Neill and George O'Neill, *Open Marriage: A New Life Style for Couples* (New York: M. Evans, 1972; reprint 1984).

42. Margalit Fox, "Nena O'Neill, 82, an Author of 'Open Marriage,' Is Dead," *New York Times*, March 26, 2006, http://www.nytimes.com/2006/03/26/books/25oneill.html.

43. Edward M. Fernandes, "The Swinging Paradigm: An Evaluation of the Marital and Sexual Satisfaction of Swingers," *Electronic Journal of Human*

Sexuality 12 (2009), https://www.psychologytoday.com/files/attachments/
134956/the-swinging-paradigm.pdf.

44. Rubin, "Alternative Lifestyles."

45. Elisabeth Sheff, "Polyamorous Families, Same-Sex Marriage, and the
Slippery Slope," *Journal of Contemporary Ethnography* 40, no. 5 (2011): 488.

46. Rubin, "Alternative Lifestyles."

47. Sheff, "Polyamorous Families," 489.

48. Sheff, "Polyamorous Families."

49. Tyler Kingkade, "Texas Tech Frat Loses Charter Following 'No Means
Yes, Yes Means Anal' Display," *Huffington Post*, October 8, 2014, http://www.
huffingtonpost.com/2014/10/08/texas-tech-frat-no-means-yes_n_5953302.
html.

50. Conor Friedersdorf, "Why One Male College Student Abandoned Affirmative Consent," *Atlantic*, October 20, 2014, http://www.theatlantic.com/
politics/archive/2014/10/why-a-college-student-abandoned-affirmative-
consent/381650/.

51. Jay Wiseman, *SM 101: A Realistic Introduction*, 2nd ed. (San Francisco:
Greenery, 1996).

52. Robert Jensen, *Getting Off: Pornography and the End of Masculinity*
(Cambridge, MA: South End Press, 2007).

53. Betty Friedan, *The Feminine Mystique* (New York: Norton, 1963).

54. For more on this debate, see Lynn S. Chancer, *Reconcilable Differences: Confronting Beauty, Pornography, and the Future of Feminism* (Berkeley: University of California Press, 1998).

55. Nikki Gloudeman, "Feminist Filmmaker Erika Lust on Why Porn Must
Change," *Huffington Post*, January 30, 2015, http://www.huffingtonpost.com/
nikki-gloudeman/why-porn-must-change_b_6571348.html.

7. VIOLENCE, AGGRESSION, AND PRIVILEGE

1. Dorothy L. Espelage, Melissa K. Holt, and V. Paul Poteat, "Individual
and Contextual Influences on Bullying," in *Handbook of Research on Schools,
Schooling, and Human Development*, ed. Judith L. Meece and Jacquelynne S.
Eccles (New York: Routledge, 2010), 146–60.

2. Derald Wing Sue, *Microaggressions in Everyday Life: Race, Gender,
and Sexual Orientation* (Hoboken, NJ: Wiley, 2010).

3. Leora Tanenbaum, *Catfight: Rivalries among Women—from Diets to
Dating, from the Boardroom to the Delivery Room* (New York: Seven Stories,
2002).

4. John Archer and Sarah M. Coyne, "An Integrated Review of Indirect, Relational, and Social Aggression," *Personality and Social Psychology Review* 9, no. 3 (2005): 212–30.

5. American Psychological Association, "Violence," http://www.apa.org/topics/violence/.

6. World Health Organization, "Definition and Typology of Violence," http://www.who.int/violenceprevention/approach/definition/en/.

7. Megan Garber, "Why the Limit to *Mean Girls* Does Not Exist," *Atlantic*, April 30, 2014, http://www.theatlantic.com/entertainment/archive/2014/04/The-limit-to-Mean-Girls-Does-Not-Exist/361432/.

8. Craig A. Anderson and Brad J. Bushman, "The Effects of Media Violence on Society," *Science* 295, no. 5564 (2002): 2377–79.

9. Sarah M. Coyne et al., "The Effects of Viewing Physical and Relational Aggression in the Media: Evidence for a Cross-Over Effect," *Journal of Experimental Social Psychology* 44, no. 6 (2008): 1551–54.

10. Coyne et al., "Effects of Viewing Physical and Relational Aggression," 1552.

11. Coyne et al., "Effects of Viewing Physical and Relational Aggression."

12. Coyne et al., "Effects of Viewing Physical and Relational Aggression."

13. Nicki R. Crick and Jennifer K. Grotpeter, "Relational Aggression, Gender, and Social-Psychological Adjustment," *Child Development* 66, no. 3 (1995): 710–22.

14. Archer and Coyne, "An Integrated Review."

15. Federal Bureau of Investigation, "Ten-Year Arrest Trends," *Crime in the United States 2012*, http://www.fbi.gov/about-us/cjis/ucr/crime-in-the-u.s/2012/crime-in-the-u.s.-2012/tables/33tabledatadecoverviewpdf.

16. Carol J. Clover, *Men, Women, and Chain Saws: Gender in the Modern Horror Film* (Princeton, NJ: Princeton University Press, 1992).

17. Please see any of the installments of Sut Jhally's *Dreamworlds* films and Terri M. Adams and Douglas B. Fuller, "The Words Have Changed but the Ideology Remains the Same: Misogynistic Lyrics in Rap Music," *Journal of Black Studies* 36, no. 6 (2006): 938–57.

18. Kurt Squire, "From Content to Context: Videogames as Designed Experience," *Educational Researcher* 35, no. 8 (2006): 19–29.

19. See Leora Tanenbaum, *I Am Not a Slut: Slut-Shaming in the Age of the Internet* (New York: Harper Perennial, 2015).

20. Amanda Hess, "A *Thot* Is Not a *Slut*: The Popular Insult Is More about Race and Class Than Sex," *Slate XXfactor*, October 16, 2014, http://www.slate.com/blogs/xx_factor/2014/10/16/a_thot_is_not_a_slut_on_popular_slurs_race_class_and_sex.html.

21. John Ortved, "Ratchet: The Rap Insult That Became a Compliment," *New York Magazine*, April 11, 2013, http://nymag.com/thecut/2013/04/ratchet-the-rap-insult-that-became-a-compliment.html.

22. William A. Smith, Tara J. Yosso, and Daniel G. Solorzano, "Racial Primes and Black Misandry on Historically White Campuses: Toward Critical Race Accountability in Educational Administration," *Educational Administration Quarterly* 43, no. 5 (2007): 559–85.

23. William A. Smith, Walter R. Allen, and Lynette L. Danley, "'Assume the Position . . . You Fit the Description': Psychosocial Experiences and Racial Battle Fatigue among African American Male College Students," *American Behavioral Scientist* 51, no. 4 (2007): 551–78.

24. Smith and colleagues include "pathological" in their definition of Black misandry, hearkening to psychotherapist George Weinberg's choice in the 1960s to flip the understanding of disease. Weinberg coined *homophobia* at a time when sexual attraction to people of one's own gender was officially defined as pathological—diseased (described in chapter 3). Phobia is pathological fear, suggesting that discomfort with queer people, rather than being queer, is the problem. Similarly, Smith and colleagues focus on pathological fear of Black men, a reverse from the common obfuscation of the problems faced by African Americans. Black culture is often misconstrued as pathological and the root of problems for African American men. Smith and colleagues identify stereotyping of Black men as the problem.

25. A Voice for Men, "Mission Statement," http://www.avoiceformen.com/policies/mission-statement/.

26. Carolyn B. Maloney and the Joint Economic Committee Democratic Staff, *Gender Pay Inequality: Consequences for Women, Families and the Economy* (Washington, DC: Joint Economic Committee United States Congress, 2016); see also Carmen DeNavas-Walt and Bernadette D. Proctor, *Income and Poverty in the United States: 2013* (Washington, DC: US Government Printing Office, 2014).

27. Maloney et al., *Gender Pay Inequality*.

28. Joan Entmacher et al., *Insecure & Unemployed: Poverty and Income among Women and Families 2000–2013* (Washington, DC: National Women's Law Center, 2014).

29. Michael S. Kimmel, *The Gendered Society*, 5th ed. (New York: Oxford University Press, 2012).

30. DeNavas-Walt and Proctor, *Income and Poverty*.

31. A Voice for Men, "Mission Statement."

32. For a review of rape shield law, see Michelle J. Anderson, "From Chastity Requirement to Sexuality License: Sexual Consent and a New Rape Shield Law," *George Washington Law Review* 70, no. 1 (2002): 51–162.

33. Paul Elam, "Challenging the Etiology of Rape," A Voice for Men, November 14, 2010, http://www.avoiceformen.com/mens-rights/false-rape-culture/challenging-the-etiology-of-rape/.

34. Sarah Begley, "Ironic Misandry: Why Feminists Pretending to Hate Men Isn't Funny," *Time*, August 12, 2014, http://time.com/3101429/misandry-misandrist-feminist-womenagainstfeminism/.

35. Ana Revenga and Sudhir Shetty, "Empowering Women Is Smart Economics," *Finance and Development* 49, no. 1 (2012): 40–43.

36. Jaime M. Grant et al., *Injustice at Every Turn: A Report of the National Transgender Discrimination Survey* (Washington, DC: National Center for Transgender Equality and National Gay and Lesbian Task Force, 2011).

37. Gary Morris, "The Rage from Nowhere? Arthur Dong's *Licensed to Kill* Interviews Murderers of Gay Men," *Bright Lights Film Journal* (August 1, 2005), http://brightlightsfilm.com/rage-nowhere-arthur-dongs-licensed-kill-interviews-murderers-gay-men/.

38. *Licensed to Kill*, directed by Arthur Dong (Deep Focus Productions, 1997), DVD.

39. United States Department of Justice, Office of Justice Programs, Office for Victims of Crime, "Responding to Transgender Victims of Sexual Assault," June 2014, http://ovc.gov/pubs/forge/sexual_numbers.html#victims.

40. Tyler Clementi Foundation, "Tyler's Story," http://www.tylerclementi.org/tylers-story.

41. Angela J. Bahns and Nyla R. Branscombe, "Effects of Legitimizing Discrimination against Homosexuals on Gay Bashing," *European Journal of Social Psychology* 41, no. 3 (2011): 388–96.

42. Centers for Disease Control and Prevention, Injury Prevention & Control: Division of Violence Prevention, "Intimate Partner Violence: Definitions," last updated July 2016, http://www.cdc.gov/violenceprevention/intimatepartnerviolence/definitions.html.

43. Callie Marie Rennison and Sarah Welchans, *Bureau of Justice Statistics Special Report: Intimate Partner Violence* (Washington, DC: US Department of Justice, 2000; reprint 2002), http://www.atria.nl/epublications/2000/intimate_partner_violence.pdf.

44. Michele C. Black et al., *The National Intimate Partner and Sexual Violence Survey (NISVS): 2010 Summary Report* (Atlanta, GA: National Center for Injury Prevention and Control, Centers for Disease Control and Prevention), 43.

45. Black et al., *National Intimate Partner and Sexual Violence*, 2.

46. Black et al., *National Intimate Partner and Sexual Violence*, 2.

47. Debby Phillips and Dorothy Henderson, "'Patient Was Hit in the Face by a Fist . . .' A Discourse Analysis of Male Violence against Women," *American Journal of Orthopsychiatry* 69, no. 1 (1999): 116–21.

48. Adrienne Rich, "Compulsory Heterosexuality and Lesbian Existence," *Signs: Journal of Women in Culture and Society* 5, no. 4 (1980): 633.

49. Rich, "Compulsory Heterosexuality," 632.

50. Rich, "Compulsory Heterosexuality," 637.

51. Chana Joffe-Walt, "Some Like It Not (on the Neck)," Episode 557: Birds & Bees, *This American Life*, May 15, 2015, http://www.thisamericanlife.org/radio-archives/episode/557/birds-bees.

52. Charlene L. Muehlenhard and Zoë D. Peterson, "Conceptualizing Sexual Violence: Socially Acceptable Coercion and Other Controversies," in *The Social Psychology of Good and Evil*, ed. Arthur G. Miller (New York: Guilford, 2004), 240–68.

53. Muehlenhard and Peterson, "Conceptualizing Sexual Violence."

54. Lara Stemple and Ilan H. Meyer, "The Sexual Victimization of Men in America: New Data Challenge Old Assumptions," *American Journal of Public Health* 104, no. 6 (2014): e20.

55. Black et al., *National Intimate Partner and Sexual Violence Survey*, 1, 2, 17.

56. Black et al., *National Intimate Partner and Sexual Violence Survey*, 24.

57. Stemple and Meyer, "Sexual Victimization of Men."

58. Diana Scully, *Understanding Sexual Violence* (New York: Routledge, 1990), 7.

59. Scully, *Understanding Sexual Violence*, 4.

60. Scully, *Understanding Sexual Violence*, 46.

61. Scully, *Understanding Sexual Violence*, 48.

62. Scully, *Understanding Sexual Violence*, 52.

63. Scully, *Understanding Sexual Violence*, 48.

64. Dianne F. Herman, "The Rape Culture," in *Seeing Ourselves: Classic, Contemporary, and Cross-Cultural Readings in Sociology*, ed. John L. Macionis and Nijole V. Benokraitis (Upper Saddle River, NJ: Prentice Hall, 1994), 49.

65. Diana L. Payne, Kimberly A. Lonsway, and Louise F. Fitzgerald, "Rape Myth Acceptance: Exploration of Its Structure and Its Measurement Using the *Illinois Rape Myth Acceptance Scale*," *Journal of Research in Personality* 33, no. 1 (1999): 49–50.

66. David Lisak and Paul M. Miller, "Repeat Rape and Multiple Offending among Undetected Rapists," *Violence and Victims* 17, no. 1 (2002).

67. Scully, *Understanding Sexual Violence*, 6.

68. Lisak and Miller, "Repeat Rape," 81.

69. Black et al., *National Intimate Partner and Sexual Violence Survey*, 21–22.

70. Lisak and Miller, "Repeat Rape," 75.

71. Lisak and Miller, "Repeat Rape," 78.

72. Lisak and Miller, "Repeat Rape," 78.

73. Lisak and Miller, "Repeat Rape," 80.

74. An important note is that the power differential means that children can never consent to sexual activity with an adult. See Jean O'Malley Halley, *The Parallel Lives of Women and Cows: Meat Markets* (New York: Palgrave Macmillan, 2012).

75. Stuart Ewen and Elizabeth Ewen, *Typecasting: On the Arts and Sciences of Human Inequality* (New York: Seven Stories Press, 2006), 299.

76. Heinz Heger, *The Men with the Pink Triangle* (Surrey, UK: Gay Men's Press, 1980).

77. Neil Miller, *Out of the Past: Gay and Lesbian History from 1869 to the Present* (New York: Alyson, 2006), 201.

78. Miller, *Out of the Past*, 201.

79. Miller, *Out of the Past*, 201.

80. Miller, *Out of the Past*, 206.

81. Miller, *Out of the Past*, 206.

82. APA Task Force on Appropriate Therapeutic Responses to Sexual Orientation, *Report of the Task Force on Appropriate Therapeutic Responses to Sexual Orientation* (Washington, DC: American Psychological Association, 2009), 119.

83. APA Task Force, *Therapeutic Responses*, 42.

84. APA Task Force, *Therapeutic Responses*, 120.

85. Leelah Alcorn's suicide note was quoted in full in multiple web logs, including J. Bryan Lowder, "Listen to Leelah Alcorn's Final Words," *Slate*, December 31, 2014, http://www.slate.com/blogs/outward/2014/12/31/leelah_alcorn_transgender_teen_from_ohio_should_be_honored_in_death.html.

86. Katy Steinmetz, "Oregon Becomes Third State to Ban Conversion Therapy on Minors," *Time*, May 19, 2015, http://time.com/3889687/oregon-conversion-therapy-ban/.

87. Lila Shapiro, "This Bill Could End 'Gay Conversion Therapy' in the U.S.," *Huffington Post*, May 19, 2015, http://www.huffingtonpost.com/2015/05/19/conversion-therapy-ban_n_7322828.html.

8. IT'S GETTING BETTER

1. Dan Avery, "Y'all Can Go Home—This 8-Year-Old Boy Won NYC Pride," *New Now Next* (blog), June 29, 2015, http://m.newnownext.com/yall-can-go-home-this-8-year-old-boy-won-nyc-pride/06/2015/.

2. Avery, "Y'all Can Go Home."

3. George Gao, "Most Americans Now Say Learning Their Child Is Gay Wouldn't Upset Them," Pew Research Center, June 29, 2015, http://www.pewresearch.org/fact-tank/2015/06/29/most-americans-now-say-learning-their-child-is-gay-wouldnt-upset-them/.

4. "Gay and Lesbian Rights," Gallup, accessed July 28, 2015, http://www.gallup.com/poll/1651/gay-lesbian-rights.aspx.

5. Ken Paxton, "Attorney General Ken Paxton: Following High Court's Flawed Ruling, Next Fight Is Religious Liberty," news release, June 26, 2015, https://www.texasattorneygeneral.gov/oagnews/release.php?id=5142.

6. Ken Paxton, "Attorney General Ken Paxton: Religious Liberties of Texas Public Officials Remain Constitutionally Protected after Obergefell v. Hodges," news release, June 28, 2015, https://www.texasattorneygeneral.gov/oagnews/release.php?id=5144.

7. Lauren McGaughy, "Texas Attorney General Says Clerks Can Refuse Same-Sex Marriage Licenses," *Houston Chronicle*, June 28, 2015, http://www.houstonchronicle.com/news/houston-texas/texas/article/Texas-attorney-general-says-clerks-can-refuse-to-6354754.php.

8. Pauline Park, interview by the author, New York City, December 9, 2013.

9. Ackerman Institute for the Family, "Gender and Family Project," accessed July 3, 2015, https://www.ackerman.org/gfp/.

10. Ackerman Institute for the Family, "The Ackerman Podcast #5: Between Pink and Blue with Jean Malpas LMHC LMFT," accessed July 3, 2015, http://ackerman.podbean.com/page/3/.

11. Emma Whitford, "Transgender Students Endure Widespread Harassment in NY Public Schools, Report Finds," *Gothamist* (blog), June 24, 2015, http://gothamist.com/2015/06/24/report_transgender_and_non-gender_c.php.

12. New York City Department of Education, "Transgender Student Guidelines," *Rules and Policies*, accessed July 2, 2015, http://schools.nyc.gov/RulesPolicies/TransgenderStudentGuidelines/default.htm.

13. Yasmeen Kahn, "For This Transgender Third-Grader, Life as a Boy Is Liberating," National Public Radio, July 5, 2015.

14. Irene Chidinma Nwoye, "New York's Bravest Is Trans FDNY Firefighter Brooke Guinan," *Village Voice*, February 24, 2015, http://www.villagevoice.com/news/new-yorks-bravest-is-trans-fdny-firefighter-brooke-guinan-6722705.

15. Nwoye, "New York's Bravest."

16. Nwoye, "New York's Bravest."

17. Nwoye, "New York's Bravest."

18. Nwoye, "New York's Bravest."

19. Jessica Valenti, "SlutWalks and the Future of Feminism," *Washington Post*, June 3, 2011, http://www.washingtonpost.com/opinions/slutwalks-and-the-future-of-feminism/2011/06/01/AGjB9LIH_story.html.

20. Rama Lakshmi, "Indian Women Alter SlutWalk to Better Match Country's Conservatism," *Washington Post*, July 23, 2011, https://www.washingtonpost.com/world/asia-pacific/indian-women-tweak-their-slutwalk/2011/07/21/gIQAlY9JTI_story.html.

21. Harsha Walia, "Slutwalk: To March or Not to March," Rabble.ca, May 18, 2011, http://rabble.ca/news/2011/05/slutwalk-march-or-not-march.

22. Walia, "Slutwalk."

23. Lakshmi, "Indian Women Alter SlutWalk."

24. Amy Shaw, "Masturbation Is for Women Too and Not Just for Men," *Everyday Feminism* (blog), July 30, 2012. http://everydayfeminism.com/2012/07/women-masturbating/.

25. It Gets Better Project, http://www.itgetsbetter.org/pages/about-it-gets-better-project/.

26. See our related arguments in Jean Halley, Amy Eshleman, and Ramya Mahadevan Vijaya, *Seeing White: An Introduction to White Privilege and Race* (Lanham, MD: Rowman & Littlefield, 2011).

27. M. V. Lee Badgett and Alyssa Schneebaum, *The Impact of Wage Equality on Sexual Orientation Poverty Gaps* (Los Angeles: Williams Institute, 2015).

28. Casey Judge, "Thrown Away for Being Gay: The Abandonment of LGBT Youth and Their Lack of Legal Recourse," *Indiana Journal of Law and Social Equality* 3, no. 2 (2015): Article 5.

29. Svati P. Shah, "Sex Work and Queer Politics in Three Acts," *Scholar & Feminist Online* 10, no. 1/2 (2011), http://sfonline.barnard.edu/a-new-queer-agenda/sex-work-and-queer-politics-in-three-acts/0/.

30. Blake Ellis, "Transgender and Struggling to Pay Medical Costs," *CNN Money*, August 22, 2013, http://money.cnn.com/2013/08/22/pf/transgender-medical-costs/.

31. Badgett and Schneebaum, *The Impact of Wage Equality*.

32. Jennifer Bendery, "It Is Now Illegal for a Federal Contractor to Fire Someone for Being LGBT," *Huffington Post*, April 8, 2015, http://www.huffingtonpost.com/2015/04/08/lgbt-job-discrimination-federal-contractors_n_7025564.html.

33. Halley, Eshleman, and Vijaya, *Seeing White*, 199.

34. Avery, "Y'all Can Go Home."

BIBLIOGRAPHY

Ackerman Institute for the Family. "The Ackerman Podcast #5: Between Pink and Blue with Jean Malpas LMHC LMFT." Accessed July 3, 2015. http://ackerman.podbean.com/page/3/.

———. "Gender and Family Project." Accessed July 3, 2015. https://www.ackerman.org/gfp/.

Adam, Barry D. "Theorizing Homophobia." *Sexualities* 1, no. 4 (1998): 387–404.

Adam, Seth, and Nick Adams. "GLAAD Responds to ABC News Interview with Bruce Jenner, Releases Tip Sheet for Journalists." April 24, 2015. http://www.glaad.org/releases/glaad-responds-abc-news-interview-bruce-jenner-releases-tip-sheet-journalists.

Adams, Terri M., and Douglas B. Fuller. "The Words Have Changed but the Ideology Remains the Same: Misogynistic Lyrics in Rap Music." *Journal of Black Studies* 36, no. 6 (2006): 938–57.

American Civil Liberties Union. "Cole v. Arkansas—Case Profile." April 7, 2011. https://www.aclu.org/lgbt-rights_hiv-aids/cole-v-arkansas-case-profile.

———. "Missouri Judge Rules That Lesbian Can Be Foster Parent." February 17, 2006. https://www.aclu.org/lgbt-rights_hiv-aids/missouri-judge-rules-lesbian-can-be-foster-parent.

———. "Nebraska's Ban on Gay Foster Parents Is Beatable." April 25, 2014. https://www.aclu.org/blog/lgbt-rights/nebraskas-ban-gay-foster-parents-beatable.

———. "Stewart and Stewart v. Heineman—Client Profiles." August 23, 2013. https://www.aclu.org/lgbt-rights/stewart-and-stewart-v-heineman-client-profiles.

American Psychological Association. "Violence." http://www.apa.org/topics/violence/.

Andersen, Margaret L., and Patricia Hill Collins. *Race, Class and Gender: An Anthology.* 7th ed. Belmont, CA: Wadsworth, 2010.

Anderson, Craig A., and Brad J. Bushman. "The Effects of Media Violence on Society." *Science* 295, no. 5564 (2002): 2377–79.

Anderson, Michelle J. "From Chastity Requirement to Sexuality License: Sexual Consent and a New Rape Shield Law." *George Washington Law Review* 70, no. 1 (2002): 51–162.

Anderson, Ryan T. *Truth Overruled: The Future of Marriage and Religious Freedom.* Washington, DC: Regnery, 2015.

APA Task Force on Appropriate Therapeutic Responses to Sexual Orientation. *Report of the Task Force on Appropriate Therapeutic Responses to Sexual Orientation.* Washington, DC: American Psychological Association, 2009.

Archer, John, and Sarah M. Coyne. "An Integrated Review of Indirect, Relational, and Social Aggression." *Personality and Social Psychology Review* 9, no. 3 (2005): 212–30.

Avery, Dan. "Y'all Can Go Home—This 8-Year-Old Boy Won NYC Pride." *New Now Next* (blog), June 29, 2015. http://m.newnownext.com/yall-can-go-home-this-8-year-old-boy-won-nyc-pride/06/2015/.

B., Hima. *Straight for the Money: Interviews with Queer Sex Workers.* 1994. DVD, 59 min.

Badgett, M. V. Lee, and Alyssa Schneebaum. *The Impact of Wage Equality on Sexual Orientation Poverty Gaps.* Los Angeles: Williams Institute, 2015.

Bahns, Angela J., and Nyla R. Branscombe. "Effects of Legitimizing Discrimination against Homosexuals on Gay Bashing." *European Journal of Social Psychology* 41, no. 3 (2011): 388–96.

Balsam, Kimberly, Bu Huang, Karen C. Fieland, Jane M. Simoni, and Karina Walters. "Culture, Trauma, and Wellness: A Comparison of Heterosexual and Lesbian, Gay, Bisexual, and Two-Spirit Native Americans." *Cultural Diversity and Ethnic Minority Psychology* 10, no. 3 (2004): 287–301.

Bartky, Sandra Lee. *Femininity and Domination: Studies in the Phenomenology of Oppression.* New York: Routledge, 1990.

Bem, Sandra Lipsitz. "Gender Schema Theory and Its Implications for Child Development: Raising Gender-Aschematic Children in a Gender-Schematic Society." *Signs* 8, no. 4 (1983): 598–616.

———. *An Unconventional Family.* New Haven, CT: Yale University Press, 1998.

Berger, Kathleen Stassen. *The Developing Person through the Life Span.* 8th ed. New York: Worth, 2012.

Berquist, Kathleen Ja Sook, M. Elizabeth Vonk, Dong Soo Kim, and Marvin D. Feit. *International Korean Adoption: A Fifty-Year History of Policy and Practice.* New York: Haworth, 2007.

Bérubé, Alan. *Coming Out under Fire: The History of Gay Men and Women in World War II.* New York: Simon & Schuster, 1990.

Black, Michele C., Kathleen C. Basile, Matthew J. Breiding, Sharon G. Smith, Mikel L. Walters, Melissa T. Merrick, Jieru Chen, and Mark R. Stevens. *The National Intimate Partner and Sexual Violence Survey (NISVS): 2010 Summary Report.* Atlanta, GA: National Center for Injury Prevention and Control, Centers for Disease Control and Prevention, 2010.

Blackmon, Douglas A. *Slavery by Another Name: The Re-Enslavement of Black Americans from the Civil War to World War II.* New York: Anchor, 2008.

Blumer, Markie L. C., and Megan J. Murphy. "Alaskan Gay Males' Couple Experiences of Societal Non-support: Coping through Families of Choice and Therapeutic Means." *Contemporary Family Therapy* 33, no. 3 (2011): 273–90.

Blumstein, Philip, and Pepper Schwartz. "The Creation of Sexuality." In *Homosexuality/Heterosexuality: Concepts of Sexual Orientation*, edited by D. P. Whirter, S. A. Sanders, and J. M. Reinisch, 307–20. New York: Oxford University Press, 1990.

Borch, Fred L. III. "The History of 'Don't Ask, Don't Tell' in the Army: How We Got to It and Why It Is What It Is." *Military Law Review* 203 (Spring 2010): 189–206.

Bordo, Susan. "The Empire of Images in Our World of Bodies." *Chronicle of Higher Education* 50, no. 17 (December 19, 2003).

Boswell, John. *Christianity, Social Tolerance, and Homosexuality.* Chicago: University of Chicago Press, 1980.

Brown, Matthew K. "Constitutional Law: First Amendment and Congress's Spending Clause Power: The Supreme Court Supports Military Recruiters and the United States Military's Discrimination against Homosexuals Despite Law Schools' Protests: Rumsfeld v. Forum for Academic & Institutional Rights." *University of Arkansas at Little Rock Law Review* 29, no. 2 (Winter 2007): 345–78.

Brownmiller, Susan. *Against Our Will: Men, Women and Rape.* New York: Ballantine, 1993.

Burrelli, David F. "An Overview of the Debate on Homosexuals in the U.S. Military." In *Gays and Lesbians in the Military: Issues, Concerns, and Contrasts*, edited by Wilbur J. Scott and Sandra Carson Stanley, 17–31. Hawthorne, NY: Aldine de Gruyter, 1994.

Butler, Judith. *Gender Trouble: Feminism and the Subversion of Identity.* New York: Routledge, 1990.

Caldwell, Gisela. "The Seventh Circuit in *Ben-Shalom v. Marsh*: Equating Speech with Conduct." *Loyola of Los Angeles Law Review* 24, no. 2 (January 1991): 421–65.

Cameron, Eric. "APA to Remove 'Gender Identity Disorder' from *DSM-5*." *Human Rights Campaign* (blog), December 4, 2012. http://www.hrc.org/blog/entry/apa-to-remove-gender-identity-disorder-from-dsm-5.

Carter, David. *Stonewall: The Riots That Sparked the Gay Revolution*. New York: St. Martin's, 2004.

Centers for Disease Control and Prevention, Injury Prevention & Control: Division of Violence Prevention. "Intimate Partner Violence: Definitions." Last updated July 2016. http://www.cdc.gov/violenceprevention/intimatepartnerviolence/definitions.html.

Chancer, Lynn S. *Reconcilable Differences: Confronting Beauty, Pornography, and the Future of Feminism*. Berkeley: University of California Press, 1998.

Chapkis, Wendy. *Live Sex Acts: Women Performing Erotic Labor*. New York: Routledge, 1997.

Cialdini, Robert B. "Crafting Normative Messages to Protect the Environment." *Current Directions in Psychological Science* 12, no. 4 (2003): 105–9.

Cialdini, Robert B., and Noah J. Goldstein. "Social Influence: Compliance and Conformity." *Annual Review of Psychology* 55 (2004): 591–621.

Cialdini, Robert B., Raymond R. Reno, and Carl A. Kallgren. "A Focus Theory of Normative Conduct: Recycling the Concept of Norms to Reduce Littering in Public Places." *Journal of Personality and Social Psychology* 58, no. 6 (1990): 1015–26.

Clinton, William J. "Statement on the Death of Pedro Zamora." *The American Presidency Project*, edited by Gerhard Peters and John T. Woolley. November 11, 1994. http://www.presidency.ucsb.edu/ws/?pid=49482.

Clover, Carol J. *Men, Women, and Chain Saws: Gender in the Modern Horror Film*. Princeton, NJ: Princeton University Press, 1992.

Committee on Lesbian and Gay Concerns. "Avoiding Heterosexual Bias in Language." American Psychological Association, September 1991. http://www.apa.org/pi/lgbt/resources/language.aspx.

Connell, R. W., and James W. Messerschmidt. "Hegemonic Masculinity: Rethinking the Concept." *Gender and Society* 19, no. 6 (2005): 829–59.

Coyne, Sarah M., David A. Nelson, Frances Lawton, Shelly Haslam, Lucy Rooney, Leigh Titterington, Hannah Trainor, Jack Remnant, and Leah Ogunlaja. "The Effects of Viewing Physical and Relational Aggression in the Media: Evidence for a Cross-Over Effect." *Journal of Experimental Social Psychology* 44, no. 6 (2008): 1551–54.

Crandall, Christian S., Amy Eshleman, and Laurie T. O'Brien. "Social Norms and the Expression and Suppression of Prejudice: The Struggle for Internalization." *Journal of Personality and Social Psychology* 82, no. 3 (2002): 359–78.

Crick, Nicki R., and Jennifer K. Grotpeter. "Relational Aggression, Gender, and Social-Psychological Adjustment." *Child Development* 66, no. 3 (1995): 710–22.

Crombie, Gail, Sandra W. Pyke, Naida Silverthorn, Alison Jones, and Sergio Piccinin. "Students' Perceptions of Their Classroom Participation and Instructor as a Function of Gender and Context." *Journal of Higher Education* 74, no. 1 (2003): 51–76.

Davidoff, Leonore. "Gender and the 'Great Divide': Public and Private in British Gender History." *Journal of Women's History* 15, no. 1 (2003): 11–27.

Davidson, Megan. "Seeking Refuge under the Umbrella: Inclusion, Exclusion, and Organizing within the Category *Transgender*." *Sexuality Research & Social Policy* 4, no. 4 (December 2007): 60–80.

Dein, Simon. "Working with Patients with Religious Beliefs." *Advances in Psychiatric Treatment* 10 (2004): 287–94.

DeNavas-Walt, Carmen, and Bernadette D. Proctor. *Income and Poverty in the United States: 2013*. Washington, DC: US Government Printing Office, 2014.

Diamond, Lisa M. "What Does Sexual Orientation Orient? A Biobehavioral Model Distinguishing Romantic Love and Sexual Desire." *Psychological Review* 110, no. 1 (2003): 173–92.

Dong, Arthur. *Licensed to Kill*. Deep Focus Productions (1997). DVD, 80 min.

Driscoll, Mark, Dava Savell, Tracy Newman, Jonathan Stark, and Ellen Degeneres. "The Puppy Episode." *Ellen*, season 4, episodes 22 and 23. Aired on ABC April 30, 1997. DVD. New York: A&E Home Video, 2006.

Dyche, Lawrence, and Luis H. Zayas. "Cross-Cultural Empathy and Training the Contemporary Psychotherapist." *Clinical Social Work Journal* 29, no. 3 (2001): 245–58.

Earlham College. "Unpacking the Invisible Knapsack II: Daily Effects of Straight Privilege." http://www.cs.earlham.edu/~hyrax/personal/files/student_res/straightprivilege.htm.

Elam, Paul. "Challenging the Etiology of Rape." A Voice for Men, November 14, 2010. http://www.avoiceformen.com/mens-rights/false-rape-culture/challenging-the-etiology-of-rape/.

Elliott, Diana B., and Tavia Simmons. *Marital Events of Americans: 2009*. Washington, DC: United States Census Bureau, 2011.

Ellis, Havelock, and John Addington Symonds. *Sexual Inversion*. London: Wilson and Macmillan, 1897.

Elsas, Louis J., Arne Ljungqvist, Malcolm A. Ferguson-Smith, Joe Leigh Simpson, Myron Genel, Alison S. Carlson, Elizabeth Ferris, Albert de la Chapelle, and Anke A. Ehrhardt. "Gender Verification of Female Athletes." *Genetics in Medicine* 2, no. 4 (2000): 249–54.

Entmacher, Joan, Katherine Gallagher Robbins, Julie Vogtman, and Anne Morrison. *Insecure & Unemployed: Poverty and Income among Women and Families 2000–2013*. Washington, DC: National Women's Law Center, 2014.

Eskridge, William N., Jr. "Gaylegal Narratives." *Stanford Law Review* 46, no. 3 (February 1994): 607–46.

Espelage, Dorothy L., Melissa K. Holt, and V. Paul Poteat. "Individual and Contextual Influences on Bullying." In *Handbook of Research on Schools, Schooling, and Human Development*, edited by Judith L. Meece and Jacquelynne S. Eccles, 146–60. New York: Routledge, 2010.

Esposito, Jennifer. "We're Here, We're Queer, but We're Just Like Heterosexuals: A Cultural Studies Analysis of Lesbian Themed Children's Books." *Educational Foundations* 23, no. 3–4 (Summer–Fall 2009): 61–78.

Eves, Alison. "Queer Theory, Butch/Femme Identities and Lesbian Space." *Sexualities* 7, no. 4 (2004): 480–96.

Ewen, Stuart. *All Consuming Images: The Politics of Style in Contemporary Culture*. New York: Basic, 1989.

———. *Captains of Consciousness: Advertising and the Social Roots of the Consumer Culture*. New York: McGraw-Hill, 1976.

Ewen, Stuart, and Elizabeth Ewen. *Typecasting: On the Arts and Sciences of Human Inequality*. New York: Seven Stories Press, 2006.

Fausto-Sterling, Anne. "The Five Sexes, Revisited." *Sciences* 40, no. 4 (2010): 18–23.

Federal Bureau of Investigation. "Ten-Year Arrest Trends." *Crime in the United States 2012*. http://www.fbi.gov/about-us/cjis/ucr/crime-in-the-u.s/2012/crime-in-the-u.s.-2012/tables/33tabledatadecoverviewpdf.

Feinberg, Leslie. *Stone Butch Blues*. Ann Arbor, MI: Firebrand, 1993.

Fernandes, Edward M. "The Swinging Paradigm: An Evaluation of the Marital and Sexual Satisfaction of Swingers." *Electronic Journal of Human Sexuality* 12 (2009). https://www.psychologytoday.com/files/attachments/134956/the-swinging-paradigm.pdf.

Fineman, Martha Albertson. *The Neutered Mother, the Sexual Family and Other Twentieth Century Tragedies*. New York: Routledge, 1995.

Finnemore, Martha, and Kathryn Sikkink. "International Norm Dynamics and Political Change." *International Organization* 52, no. 4 (1998): 887–917.

Fitzpatrick, John C., ed. *The Writings of George Washington*. Washington, DC: United States Government Printing Office, 1934. http://etext.virginia.edu/washington.

Foucault, Michel. *Discipline and Punish: The Birth of the Prison*. New York: Vintage, 1977.

———. *The History of Sexuality: An Introduction*. Vol. 1. New York: Vintage, 1978.

Friedan, Betty. *The Feminine Mystique*. New York: Norton, 1963.

Gaertner, Samuel L., and John F. Dovidio. "The Aversive Form of Racism." In *Prejudice, Discrimination, and Racism*, edited by John F. Dovidio and Samuel L. Gaertner, 61–89. Orlando, FL: Academic, 1986.

Gamache, Peter, and Katherine J. Lazear. *Asset-Based Approaches for Lesbian, Gay, Bisexual, Transgender, Questioning, Intersex, and Two-Spirit (LGBTQI2-S)*. FMHI pub. no. 252. Tampa, FL: University of South Florida, College of Behavioral and Community Sciences, Louis de la Parte Florida Mental Health Institute, Research and Training Center for Children's Mental Health, 2009.

Gay, Peter. *The Tender Passion: The Bourgeois Experience*. Vol. 2. New York: Oxford University Press, 1986.

Gilder, George. *Men and Marriage*. Gretna, LA: Pelican, 1986.

GLAAD. *GLAAD Media Reference Guide*. 9th ed. August 2014. http://www.glaad.org/reference.

Goffman, Erving. *Stigma: Notes on the Management of Spoiled Identity*. Englewood Cliffs, NJ: Prentice Hall, 1963.

Goldbaum, Gary, Thomas Perdue, and Donna Higgins. "Non-Gay-Identifying Men Who Have Sex with Men: Formative Research Results from Seattle, Washington." *Public Health Reports* 111, Suppl. 1 (1996): 36–40.

Goldberg, Michelle. "Awakenings: On Margaret Sanger." *Nation*, February 27, 2012. http://www.thenation.com/article/166121/awakenings-margaret-sanger#.

Grant, Jaime M., Lisa A. Mottet, Justin Tanis, Jack Harrison, Jody L. Herman, and Mara Keisling. *Injustice at Every Turn: A Report of the National Transgender Discrimination Survey*. Washington, DC: National Center for Transgender Equality and National Gay and Lesbian Task Force, 2011.

Gumbleton, Thomas. "All Races, Sexual Orientations Welcome at Christ's Table." *Catholic Reporter*, January 6, 2011. http://ncronline.org/blogs/peace-pulpit/all-races-sexual-orientations-welcome-christs-table.

Hall, Radclyffe. *The Well of Loneliness*. New York: Covici Friede, 1930.

Halley, Jean O'Malley. *Boundaries of Touch: Parenting and Adult-Child Intimacy*. Chicago: University of Illinois Press, 2007.

———. *The Parallel Lives of Women and Cows: Meat Markets*. New York: Palgrave Macmillan, 2012.

Halley, Jean, Amy Eshleman, and Ramya Mahadevan Vijaya. *Seeing White: An Introduction to White Privilege and Race*. Lanham, MD: Rowman & Littlefield, 2011.

Hammack, Phillip L. "The Life Course Development of Human Sexual Orientation: An Integrative Paradigm." *Human Development* 48 (2005): 267–90.

Heger, Heinz. *The Men with the Pink Triangle*. Surrey, UK: Gay Men's Press, 1980.

Henslin, James M. *Sociology: A Down-to-Earth Approach*. 12th ed. New York: Pearson, 2013.

Herek, Gregory M. "Beyond 'Homophobia': Thinking about Sexual Prejudice and Stigma in the Twenty-First Century." *Sexuality Research & Social Policy* 1, no. 2 (2004): 6–24.

———. "On Heterosexual Masculinity: Some Psychical Consequences of the Social Construction of Gender and Sexuality." *American Behavioral Scientist* 29, no. 5 (1986): 563–77.

Herman, Dianne F. "The Rape Culture." In *Seeing Ourselves: Classic, Contemporary, and Cross-Cultural Readings in Sociology*, edited by John L. Macionis and Nijole V. Benokraitis, 45–53. Upper Saddle River, NJ: Prentice Hall, 1994.

Hollway, Wendy. "V. Beyond Sex Differences: A Project for Feminist Psychology." *Feminism & Psychology* 4, no. 4 (1994): 538–46.

Human Rights Campaign. "An Overview of Federal Rights and Protections Granted to Married Couples." http://www.hrc.org/resources/entry/an-overview-of-federal-rights-and-protections-granted-to-married-couples.

———. "Stances of Faiths on LGBT Issues: Islam." http://www.hrc.org/resources/entry/stances-of-faiths-on-lgbt-issues-islam.

———. "Stances of Faiths on LGBT Issues: Judaism." http://www.hrc.org/resources/entry/stances-of-faiths-on-lgbt-issues-judaism.

Huppin, Mark, and Neil Malamuth. "The Obscenity Conundrum, Contingent Harms, and Constitutional Consistency." *Stanford Law & Policy Review* 23, no. 1 (2012): 65–100.

Hyde, Janet Shibley. "Gender Similarities and Differences." *Annual Review of Psychology* 65 (2014): 373–98.

———. "The Gender Similarities Hypothesis." *American Psychologist* 60, no. 6 (2005): 581–92.

"In Her Own Image: Transgender Activist Pauline Park." *The Gully*, July 2, 2002. http://www.thegully.com/essays/gaymundo/020702_transgender_p_park.html.

Jensen, Robert. *Getting Off: Pornography and the End of Masculinity*. Cambridge, MA: South End Press, 2007.

Johnson, Julia R. "Cisgender Privilege, Intersectionality, and the Criminalization of CeCe McDonald: Why Intercultural Communication Needs Transgender Studies." *Journal of International and Intercultural Communication* 6, no. 2 (2013): 135–44.

Jones, Nash. "Bridging the Gap—Trans°: What Does the Asterisk Mean and Why Is It Used?" Q Center, August 18, 2013. http://www.pdxqcenter.org/bridging-the-gap-trans-what-does-the-asterisk-mean-and-why-is-it-used/.

Judge, Casey. "Thrown Away for Being Gay: The Abandonment of LGBT Youth and Their Lack of Legal Recourse." *Indiana Journal of Law and Social Equality* 3, no. 2 (2015): Article 5.

Kammeyer, Kenneth. *The Hypersexual Society: Sexual Discourse, Erotica, and Pornography in America Today*. New York: Palgrave Macmillan, 2008.

Kane, Emily W. "'No Way My Boys Are Going to Be Like That!' Parents' Responses to Children's Gender Nonconformity." *Gender & Society* 20, no. 2 (2006): 149–76.

Kane, Melinda D. "Timing Matters: Shifts in the Causal Determinants of Sodomy Law Decriminalization, 1961–1998." *Social Problems* 54, no. 2 (2007): 211–39.

Karslake, Daniel G. *For the Bible Tells Me So*, 2007. First Run Features. DVD, 95 min.

Katz, Jackson. "Reconstructing Masculinity in the Locker Room: The Mentors in Violence Prevention Project." *Harvard Educational Review* 65, no. 2 (1995): 163–74.

Katz, Jonathan Ned. *The Invention of Heterosexuality*. Chicago: University of Chicago Press, 1995.

Kim, Eunjung. "Asexuality in Disability Narratives." *Sexualities* 14, no. 4 (2011): 479–93.

Kim, Hosu. "Television Mothers: Korean Birthmothers Lost and Found in the Search-and-Reunion Narratives." *Cultural Studies/Critical Methodologies* 12, no. 5 (October 2012): 438–49.

Kimmel, Michael S. *The Gendered Society*. 5th ed. New York: Oxford University Press, 2012.

Kinsey, Alfred C., Wardell B. Pomeroy, Clyde E. Martin, and Paul H. Gebhard. *Sexual Behavior in the Human Female*. Philadelphia: Saunders, 1953.

———. *Sexual Behavior in the Human Male*. Philadelphia: Saunders, 1948.

Kuhnle, Ursula, and Wolfgang Krahl. "The Impact of Culture on Sex Assignment and Gender Development in Intersex Patients." *Perspectives in Biology and Medicine* 45, no. 1 (2002): 85–103.

Leichliter, Jami S., Anjani Chandra, Nicole Liddon, Kevin A. Fenton, and Sevgi O. Aral. "Prevalence and Correlates of Heterosexual Anal and Oral Sex in Adolescents and Adults in the United States." *Journal of Infectious Diseases* 196, no. 12 (2007): 1852–59.

Leigh, Carol, a.k.a. Scarlot Harlot. "Inventing Sex Work." In *Whores and Other Feminists*, edited by Jill Nagle, 223–31. New York: Routledge, 1997.

Linz, Daniel G., Edward Donnerstein, and Steven Penrod. "Effects of Long-Term Exposure to Violent and Sexually Degrading Depictions of Women." *Journal of Personality and Social Psychology* 55, no. 5 (1988): 758–88.

Lisak, David, and Paul M. Miller. "Repeat Rape and Multiple Offending among Undetected Rapists." *Violence and Victims* 17, no. 1 (2002): 73–84.

Lorber, Judith. "Believing Is Seeing: Biology as Ideology." *Gender and Society* 7, no. 4 (December 1993): 568–81.

Lorde, Audre. "The Master's Tools Will Never Dismantle the Master's House." In *This Bridge Called My Back: Writings by Radical Women of Color*, edited by Cherríe Moraga and Gloria Anzaldúa, 99. Latham, NY: Kitchen Table: Women of Color Press, 1981. Reprint 1983.

———. "An Open Letter to Mary Daly." In *This Bridge Called My Back: Writings by Radical Women of Color*, edited by Cherríe Moraga and Gloria Anzaldúa, 94–97. Latham, NY: Kitchen Table: Women of Color Press, 1981. Reprint 1983.

———. *Sister Outsider: Essays and Speeches*. Freedom, CA: Crossing, 1984.

Lowry, Rich. "The Wages of Polygamy." *National Review*, April 22, 2008. http://www.nationalreview.com/article/224262/big-trouble-rich-lowry.

Lucchese, Danielle. "Female or Not? Relational Aggression, Mixed Gender Messages and Disability Limitations." *Wagner College Forum for Undergraduate Research* 11, no. 2 (2013): 79–86.

Lundberg, Shelly, and Robert A. Pollack. "The Evolving Role of Marriage: 1950–2010." *Future of Children* 25, no. 2 (August 2015): 29–50.

Maccoby, Eleanor E., and Carol N. Jacklin. *The Psychology of Sex Differences*. Stanford, CA: Stanford University Press, 1974.

Maloney, Carolyn B., and the Joint Economic Committee Democratic Staff. *Gender Pay Inequality: Consequences for Women, Families and the Economy*. Washington, DC: Joint Economic Committee United States Congress, 2016.

March, James G., and Johan P. Olsen. "The Institutional Dynamics of International Political Orders." *International Organization* 52, no. 4 (1998): 943–69.

McCabe, Janice, Emily Fairchild, Liz Grauerholz, Bernice A. Pescosolido, and Daniel Tope. "Gender in Twentieth-Century Children's Books: Patterns of Disparity in Titles and Central Characters." *Gender & Society* 25, no. 2 (April 2011): 197–226.

McIntosh, Peggy. "White Privilege: Unpacking the Invisible Knapsack." In *Race, Class, & Gender: An Anthology*, 6th ed., edited by Margaret L. Andersen and Patricia Hill Collins, 98–102. Belmont, CA: Wadsworth, 2007.

McLeod, Kimberley. "Sticks, Stones and Slurs: Does 'Reclaiming' Words Work?" *Ebony*, March 14, 2012. http://www.ebony.com/news-views/sticks-stones-and-slurs.

McMahon-Howard, Jennifer, Jody Clay-Warner, and Linda Renzulli. "Criminalizing Spousal Rape: The Diffusion of Legal Reforms." *Sociological Perspectives* 52, no. 4 (Winter 2009): 505–31.

McRuer, Robert. "Compulsory Able-Bodiedness and Queer/Disabled Existence." In *The Disability Studies Reader*, 4th ed., edited by Lennard J. Davis, 369–79. New York: Routledge, 2013.

Mead, Margaret. *Sex and Temperament in Three Primitive Societies*. New York: William Morrow, 1935. Reprint 1963.

Miller, Alyson. "Unsuited to Age Group: The Scandals of Children's Literature." *College Literature* 41, no. 2 (2014): 120–40.

Miller, Neil. *Out of the Past: Gay and Lesbian History from 1869 to the Present*. New York: Alyson, 2006.

Moraga, Cherríe, and Gloria E. Anzaldúa, eds. *This Bridge Called My Back: Writings by Radical Women of Color*. Lanthan, NY: Kitchen Table: Women of Color Press, 1981. Reprint 1983.

Morgan, Ted. "The Newport Scandal." In *Gay Warriors: A Documentary History from the Ancient World to the Present*, edited by B. R. Burg, chap. 7. New York: New York University Press, 2002.

Morris, Gary. "The Rage from Nowhere? Arthur Dong's *Licensed to Kill* Interviews Murderers of Gay Men." *Bright Lights Film Journal* (August 1, 2005). http://brightlightsfilm.com/rage-nowhere-arthur-dongs-licensed-kill-interviews-murderers-gay-men/.

Muehlenhard, Charlene L., and Zoë D. Peterson. "Conceptualizing Sexual Violence: Socially Acceptable Coercion and Other Controversies." In *The Social Psychology of Good and Evil*, edited by Arthur G. Miller, 240–68. New York: Guilford, 2004.

———. "Distinguishing between *Sex* and *Gender*: History, Current Conceptualizations, and Implications." *Sex Roles* 64, no. 11/12 (2011): 791–803.

Nadal, Kevin L. *That's So Gay! Microaggressions and the Lesbian, Gay, Bisexual, and Transgender Community*. Washington, DC: American Psychological Association, 2013.

NCAA Office of Inclusion. "NCAA Inclusion of Transgender Student-Athletes." 2011. https:/
/www.ncaa.org/sites/default/files/Transgender_Handbook_2011_Final.pdf.

Nestle, Joan. "A Fem's Feminist History." In *The Feminist Memoir Project: Voices from
Women's Liberation*, edited by Rachel Blau DuPlessis and Ann Snitow. 338–49. New
York: Three Rivers, 1998.

Newman, Kim. *Nightmare Movies: A Critical History of the Horror Film, 1968–88*. New ed.
London: Bloomsbury, 1988.

New York City Commission on Human Rights. "Guidelines Regarding 'Gender Identity'
Discrimination, a Form of Gender Discrimination Prohibited by the New York City
Human Rights Law." New York: New York City Commission on Human Rights, 2004.

New York City Department of Education. "Transgender Student Guidelines." *Rules and
Policies*. Accessed July 2, 2015. http://schools.nyc.gov/RulesPolicies/TransgenderStudent
Guidelines/default.htm.

Noriega, Chon. "'Something's Missing Here!': Homosexuality and Film Reviews during the
Production Code Era, 1934–1962." *Cinema Journal* 30, no. 1 (Autumn 1990): 20–41.

Nussbaum, Martha. "A Right to Marry? Same-Sex Marriage and Constitutional Law." *Dissent: A Quarterly of Politics and Culture* (Summer 2009): 43–55.

Nygren, Eric. "Happy Loving Day!" (blog). American Civil Liberties Union of Washington
State, June 13, 2001. https://aclu-wa.org/blog/happy-loving-day.

O'Neill, Nena, and George O'Neill. *Open Marriage: A New Life Style for Couples*. New
York: M. Evans, 1972. Reprint 1984.

Park, Pauline. "Homeward Bound: The Journey of a Transgendered Korean Adoptee." In
Homelands: Women's Journeys across Race, Place, and Time, edited by Patricia Justine
Tumang and Jenesha de Rivera, 125–34. Emoryville, CA: Seal, 2006.

Paxton, Ken. "Attorney General Ken Paxton: Following High Court's Flawed Ruling, Next
Fight Is Religious Liberty." News release, June 26, 2015. https://www.
texasattorneygeneral.gov/oagnews/release.php?id=5142.

———. "Attorney General Ken Paxton: Religious Liberties of Texas Public Officials Remain
Constitutionally Protected after *Obergefell v. Hodges*." News release, June 28, 2015.
https://www.texasattorneygeneral.gov/oagnews/release.php?id=5144.

Payne, Diana L., Kimberly A. Lonsway, and Louise F. Fitzgerald. "Rape Myth Acceptance:
Exploration of Its Structure and Its Measurement Using the *Illinois Rape Myth Acceptance Scale*." *Journal of Research in Personality* 33, no. 1 (1999): 27–68.

Peplau, Letitia Anne, and Linda D. Garnets. "A New Paradigm for Understanding Women's
Sexuality and Sexual Orientation." *Journal of Social Issues* 56, no. 2 (2000): 329–50.

Perry, D., K. Walder, T. Hendler, and S. G. Shamay-Tsoory. "The Gender You Are and the
Gender You Like: Sexual Preference and Empathic Neural Responses." *Brain Research*
1534 (2013): 66–75.

Phillips, Debby, and Dorothy Henderson. "'Patient Was Hit in the Face by a Fist . . .' A
Discourse Analysis of Male Violence against Women." *American Journal of Orthopsychiatry* 69, no. 1 (1999): 116–21.

Pollack, William. *Real Boys: Rescuing Our Sons from the Myths of Boyhood*. New York:
Henry Holt, 1998.

Pomeroy, Wardell B. *Dr. Kinsey and the Institute for Sex Research*. New York: Harper &
Row, 1972.

Prager, Dennis. "Four Legacies of Feminism: They Have Made Life—and Life for Wom-
en—Worse." *National Review*, November 1, 2011. http://www.nationalreview.com/article/
281795/four-legacies-feminism-dennis-prager.

Purandare, Mrinalini. "Transgender: A Psychosocial Profile." *Journal of Psychosocial Research* 8, no. 1 (2013): 61–69.

Radner, Hilary. "Pretty Is as Pretty Does: Free Enterprise and the Marriage Plot." In *Film
Theory Goes to the Movies: Cultural Analysis of Contemporary Film*, edited by Jim
Collins, Ava Preacher Collins, and Hilary Radner, 56–76. New York: Routledge, 1993.

Rennison, Callie Marie, and Sarah Welchans. *Bureau of Justice Statistics Special Report:
Intimate Partner Violence*. Washington, DC: US Department of Justice, 2000. Reprint
2002. http://www.atria.nl/epublications/2000/intimate_partner_violence.pdf.

Revenga, Ana, and Sudhir Shetty. "Empowering Women Is Smart Economics." *Finance and Development* 49, no. 1 (2012): 40–43.

Rich, Adrienne. "Compulsory Heterosexuality and Lesbian Existence." *Signs: Journal of Women in Culture and Society* 5, no. 4 (1980): 631–60.

Risman, Barbara J. *Gender Vertigo: American Families in Transition.* New Haven, CT: Yale University Press, 1998.

Rogin, Michael. "'The Sword Became a Flashing Vision': D. W. Griffith's *The Birth of a Nation.*" *Representations* 9 (Winter 1985): 150–95.

Rosario, Margaret, Eric W. Schrimshaw, and Joyce Hunter. "Ethnic/Racial Differences in the Coming-Out Process of Lesbian, Gay, and Bisexual Youths: A Comparison of Sexual Identity Development over Time." *Cultural Diversity and Ethnic Minority Psychology* 10, no. 3 (2004): 215–28.

Rose, Tricia. *The Hip Hop Wars: What We Talk about When We Talk about Hip Hop—and Why It Matters.* New York: Basic Civitas, 2008.

Rubin, Gayle. "The Traffic in Women: Notes on the 'Political Economy' of Sex." In *Toward an Anthropology of Women,* edited by Rayna Reiter, 157–210. New York: Monthly Review Press, 1975.

Rubin, Roger H. "Alternative Lifestyles Revisited, or Whatever Happened to Swingers, Group Marriages, and Communes?" *Journal of Family Studies* 22, no. 6 (2001): 711–26.

Russo, Vito. *The Celluloid Closet: Homosexuality in the Movies.* Rev. ed. New York: Harper & Row, 1987.

Savage, Dan. "PGP: 'Wise in Theory but Obnoxious in Practice." *The Stranger* (blog), July 10, 2013. http://slog.thestranger.com/slog/archives/2013/07/10/pgp-wise-in-theory-but-obnoxious-in-practice.

Schachter, Stanley. "Deviation, Rejection, and Communication." *Journal of Abnormal and Social Psychology* 46, no. 2 (1951): 190–207.

Scholinski, Daphne. *The Last Time I Wore a Dress: A Memoir.* With Jane Meredith Adams. New York: Riverhead, 1997.

Scully, Diana. *Understanding Sexual Violence.* New York: Routledge, 1990.

Shah, Svati P. "Sex Work and Queer Politics in Three Acts." *Scholar & Feminist Online* 10, no. 1/2 (2011). http://sfonline.barnard.edu/a-new-queer-agenda/sex-work-and-queer-politics-in-three-acts/0/.

Shaw, Amy. "Masturbation Is for Women Too and Not Just for Men." *Everyday Feminism* (blog), July 30, 2012. http://everydayfeminism.com/2012/07/women-masturbating/.

Sheff, Elisabeth. "Polyamorous Families, Same-Sex Marriage, and the Slippery Slope." *Journal of Contemporary Ethnography* 40, no. 5 (2011): 487–520.

Sherif, Muzafer. *The Psychology of Social Norms.* Oxford: Harper, 1936.

Shilts, Randy. *Conduct Unbecoming: Gays & Lesbians in the U.S. Military.* New York: St. Martin's, 1993.

Shneer, David, and Caryn Aviv. *American Queer: Then and Now.* Boulder, CO: Paradigm, 2006.

Shostak, Arthur B. "Oral Sex: New Standard of Intimacy and Old Index of Troubled Sexuality." *Deviant Behavior* 2, no. 2 (1981): 127–44.

Smith, Barbara. "Racism and Women's Studies." *Frontiers: A Journal of Women's Studies* 5, no. 1 (Spring 1980): 48–49.

Smith, William A., Walter R. Allen, and Lynette L. Danley, "'Assume the Position . . . You Fit the Description': Psychosocial Experiences and Racial Battle Fatigue among African American Male College Students." *American Behavioral Scientist* 51, no. 4 (2007): 551–78.

Smith, William A., Tara J. Yosso, and Daniel G. Solorzano. "Racial Primes and Black Misandry on Historically White Campuses: Toward Critical Race Accountability in Educational Administration." *Educational Administration Quarterly* 43, no. 5 (2007): 559–85.

Squire, Kurt. "From Content to Context: Videogames as Designed Experience." *Educational Researcher* 35, no. 8 (2006): 19–29.

Stemple, Lara, and Ilan H. Meyer. "The Sexual Victimization of Men in America: New Data Challenge Old Assumptions." *American Journal of Public Health* 104, no. 6 (2014): e19–e26.

"Stop US Aid to 'Israeli' Occupation." *No Tax Dollars to Israel* (blog), February 15, 2014. http://www.notaxdollarstoisrael.com/2014/02/15/stop-us-aid-to-israeli-occupation/.

Sue, Derald Wing. *Microaggressions in Everyday Life: Race, Gender, and Sexual Orientation*. Hoboken, NJ: Wiley, 2010.

Sullivan, Nikki. *A Critical Introduction to Queer Theory*. New York: New York University Press, 2003.

Sycamore, Mattilda (a.k.a. Matt) Bernstein, ed. *Nobody Passes: Rejecting the Rules of Gender and Conformity*. Emeryville, CA: Seal Press, 2006.

Tanenbaum, Leora. *Catfight: Rivalries among Women—from Diets to Dating, from the Boardroom to the Delivery Room*. New York: Seven Stories, 2002.

———. *I Am Not a Slut: Slut-Shaming in the Age of the Internet*. New York: Harper Perennial, 2015.

Turner, John C. *Social Influence*. Pacific Grove, CA: Brooks/Cole, 1991.

Tyler Clementi Foundation. "Tyler's Story." http://www.tylerclementi.org/tylers-story.

Unger, Rhoda K. "Toward a Redefinition of Sex and Gender." *American Psychologist* 34, no. 11 (1979): 1084–94.

United States Department of Justice, Office of Justice Programs, Office for Victims of Crime. "Responding to Transgender Victims of Sexual Assault," June 2014. http://ovc.gov/pubs/forge/sexual_numbers.html#victims.

United States General Accounting Office. "Defense Force Management DOD's Policy on Homosexuality: Report to Congressional Requesters." Washington, DC: US General Accounting Office, June 1992.

US National Library of Medicine. "Turner Syndrome." *Genetics Home Reference*. http://ghr.nlm.nih.gov/condition/turner-syndrome.

US Naval Institute. "Key Dates in U.S. Policy on Gay Men and Women in Military Service." http://www.usni.org/news-and-features/dont-ask-dont-tell/timeline.

Vasey, Paul H., and Nancy H. Bartlett. "What Can the Samoan 'Fa'afafine' Teach Us about the Western Concept of Gender Identity Disorder in Childhood?" *Perspectives in Biology and Medicine* 50, no. 4 (2007): 481–90.

Wake, Naoko. "The Military, Psychiatry, and 'Unfit' Soldiers, 1939–1942." *Journal of the History of Medicine and Allied Sciences* 62, no. 4 (October 2007): 461–94.

Wallace, Mark I. "Postmodern Biblicism: The Challenge of René Girard for Contemporary Theology." *Modern Theology* 5, no. 4 (1989): 309–25.

Warner, Michael. "Fear of a Queer Planet." *Social Text*, no. 29 (1991): 3–17.

Webley, Kayla. "Indiana High Schoolers Push to Ban Gay Classmates from 'Traditional' Prom." *Time*, February 11, 2013. http://newsfeed.time.com/2013/02/11/indiana-high-schoolers-push-to-ban-gay-classmates-from-traditional-prom/.

West, Candace, and Don H. Zimmerman. "Doing Gender." *Gender & Society* 1, no. 2 (June 1987): 125–51.

Weston, Kath. *Families We Choose: Lesbians, Gays, Kinship*. New York: Columbia University Press, 1991.

Whitford, Emma. "Transgender Students Endure Widespread Harassment in NY Public Schools, Report Finds." *Gothamist* (blog), June 24, 2015. http://gothamist.com/2015/06/24/report_transgender_and_non-gender_c.php.

Wiseman, Jay. *SM 101: A Realistic Introduction*. 2nd ed. San Francisco: Greenery, 1996.

World Health Organization. "Definition and Typology of Violence." http://www.who.int/violenceprevention/approach/definition/en/.

Wyman, Leah M., and George N. Dionisopoulos. "Transcending the Virgin/Whore Dichotomy: Telling Mina's Story in *Bram Stoker's Dracula*." *Women's Studies in Communication* 23, no. 2 (2000): 209–37.

Yoder, Janice D. *Women and Gender: Transforming Psychology*. Upper Saddle River, NJ: Prentice Hall, 1999.

Zucker, Kenneth J., and Peggy T. Cohen-Kettenis. "Gender Identity Disorder in Children and Adolescents." In *Handbook of Sexual and Gender Identity Disorders*, edited by David L. Rowland and Luca Incrocci, 380–422. Hoboken, NJ: Wiley, 2008.

INDEX

ABOUT THE AUTHORS

Jean Halley is an associate professor of sociology at the College of Staten Island of the City University of New York. She earned her doctorate in sociology at the Graduate Center of the City University of New York and her master's degree in theology at Harvard University. Her book about touching children, breastfeeding, children's sleep, and gender and heteronormativity, *Boundaries of Touch: Parenting and Adult-Child Intimacy*, was published in July 2007. She assisted Patricia Ticineto Clough in editing *The Affective Turn: Theorizing the Social* (2007). Halley's most recent book, *The Parallel Lives of Women and Cows: Meat Markets*, a mix of memoir and social history of cattle ranching in the United States, came out in November 2012. With Amy Eshleman and Ramya Vijaya, Halley coauthored *Seeing White: An Introduction to White Privilege and Race*, published by Rowman & Littlefield in 2011. Halley is currently writing a book about horses and the girls who love them, *Horse Crazy: Girls and the Lives of Horses*.

Amy Eshleman, a professor of psychology at Wagner College, regularly teaches courses on gender, sexuality, race, and class in which she shares her research on expressions of prejudice with students. She holds a PhD from the University of Kansas. With Jean Halley and Ramya Vijaya, Eshleman coauthored *Seeing White: An Introduction to White Privilege and Race*, published by Rowman & Littlefield in 2011.